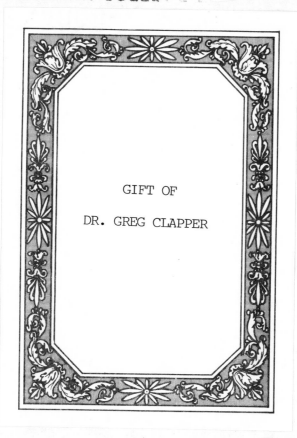

CHRIST AND THE CHRISTIAN MOVEMENT

Jesus in the New Testament, the Creeds and Modern Theology

CHRIST AND THE CHRISTIAN MOVEMENT

Jesus in the New Testament, the Creeds and Modern Theology

by

Leland Jennings White

ALBA · HOUSE   NEW · YORK

SOCIETY OF ST. PAUL, 2187 VICTORY BLVD., STATEN ISLAND, NEW YORK 10314

Library of Congress Cataloging in Publication Data

White, Leland Jennings.
  Christ and the Christian movement.

  Bibliography: p.
  1. Jesus Christ—History of doctrines. 2. Jesus
Christ—Person and offices. I. Title.
BT198.W46   1985   232'.09   85-11190
ISBN 0-8189-0484-4

Designed, printed and bound in the United States of
America by the Fathers and Brothers of the
Society of St. Paul, 2187 Victory Boulevard,
Staten Island, New York 10314, as part of their
communications apostolate.

---

1 2 3 4 5 6 7 8 9 (Current Printing: first digit)

He was a poet whose whole life was a poem.
He was not so much a minstrel merely singing his
own songs as a dramatist capable of acting the
whole of his own play.
The things he said were more imaginative than the
things he wrote.
The things he did were more imaginative than the
things he said.
. . . St. Francis walked the world like the Pardon of
God.
His appearance marked the moment when men could be
reconciled not only to God but to nature,
and most difficult of all,
to themselves.

G. K. Chesterton

PREFACE

This book was written in the course of teaching upper level undergraduate students. Its purpose is to present the more fundamental Christian interpretations of the person and work of Jesus against the background of the Christian movement's passage through successive cultural situations.

My primary objective, to survey the biblical and dogmatic materials, has survived more than a decade of research and writing. I remain as convinced as ever that theological curricula rightly dedicate a full course to such a study, which clarifies how Christians not only follow in the footsteps of Jesus of Nazareth but believe in him as the Living Christ and Son of God.

But my secondary objective, to provide background explaining how Christ came to be understood in so many different ways, has undergone a subtle shift. Initially, I was satisfied to do what many others have done, to show the historical progress from the New Testament, through the Fathers and ecumenical councils to contemporary theology. I am increasingly persuaded that, while history explains a great deal, a more ample analysis of culture explains more. Over time, instead of asking how different Christologies arose, my question became, what did these different Christologies mean for their creators?

What draws the attention of a given group of people?

What kind of questions do they raise? How do they create
and recreate their inherited religious symbols? These are
matters of culture, or cultural history, which better accounts
for motives, for the deeper experiences that make people
and movements change, than do mere historical events and
personalities.

Growing sensitivity to the cultural issue did more than
change my questions. It led me to bracket, if not deny, the
presumption of historically minded modern westerners that
the newer forms of theological reflection were always the
result of progress or, alternately, decline. The historian
recreates a past that is relatively meaningful in terms of the
present. To understand how we reached this juncture in
time, to assess inherited assets and liabilities is our real
motive for history. The student of culture, on the other
hand, tries to recreate different worlds to understand those
who inhabit them, on their own terms.

The more we enter into these worlds, the more we shall
recognize that the people involved lived a full life, a grace-
filled life. Such a life is always more than a stage in human
development or a phase in the development of doctrine.
The apostolic community was not waiting for Nicaea any
more than Thomas Aquinas prepared the way for Karl
Barth.

The payoff is clear. The cultural perspective encourages us to accept cultural diversity as a fact, and as a source
of enrichment. It prepares us to live with the enormous
cultural diversity of the contemporary world and to
welcome critically the new expressions of Christian faith
that come from those who often seem to be "strangers and
aliens." For perhaps the first time we have both the opportunity and the challenge to make the Christian Church a
truly world-wide movement. Indeed, we may now seriously
try to live up to our ancient calling to be "strangers and

aliens no longer . . . [but] fellow citizens . . . and members of the household of God" (Ep 2:19).

To acknowledge diversity — even more, to account for conflict in expressions of faith — we shall require an ever broader vision of the Church itself. For this reason I have chosen to speak more often of *the Christian Movement* than of *the Church*. By no means do I wish to downplay the significance of the concretely historical Church in the interest of a more abstract ideal. But the concrete meanings we typically attach to the word *Church* are too narrow.

When we say "the Church teaches," just as when we say "the gospel says," we need to become more keenly aware that the "Church" is that whole body to which Christ gives life and purpose, just as "the gospel" is that which Christ teaches, expressed in the *gospels* of Matthew, Mark, Luke and John, but nonetheless a more comprehensive reality. The churches in Matthew or Paul, and in Rome, Alexandria, Chicago or Recife express the varied possibilities of life and faith of the movement of Christ and his followers through our world. Chapter One develops these notions to give the contemporary Christian both an orientation and a theoretical foundation for the Christological changes recorded in the rest of the book.

Chapters Two and Three present the Christologies of the New Testament from two perspectives. First, the Christological statements are seen in terms of the changing timeframes of the early disciples from Easter to the end of the apostolic period. Then, the changes are placed in the differing contexts of the Christian community's movement from the Jewish world to the Hellenistic Roman Empire.

That movement into the Gentile world is further developed in Chapters Four, Five and Six. First, the effort to speak of Christ in terms comprehensible to Hellenistic thinkers is outlined in the Christologies of Tertullian and

Origen. Second, the limitations of these philosophically oriented Christologies are demonstrated in the Arian controversy. At this point, the Christian movement first demonstrated its capacity to play a public role in the political life of the empire at Nicaea. Finally, the early synthesis of faith in Jesus as truly God and truly human arose in a series of controversies in which the Church developed a relatively coherent logic for its statements of faith at Chalcedon.

The synthesis achieved at Chalcedon provided the basis for theological reflection as well as Church life until the dawn of what may be called "modernity." If we see our world today as "modern," the challenge to post-Chalcedonian Christianity is two-fold. First is the challenge of change itself. As modern people we have come to see that we have ourselves constructed the world, the everyday reality, in which we live. What we have made, we may re-make or change. Change does not just happen. It has become our responsibility.

Second is the challenge already mentioned of a much more culturally diverse yet unified world. In less than a century, communications, transportation and even the nuclear threat have reduced humanity to a neighborhood. We know what our neighbors are doing and they are aware of our actions.

Chapters Seven and Eight show the initial responses of modern theologians to these two challenges. Facing the first challenge made us critical of the synthesis we achieved. The second challenge is to face others, to hear new questions, indeed to hear a different kind of questioning than even self-critical moderns are inclined to admit.

Our questions have become ever more fundamental. Fully developed answers appear to lie on a rather distant horizon. But we have a history of successful questioning behind us in Christology. Even more, we are today reliving an old experience: once again the Christian movement is reaching out to include everything and everybody that is a part of God's world. What questions we should now raise about Christ, and what answers should be given may lie beyond our present imagination. Nonetheless, modern theology reflects the Church's concern to follow Christ in outreach on behalf of the Father's will to make of humankind a true family.

In presenting such a panoramic sketch of an historic experience still in progress, I have obviously drawn on the specialized studies of many others. In so doing, whether for pedagogical purposes or for lack of personal expertise in all the specialties involved, some over-simplification is inevitable. The risk of over-simplification is worth taking in order to integrate the work of many experts and make that work available for the non-expert. My purpose is to drive the reader from this survey to its sources, some of which are included in the appendices, and to the experts themselves.

Because I have argued throughout that statements of faith reflect the communities which make them, it is appropriate that I at least sketch my own background. Bear in mind that I am a Southerner and a Catholic. It is somewhat unusual to combine these two traditions. What is common to both is the large role assigned to tradition itself and the ever-present awareness of the reality of symbols. No doubt, this shapes my perspective on both Christ and the Christian movement. More than others, I am inclined to assume that our symbols shape our lives, and that our symbols are the products of traditions.

To change the meaning of our symbols too slowly or too rapidly strikes me as both difficult and dangerous. To do so without questioning what they meant goes against my grain. I envy and admire those who can move day by day into the future with fewer questions about our past. The everyday tactics of the Christian movement's ministry to the world is usually best entrusted to such people. But to imagine overall strategies capable of meeting our longer-term service to God's family, our ministry must involve both living with often complicated questions and a willingness to propose rather than impose answers.

In fulfilling such a ministry in this book in particular, I have been assisted by far too many people to mention here. Nonetheless, credit, but not blame, for what is positive in this work should be given to the following: Father Bernard Lonergan of the Gregorian University, whose lectures in Christology I followed as a student; Dean Alex Brunet of St. John's Provincial Seminary, who greatly encouraged me as a beginning instructor to take theological research seriously; Professor Thomas Langford of Duke University, who led me through the Barthian corpus to the conviction that Christology is at the heart of our theology; Professors Frederick Herzog of Duke University and Bruce Malina of Creighton University, who helped me frame the issues of political and cultural context; Dean David Bossman of Siena College and St. Bonaventure University, who has read and criticized the many versions of this text in too many ways to recount.

Finally, acknowledging the support of my colleagues in the Theology Department at St. John's University, I wish to thank Father Jeffrey Micker of Alba House for many helpful suggestions that have made this, I hope, a far more readable book, as well as Mr. Howard Angione, Ms. Frances McNamara and Ms. Virginia Clark, who painstakingly edited the final typescript.

Leland J. White
St. John's University
New York, New York

ACKNOWLEDGMENTS

The scripture quotations in this publication are from *The New American Bible*, copyrighted 1970 by the Confraternity of Christian Doctrine, Washington, D.C. unless otherwise noted.

Acknowledgment is made to the following for permission to use copyrighted materials:

Darton, Longman & Todd Ltd. and Doubleday and Company, Inc. for texts from *The Jerusalem Bible*.

Society for Promoting Christian Knowledge for texts from *Tertullian's Treatise Against Praxeas*, edited and translated by Ernest Evans.

The Newman Press for text from *Tertullian's, The Treatise Against Hermogenes*, translated by J. H. Waszink.

Society for Promoting Christian Knowledge for texts from *Origen on First Principles*, translated by G. W. Butterworth.

Wm. B. Eerdmans Publishing Co. for texts from *A Select Library of Nicene and Post-Nicene Fathers, Vol. III: Theodoret, Jerome, Gennadius, Rufinus: Historical Writings, etc.; Vol. IV: St. Athanasius: Select Works and Letters*, edited by Philip Schaff and Henry Wace.

Doubleday & Company, Inc. for texts from *Creeds of the Churches: A Reader in Christian Doctrine from the Bible to the Present*, edited by John H. Leith.

Macmillan Publishing Co., Inc. for text from *On the Incarnation: The Treatise De Incarnatione Verbi* by St. Athanasius, translated and edited by Sister Penelope Lawson.

Cambridge University Press for text from *Documents in Early Christian Thought*, edited by Maurice Wiles and Mark Santer.

The Newman Press for texts from *Christ and His Mission: Christology and Soteriology*, edited by James M. Carmody and Thomas E. Clarke.

The Westminster Press for text from *Christology of the Later Fathers* edited by Edward Rochie Hardy and Cyril C. Richardson.

CONTENTS

Chapter One:

Christ and the Christian Movement

Chapter Two:

Across Time: New Testament Frameworks

Chapter Three:

From the Land of Israel to the Hellenistic World

Chapter Four:

Into the Mainstream of Hellenistic Culture

Chapter Five:

Into the World of Imperial Politics: Nicaea's Enduring Legacy

APPENDICES

CHRIST AND THE CHRISTIAN MOVEMENT

Jesus in the New Testament, the Creeds and Modern Theology

CHAPTER ONE

CHRIST AND THE CHRISTIAN MOVEMENT

Questions to think about:

— *Why should we see the Church as a movement?*
— *How open to adaptation is our sense of Christian identity?*
— *Why do Christians use different criteria to express belief?*
— *What does it mean to say doctrine changes?*
— *How is the heart of Christian experience disclosed?*

Americans have always been on the move. At its beginning Christianity was similarly mobile. During this past century American Christians especially have been challenged by the enormous changes in both the Church and the world. Conscious of accelerating change, directly or sometimes indirectly we hear an ancient question. Who do we say that Christ is? We seek assurance that the Church that follows this Christ will be adequate in the face of unprecedented change.

Change in believers' affirmations of Christ is not new, even if Christians of the past did not notice change as poignantly as we do today. To adequately appreciate how such change occurred, it is helpful to see the Church as a movement rather than as an institution. In its effort to speak about Jesus of Nazareth, the Christian movement over time has *learned* a great deal. At the same time, it has constantly been *rediscovering* the same Christ in its faith life. The Christian movement is thus the context for comprehending both stability and adaptability in witness to Christ through the ages.

1. Starting Point: The Church as a Movement

To speak of the Church as a *movement* is not to dismiss other rich images of the Church as *Body of Christ, People of God, Communion* or *Bride of Christ* or to question its character as an *institution.* Calling the Church the *Christian movement* focuses attention on its purpose or mission throughout history. For a *movement* is a series of organized activities by persons working concertedly for common goals. Thus, we recognize an important fact. The Christian movement existed before the Church acquired its formal organization. Therefore, the institutional model is less comprehensive than the movement model.

The movement model describes the Church better than other social models. For instance, social scientists argue that the Church spread throughout the world can be categorized as a *community* only in an analogous sense. Its members are too dispersed to interact on a face to face, communal level. Moreover, the community model for the Church ironically ignores a central belief, that the Church shares a communion over time with all the saints who have gone before us. Next, sociologists themselves often analyze the Church as a *voluntary association,* because this shows how it functions in a free society. Yet most Christians believe that it is more than voluntary because the Church was created independently of the initiatives of believers past or present.

What the Church always has been is thus better understood by the idea of a movement. The Church is a series of activities by Christ and Christians organized to bring to fulfillment Christ's own mission in the world. This is what the term *Christian movement* means.

ACCOUNTING FOR HISTORICAL CHANGE: Taking the *Christian movement* model as our starting point, we become better able to see the significance of history. True, when we see the Church as an institution we are aware of an organization that has maintained itself through the centuries. Nonetheless, every day we become more aware that today's organization is in many ways different from the past. People frequently have questioned the claims made for this or that feature of the organization. Is its hierarchical structure necessary? Is the way Church leaders use power legitimate? If we focus on activities and actions, such questions arise later and in historical perspective.

Different actions can be interpreted as directed to the same mission, and the differences more readily accepted because of historical circumstances. In such a scheme of things, the organization that carries out the actions is seen as legitimate because it serves the common mission. Instead of having to argue that the Church has the power to give grace, we acknowledge that where grace becomes present, the Church or the Christian movement is effective. Historically, we find that the Christian movement has carried out its mission in a variety of ways, with changeable structures and forms of organization.

Different Statements of Belief: One of the great insights of contemporary studies of communication and language is that all statements presuppose a particular setting. In fact, studies have helped us understand how different *spoken* statements are from *written* ones. We are somewhat more sensitive now to the fact, for example, that tone of voice, inflection, gestures, posture and even the anticipated reaction of the hearer contribute to the meaning of a spoken statement. Ex-President Nixon was perceptive when he tried to prevent the Watergate investigators from listening to his taped conversations. The spoken voice clarifies meanings that are inevitably obscure and open to wider interpretation in a written transcript.

Many things do not have to be said when one is communicating in person. We may abbreviate our spoken statement because the immediate setting clarifies its meaning. When we speak to one person, we talk differently than when we speak to another, or to a large group, or to a person miles apart by telephone. Sometimes we make a fuller statement, at other times a completely different one. When we put our statements into writing, all these differences are magnified many times over. Indeed, cultures that rely on the spoken word, unlike our own, tend to distrust the written statement. In particular, such people feel a written contract is less reliable than an oral agreement. They believe written words will be interpreted in a rigorously literal fashion in order to circumvent the real intent of the agreement.

Written statements tend to become more and more detailed in order to clarify questions of precisely who, what, why, when, where and under what circumstances. Such details as these are generally presupposed in oral statements. Of course, this needed clarification is endless and never quite satisfactory. Moreover, what may clarify a point for one audience only creates a new problem for another one.

When we are trying to explain what an ancient text means, we have to ask: for whom? For the writer, the copyist, the reader in another country or another period of history? We must decipher everything each of these individuals might have presupposed about the words utilized, if we want to interpret the text adequately. Often enough, we impose our own presuppositions, misinterpreting the original meaning. But whether the original statement is rightly, wrongly, or partially understood, all these activities, whether done by ordinary readers or by critical scholars, are evidence that the same statement does not mean the same thing in a different setting. A new statement is required to approximate the originally intended meaning. Fundamentally, this is why different statements of faith arise in every setting where people encounter God through Christ.

Stable Identity with Adaptability: Again, as a movement, the Church's goal offers stable identity at the same time that it justifies continual adaptation of statements of faith. For in the movement perspective, Christian identity is determined by the call God has given through Jesus to reconcile humanity with God and one another.

The continuing adaptation in forms of organization, as well as statements of faith, identifies the Church with the pattern of God's outreach in Jesus. In Jesus, God's will to save was concretely expressed in a particular human life in a definite time and place, under one set of social and cultural conditions. Although Jesus preached the kingdom of God, he did not leave his own message in fixed written form. Moreover, the heart of the proclamation about Jesus revolves around actions, his death and resurrection. Without careful adaptation, the identity of Jesus' followers with his work of reconciliation would have taken on a different meaning very quickly.

One example illustrates how stable identity required adaptation of the message almost immediately. When the disciples proclaimed to Jews in Jerusalem, "The God of Abraham . . . the God of our fathers, has glorified his Servant Jesus, whom you handed over and disowned" (Ac 3:13), they were making a plea for reconciliation between themselves and their fellow Jews. To use substantially the same message with Gentiles would have meant something altogether different. In the Gentile context the same formula might be understood to say: "The God of the Israelites has glorified his Servant Jesus whom the Jews themselves betrayed and disowned." Gentiles would hear an accusation against the Jews, and be led to blame Jews for Jesus' death, creating obstacles to reconciliation between Jews and Gentiles. Those called to a mission of reconciliation would have become agents of animosity. Often enough this happened. Fortunately, the statement of faith was adapted so that the Christian movement did not totally betray its identity as the agent of Christ's reconciling mission.

This chapter's theory for evaluating change and adaptation is worked out implicitly in all the following chapters in terms of Christian reflection on the identity of Christ. Readers more immediately interested in the Christological issues than in these theoretical foundations may want to go immediately to Chapter Two, and work their way through the concrete examples of change in Christology in the rest of the book. At the end of the book, these readers may find themselves asking: Has something been lost in all this change? How do we evaluate what Christians made of Christ? At that point, they might return to what follows in this chapter for an explanation. For those more comfortable with advance explanation, it is better to read what follows now.

2. The Contemporary Challenge to Christian Identity

After two thousand years, the earliest adaptations appear relatively simple matters even though study of the New Testament provides a great deal of evidence to the contrary.

The challenge today is greater. The contemporary Christian is confronted with a great variety of statements about who Christ is. These statements present images derived from various settings for different purposes, and having somewhat different meanings today. Are these statements interchangeable? Do the images presented make a difference? If so, what difference do they make? Finally, are there any criteria, standards by which we can decide among these images, to shape our own statement?

We look for criteria because adaptation continues. For example, in many Churches, images of the risen and glorified Christ have replaced the crucified and suffering Jesus. In contemporary scriptural translations, a somewhat "sacred" vocabulary has given way to a more direct and plain-spoken reporting of Jesus' words and deeds. Finally, adaptation reaches into public worship. Catholics, who once spoke of Christ "enthroned on the altar," are more likely today to speak of Jesus sharing himself in the meal of the Christian family. Indeed, the liturgical formulas of most of the major Christian Churches refer far more frequently to "Christ our Brother" than ever before. Even if we find the adaptations more meaningful, we want criteria for deciding among all the possibilities that tradition and our own imagination now provide.

Criteria and Sources: On a typical Sunday the contemporary Christian will hear a gospel reading proclaiming the words and deeds of Jesus of Nazareth. Likewise, the worshipper will recite the creed which speaks of the Son as "begotten not made, one in Being with the Father." Then, with perhaps some guidance from the preached word, the believer re-enters the everyday world to confront family, business, social and political life as a follower of Christ. The three criteria for deciding among statements of Christian faith are easy enough to identify: gospel, creed and mission in the world. Christians have learned all they know of Jesus and their own identity as Christians from these three.

If identifying the criteria and sources is relatively easy, relating one to another is more complex. Three ways of relating the sources, for making them function as criteria are common. Each of these approaches makes one source the criterion by which the others are understood.

Many assume that the meaning of the gospel and the demands of mission to others can be fully interpreted in terms of the creed. For instance, they hear a gospel account of Jesus asking a question, or saying that he does not know something, or that he is hungry or thirsty. They presume that all these indications of ordinary human limitations represent only poetic or dramatic demonstrations of how a divine person reached out to humans. The gospel accounts are filtered through the creedal statement of the Son's divine eternity, omniscience and omnipotence.

Others focus on the New Testament portrait of Jesus. When they do this consistently, taking the critical perspective of modern scholarship, they find portraits by Mark, by Matthew and by others. The faith portraits fashioned by early believers proclaim that the way Jesus lived leads to new, prevailing life. Jesus emerges from the gospel pages as our guide and teacher in word and deed.

Yet, the Jesus of history remains a question mark. Some assume that life always presents roughly the same opportunities and problems and always requires the same responses. For these, Jesus' words and deeds become models to be applied in everyday life. In other cases, his words and deeds are understood as responses of one person in a distant and different culture. Then they are taken to be only one — however good — culturally conditioned response to life. In either case, the gospels are read without the clarification of the creedal affirmation that in Jesus the divine and the human, the limited and the unlimited achieve a harmony.

Some people find a full agenda in life itself. The newspaper they pick up before or after Church details the problems for which Christian living must provide the answer. The more immediate the problems to be solved, the wounds to be bandaged, the mouths to be filled or the alienated to be reconciled, so much more urgently must such believers insist that our deeds are extensions and continuations of the work of Jesus. Not unlike those who take their agenda from the newspaper, some find a full agenda in domestic life. Issues are defined in advance of any serious confrontation with the Jesus of the New Testament or the Christ of the creeds. The contemporary concern for vital family life or for world peace is read into the words of Jesus and the faith of the Christian community.

Criteria Fit Within Basic Models: Overcoming the tendency to emphasize one source at the expense of the others is not common. Each source evokes relatively distinct and powerful images of Christ and the Christian life. Each image is inevitably associated with an extended perceptual pattern in which God, the Church and much of the religious meaning and values of both social and individual life are included. This whole pattern serves as a model, a simple and mostly unconscious strategic plan, for resolving a variety of questions of meaning and value in one's life.

Each time the model helps sort out issues in one area, its potential influence in other areas is enhanced. Thus, a person's criterion for Christology is re-enforced when the same criterion is applied to a question of economic justice. Christian individuals and communities become set with one model, with one over-riding criterion, and all data from other sources is filtered through the chosen model. Corresponding to our three criteria and sources are three basic models for religious thinking and judgment.

MODEL A: Christ is understood in terms of the analytical clarity of the creeds, and his divine status and nature become the focal concern. Simultaneously, the Christian will understand God as the source of order, as the explanation for all that takes place in the world. Likewise, the Church will be — like Christ — a point of contact between the divine and the human realms, providing fairly reliable practices and rules for relating to God and one's fellow human beings. The old catechisms met the needs of this model. Even though catechisms are out of vogue, the question-answer approach, with clear statements and rules for every significant issue, remains attractive to people with this model of belief.

MODEL B: When Christ is understood in terms of the words and deeds narrated in the gospels, he is heard addressing the Christian, whether personally or through the evangelists. The complex challenge of his life as a model for Christian discipleship is better appreciated. Then the Christian will see God as the one who sustained Jesus through human ambiguities that included death. The Church is more likely to be seen as a people on pilgrimage, relying on God, but living by ad hoc arrangements as it awaits the fulfillment of the promise of the kingdom. Persons and communities operating according to this model are less likely to expect answers for every conceivable question. Good preaching and meditative reading and study of the scriptures provide the suggestions and guidance they need to live out their hope. Indeed, they are not surprised when the proclamation or study of the word opens up new questions rather than settling old ones. The search for truth and the challenge to follow Christ are satisfying in themselves.

MODEL C: When Christ is understood in terms of contemporary cries for healing and salvation, his role as Savior, perhaps reinterpreted today as Servant, will be central. Given this focus the Christian will envision God as the one who provides what humans think they need. The servant Church will be characterized by openness and availability to all who show need. Demonstrated commitment to the service of others will be the supreme value for those guided by the criterion of mission in the world. The most characteristic expression of this model is found in contemporary social-religious causes such as the peace movement or the civil rights movement and in earlier religious orders which concentrated on charitable activity.

CONFLICT AMONG MODELS: Each model has its own strengths and weaknesses. But the strengths are felt largely by those who follow a given model, while the weaknesses are observed by those who follow another model. The need for a more comprehensive view than each model presents is felt only sporadically. People who describe their Christianity according to one of these models, encounter others with a different model. Misunderstanding and conflict result. To overcome the conflict each side needs to see its own position and that of the other side more comprehensively. Each must step back for the moment from their respective strategies which they otherwise find so helpful.

But stepping back from the model and its commitments to gain a more comprehensive view is all the more difficult because conflict usually involves only a detail in the overall pattern. For example, must Christian missions always aim at baptizing non-Christians? Is sacramental ministry the heart of pastoral responsibility? When such conflicts arise, each side devises arguments from the same sources, gospel, creeds and mission to defend its point of view. But each filters the data in the sources through its own model.

Neither side recognizes the systematic character of the conflict, because neither recognizes how the models operate or how they relate to one another (see Dulles 1974: p. 197). Avery Dulles has described this situation with special reference to theological models for the Church, observing that different models lead to "polarization, mutual incomprehension, inability to communicate, frustration, and discouragement" (1974: p. 36).

3. The Christian Movement Offers A Comprehensive Viewpoint

Left to themselves, the sources, gospel, creeds and mission become separated and ultimately divisive criteria. They are central features in models that are not fundamental. The more fundamental model of the Church as Christian movement is comprehensive. The Christian movement model provides a comprehensive view of the sources. Gospel, creeds and mission are each better appreciated as expressions and products of the Christian movement, i.e. products of the activities of Christ and Christians working towards the fulfillment of Christ's mission in the world. Each is therefore to be interpreted in light of that movement, rather than taken as an independent criterion.

Gospel as Expression of Christian Movement: Together with other New Testament writings our written gospels are products of the preaching of the gospel, the good news about Jesus. We know, of course, that Paul spoke of the gospel before there were any written gospels. His letters are expressions of this good news. Likewise, we may be aware that traditions about Jesus and his teaching were passed down orally and in some writings before these traditions were put together in the present gospels.

We are less generally aware that the New Testament

writings remained subordinate to the proclaimed word in the Church for several centuries. In their preaching the earliest disciples used the Jewish Bible to interpret the meaning of Jesus' work, supplementing the inherited scriptures with remembered sayings of Jesus. As the gospel traditions took written form, these writings were cited along with the Jewish scriptures in preaching. In preaching they used these texts freely, now supplementing these Christian scriptures with other sources and combining them to suit their own needs.

Possibly the early Church, up to perhaps the fourth century, saw the written gospels more as outlines or notes that were useful in proclaiming "the gospel" (see Sundberg: p. 137). The modern person does not subordinate texts to oral tradition because the printing press made books readily available, encouraging us to depend on them and elevating the written word over the spoken word. But ancient people, primarily dependent on oral communication, tended to use the written text as a guide to memory. It was important for such people to have the text presented, we might almost say acted out, by an interpreter. Reading was not a job for amateurs or ordinary lay persons, but for the theologically competent.

Although in modern times Catholic authorities were undoubtedly far too hesitant to let lay persons read the Bible, their hesitation reflected a recognition that the text represented the Church's faith in a rather condensed form. This sensitivity appears in the attitude of other religious traditions to their scriptures. For example, among Moslems translation of the Koran is forbidden or discouraged, reflecting in part the conviction that its meaning is really known only by members of the religious community. Protestants also have retained some form of the tradition that the most important level of meaning in the Bible cannot be grasped through a literal interpretation of the text. They understand the importance of Christological and spiritual understandings.

Apparently the gospel, as important as it is, must be seen as the expression of the Christian movement, not as its foundation. I have consciously avoided saying that the gospel is an "expression of the faith of Christians." This would imply that the members of the Church created their faith on their own. The expression "Christian movement" refers to the interaction of Christ and Christians, and the gospels are understood as expressions of the actions of *both* working in concert. Read in this sense, the gospels help us experience the movement as it now functions in the world rather than merely to learn about its past history.

Creeds as Expressions of the Christian Movement: The average Christian is familiar with the creed because of its place in worship. Yet, he is likely to have had the creed explained not as prayer, but rather as a statement of doctrines. Religious educators past and present have broken these confessions (the word means *acknowledgment, acclamation*) of faith into individual articles of belief. Then, they detailed the theological content of virtually every word. Thus, the creed often appeared to be more a legal description than a prayerful response. This approach froze the creed at one stage of its history and obscured its full significance within the Christian movement, past and present.

Throughout the New Testament there are short creedal statements, acclamations such as "Jesus is Lord." Such acclamations are prayerful responses to the proclamation of the gospel, to the presence of Christ within the Church and in the eucharistic celebration, and the convert's response to the scrutiny before admission into the Church through baptism.

To appreciate these creedal acclamations, it is helpful to keep in mind two ways in which "faith" is understood. "Faith" first means "trust or personal commitment." This is faith *in* someone. Secondly, "faith," or better "belief," refers to "things believed." This is faith *that* such and such is true. In the context of the eucharist and baptism, the confession of faith is a statement of affiliation, affirming commitment to God and fellowship with Christ and the Christian community. The Nicene Creed and the Apostles' Creed are pledges of solidarity with the Christian movement. *Faith in* takes precedence over *what is believed.*

Taken apart, analyzed article by article, the creed served the solidarity of the Christian movement in another important but secondary way. When controversy arose over more precise ways of stating Christian belief, especially when the controversy threatened the unity of the Church, some areas of the creed were restated with greater precision. The elaborated statements left the more fundamental statements intact. This suggests that disputed questions were in some real sense secondary. Also the most significant elaborations were designed to guide discussion of questions of belief rather than to answer the questions.

Unfortunately, the creed has often been used as a weapon to claim victory for one interpretation rather than as a help in building consensus. Moreover, after the victory of one camp was achieved, by breaking communion with the other, it was always necessary to explain the break. The explanation had to be found in ever more minute analysis of the articles relating to the dispute.

Perhaps the most serious casualty of the controversial use of the creed is not the unity of Christians, but rather Christian readiness to reformulate their faith acclamations in new situations. Oddly enough, we acclaim Christ's *presence* in the community celebrations, and his *ongoing* work with us, but tend not to relate Christ to events or experiences in the contemporary world. Therefore it is difficult to get across the meaning of the creed to contemporary Christians, and effectively express commitment to the objectives of the Christian movement.

In language appropriate to their time, the ancient formulas affirmed that God was at work in Jesus and his Church. The creed did more than record facts out of the past or before time. It also affirmed the present meaning of the Christian movement.

Mission Concerns as Expressions of Christian Movement: Few themes are repeated in so many ways in Christian vocabulary as the idea of *mission*. Our English word is from the Latin verb *to send*. Jesus is spoken of as *sent from God*. The word *apostle* comes from the Greek verb *to send*. The Risen Lord promised to *send* his Spirit to his disciples. A quick reading of the New Testament would show that the most significant controversies involved the limits and methods of the mission of Jesus' disciples. In short, a rather comprehensive theological interpretation could be built around this theme. Why are we sent? Where are we sent? How are we to carry out the mission? These questions are central and recurring.

Characterizing the Church as "people sent" has significant implications. First, it makes clear that the initiative for the movement is from God. This is clear even on linguistic grounds. When we find passive voice constructions in the Bible, the implied subject is usually God. Constructions such as "*being* sent" imply that God sends. Likewise, "*being* called" (the root verb in the word "Church" in Hebrew, Greek and Latin), implies that God has given the call. The Christian agenda does not come primarily from those sent, but from God. Sometimes recent proponents of the Servant Church model are criticized for taking their agenda from the world. The critics argue that this deprives the Church of control over its own life and identity. The language of mission implies that in setting its course the Church's initiative and control are already limited by its origin.

Second, the theme of mission presupposes and encourages movement, mobility. The journey or pilgrimage is a recurrent theme in religious traditions. Yet themes of this type play an extraordinary role in both ancient Israel and early Christianity. The Exodus, the going out from Egypt, was the constitutive element in the Hebrew tradition, not the possession of the promised land (Sanders 1972: pp. 25-28). Likewise, Christians described themselves as "resident aliens and visiting strangers" having no fixed home (1 P 2:11; see Elliott 1981). External forces such as exile and persecution may partially account for the predilection for terms that made a virtue of transiency. Yet such explanations account better for resignation in the face of apparent failure rather than the aggressive outreach that took place. Later Israel settled down for centuries in Jerusalem as Christianity did finally in Rome. But the original centers, for Israel the mount in Sinai left behind unmarked, and for Christians the Jerusalem largely abandoned until Constantine, became points of departure not centers of return or pilgrimage.

What is the meaning of this extraordinary emphasis on mission in the Church? Two possibilities must be considered. First, mission may represent an effort to extend and propagate the Church. This is the conventional understanding of missionary efforts. Second, mission may be seen as the activity by which the Church comes into being and exists as Church. In being sent the Church is what it is, rather than merely extending its influence and message. To be sent or called out by God is to be Church. Clearly, this second understanding of the meaning of mission is the one that accounts for the emphasis on mission in the Christian movement. Apart from mission the Church does not really exist; where mission occurs the living Church is present.

Thus, the movement of Christ and Christians into the world is the activity by which Christ's mission reaches its goal. Precisely in outreach, rather than by means of outreach, the human family is drawn together with the Father. As others are drawn into the Christian movement, the movement achieves its purpose, which is to include all. Therefore the demands of each particular stage of missionary outreach are ultimately subordinate to this fundamental demand of the ongoing mission or movement. No stage of the mission may be seen to create patterns of belief or practice which exclude in principle other stages in outreach and mission.

The mission to the Gentiles raised questions about practices and beliefs of the Christian movement among its earliest Jewish adherents. When Peter heard the voice saying "What God has purified you are not to call unclean" (Ac 10:15), and accepted the Roman centurion Cornelius into the movement, the strategies of the Jewish mission were relativized. Also the success of the Gentile mission raised for Marcion (d. c. 160 C.E.) the question of whether God as revealed by Jesus had made irrelevant or unacceptable all that had been revealed from Moses until Jesus. In accepting the Jewish Bible as its own scriptures, and rejecting Marcion's insinuation of a break in the divine outreach to humans, the strategies of the Gentile mission were in turn relativized. At this second stage, the Christian movement recognized a clear limit to strategies for which Christians might claim authorship.

Each stage of mission then stands under a single criterion. Is it compatible, or in what way might it be made compatible with the ongoing Christian movement? Past statements of belief as well as patterns of action stand to be corrected in the light of present and future possibilities of outreach. But these present and future possibilities must be fulfilled in a way that does not cut off from the movement those whom Christ and Christians have already reached. Mission comes close to serving as a foundational criterion for Christian identity. But mission itself is nonetheless only properly understood, as are gospel and creed, when it is seen as an expression of the movement to include all in the family of God.

4. Has Christology Changed or Developed?

The changes that have occurred in statements of belief about Christ over the centuries have prompted, especially in modern times, the opinion that Christology has developed. What is meant by development must be carefully scrutinized. Whether development is indeed the best description of what has occurred in Christology needs more attention than is often given.

DOES DOCTRINE DEVELOP? Theologians have commonly begun with the question of whether doctrine develops, sometimes even more specifically with the issue of whether dogma is reformable. (The basic difference between *doctrine* and *dogma* is that doctrine is the common teaching of the Christian movement while dogma is the limited portion of doctrine officially defined by Church authorities.) To protect the a priori principle that what is defined in one age may not be rejected in another, it is argued that changes in Christological doctrine must represent development, or be simply rejected as heresy. The basic model here is that dogmas (or doctrines that have achieved the status of dogma) are, as it were, the seed from which doctrine and appropriate theological reflection on Christ grow.

Unfortunately, this model does not describe what actually happened in the history of the Christian movement's long-term effort to state its belief about Christ. The dogmatic statements come relatively late, after the passage of a quarter millennium. Are we to say that the kernel of these dogmas lay within the consciousness of the early Church, however obscurely? The later Church did not justify its own formulations simply on the ground that they had developed from apostolic ideas. At the early councils, certainly, Church leaders were aware that the seed of apostolic ideas had produced both heresy and sound teaching. The councils were intent on pruning away the first and nourishing the second. On this basis, it would certainly seem more appropriate to say that dogma began (and perhaps also doctrine changed) in order to check or to channel development rather than by a natural process of development.

Moreover, the growing seed model of doctrinal change, which was introduced ostensibly to honor the contribution of the apostolic age and the sanctity of the conciliar decrees, unintentionally belittles these two foundations. It maintains that what the dogmas teach was more obscurely taught by the apostles. Also, it assumes that post-conciliar theological development must always be an effort to elucidate and communicate the previously less clear, and thus somewhat defective dogmatic teaching of the councils. Ironically, to say that dogmas are the seed of authentic Christian teaching is to say also that they are only the seed. This implies that the later teaching is the fruit, the better part of the whole tradition. This approach is a theological version of the modern conviction that by the process of evolution we are superior to all our predecessors.

A Christian Movement Model for Change: Although change may be development and it also may be decay, change does not have to be either. One-sided attention has been given in both the past and the present to dogmatic statements at the expense of those who made and used them. Change may more rightly be seen as the fruit of different people speaking about the same reality. A different statement need not be better or worse to express a new insight. The new insights come from the newness of vision and perspective of those making the statements.

VERBAL SYMBOLS: Again, contemporary linguistic studies make us increasingly aware that statements are verbal symbols by which people express and communicate their understandings and values. All people use a variety of symbols for such expression and communication. In religious life non-verbal symbols include silence, song, art, sacramental celebrations, and various forms of physical and affective outreach to others. The initial reason for employing verbal symbols is to compensate for meanings, i.e. understandings and values, that are in danger of being lost. We put our attitude into words when we find more immediate expression inadequate. We have changed from one mode of expression to another, rather than developed our ideas.

Of course, the initial reason for resorting to verbal symbols does not say everything about the reasons for speech, or the consequences of using language. Anyone who tries to use oils to picture something discovers that the paints open up possibilities for picturing things not yet seen. The new medium creates its own realities. Words function in the same way that other symbols do, only with far greater power. Just as painting a sunset allows us to see real sunsets differently than before, so verbal symbols open up new vistas on our understanding of the people and things to which they refer. They start out to state our experience, and proceed to reshape it.

MEDIA FOR EXPERIENCE: Symbols remain media for human experience. They first mediate what has been experienced. Then, they evoke new experiences. But these experiences are not contained in the media themselves, the symbols. The experiences are in the humans. If the symbol makes no connection with a person's experience, it is powerless. If the symbol is verbal and recorded in a text for others to use later, the symbol will connect with their experience or be meaningless. When it connects with their experience, the question must always be raised as to how well their experience matches the experience that generated the symbols in the first place. Making a meaningful connection is both uncertain and almost never exact. At best we partially miss the original point of the symbols, at worst we see no point at all.

In the arts it often makes little difference. We admire ancient statues of pagan gods, which were intended to evoke worship, as works of art rather than as religious objects. We will never quite understand their creators, even though we appreciate their artistic skill. Modern artists often assume that their works not only can be given meanings they never intended, but they insist that they mean whatever those who enjoy them want them to mean.

Even literary works are widely conceded to have a largely indeterminate meaning — that is, meanings determined by their authors and audience in accord with virtually unrestricted experiential backgrounds. Thus, the author of a lyric poem about Porgy rewrote his character's story into a novel, transformed it further into a play, before collaborating in a further transformation that became the opera "Porgy and Bess." Dubose Heyward was not bothered that the character changed, because the modern artist knows that in every presentation there is a new audience with a new set of experiences.

In religion, we seek a more stable basis for understanding and evaluating our place in the universe. Historical religions like Christianity are solidly based upon a definite person and a series of events. Here the indeterminate meaning of the arts is insufficient. Nonetheless, the way humans use symbols, including verbal symbols, does not change when the intentions for using them change. Thus the stability we seek does not lie in the symbols themselves, but in those who use them. Our stability lies in the Christian movement. This movement acts and lives out a fundamentally common experience across cultures and centuries. This experience ties together a variety of symbols, including the statements of belief.

LEARNING AND DISCOVERY: The relative freedom with which the Christian movement expressess itself now with one symbol, again with another is explained by the way learning and discovery relate to each other. Learning and discovery are different but complementary processes. In the process of learning we acquire the data, the procedures and conclusions left by others. In the process of discovery the bits and pieces of the data fall into place in terms of our own experience.

With a more elaborate argument than we need now, Avery Dulles explains how this dual process permits an interplay between authority and personal insight not only in religion but in scientific thought (1982: ch. 2). The acquisition of data, learning, is cumulative, for both individuals and learning communitites, the Church included. To speak of a growth of data, and thus also of doctrinal data is appropriate. The authority of the gospels and Church traditions rests on the necessity that later learners have for doctrinal data as a starting point for their discovery of meaning.

However, the discovery of meaning itself is not cumulative. When we integrate the doctrinal data with our experience, we have discovered meaning. But we cannot transfer this meaning to someone else as discovery or insight. Transferred to someone else, discovery becomes only a new form of data. In other words, discovery is not transferable from one mind to another. It is radically the experience of the person with the insight or discovery.

This distinction places all generations of the Christian movement on the same footing. The discovery or insight into how whatever is symbolized (in any way, whether verbally or not) connects with one's experience of Christ is not transmissible. How we understand and see the data, as an expression of our radical identification with Christ in his mission to the world, is not an experience transmitted from one Christian to another, or from the Church to Christians. We, and the Church as well, make available to others only data, learning. For us the data have been integrated and have become a medium for expressing a discovery.

But the data await personal discovery, grace, to actually come to life. Personal understanding takes place at this level of discovery, rather than at the level of learning. If development of doctrine refers to doctrinal data, which the Christian movement has developed in its different ways of speaking of Christ, we are talking about accumulated learning. In this sense, Christological development has taken place. But if development of doctrine refers to doctrinal understanding, the integration of the significance of the data with our experience of Christ, the claim for development is invalid. Certainly, there is no way of claiming that the accumulated doctrinal data create a uniformly developing depth of understanding.

5. Discovery as a Source of Doctrinal Change

Traditionally, studies of Christology focus attention on development of the doctrinal data. Likewise, they concentrate attention on the issues explicitly raised by the data. The first question is always how the Church came to its conviction or achieved its clarity about Jesus' divinity. Then, attention turns to the question of how it managed to relate Jesus' divinity with his full humanity. Change is described as growing clarity in answering these questions. Many argue that the questions arose when various heretics cast doubt on, or denied earlier Christian belief in Jesus' divinity. My own studies more than a decade ago began along these traditional lines.

I have already indicated that the model of doctrinal development does not do justice to the faith experience of the Christian movement. Doctrinal development describes growth in data, conclusions reached at the level of learning. But the Christian movement is energized and stimulated by a series of experiences at the level of discovery. Thus, we would better understand the change in affirmations made by Christians about Christ as responses to their experience at the level of discovery rather than in the data produced by learning. Discovery, a process in which data is integrated in terms of experience, changes the believer's understanding and expression of belief.

By perceiving doctrinal change as response to discovery, our understanding of the process is enriched. The Christian movement expresses its own inner life rather than simply reacting to outside forces or to members operating outside of its frame of reference. Adaptation in formulas arises to express its fundamental convictions rather than as mere expediency. But adaptation in formulas also manifests a realization that its experience transcends all the ways in which it might express its experience.

In this light, moreover, we judge more postively those who forced issues by statements later judged to be either inadequate or heretical. As many acknowledge, these statements became negative measures of effective expression of the Christian experience. Heresy helped the Christian movement clarify its symbols, not only to express its life, but even to generate new life. Even heresy is a witness to the inner vitality of the Christian movement, not merely its negative counterpoint. The heretic draws the wrong lines in his picture of Christian experience. Nonetheless, by trying to sketch some lines, he tells us there is something there to be portrayed. Often the faulty symbol portrays aspects of the experience particularly difficult for the Christian movement to grasp, and therefore avoided by those with less courage than the heretic.

Thus, the faith experience of the heretic and the more orthodox probably have more in common than we have previously thought. We do not acknowledge this out of a sentimental desire to smooth over differences. It is also more than an acknowledgment that both sides might hold a large number of statements in common. Instead, we finally realize that both are trying to express a common experience. What was done badly by the side *committing* the misstatement may have been *omitted* by the other side. This only shows how often we learn more from a mistake than from a success.

DISCLOSING MYSTERY: What we learn from a mistake, or from heresy, is not the answer to a question, or the solution to a problem, but rather awareness of where the difficulty arises. Bernard Lonergan has called this aware—

ness an *inverse insight* (pp. 19-25). In the inverse insight we go beyond the point where we realize we do not know the answer, or have to correct an earlier answer. The most significant feature of the inverse insight is that, having sized up the data from various perspectives, we realize that patterns of human reasoning and reflection can not produce an adequate interpretation of the data. In religious terms, we encounter mystery.

Mystery is generally taken to be commonplace in theology. In so far as theology concerns God it inevitably deals with mystery. There is no proper analogy or basis for interpretation within human experience for God. However, much that has been called mysterious in religious tradition is only the result of a false mystification or simple misunderstanding. In such cases, an adequate interpretation of the data is possible. On the other hand, to locate points at which no conceivable method of finite inquiry could lead to understanding is to encounter true mystery.

In the process of discovery, the Christian movement encounters mystery when it not only knows that a particular symbol or statement is inadequate to express its experience, but when it also knows that no symbol or statement is adequate. To say "God is not bound to the limits of time" simply means that our time concepts cannot be applied to an eternal being. This does not qualify as mystery. However strange, we can logically deny temporal characteristics to a given reality. We identify a mystery when we recognize that a given reality is misconstrued whether we affirm *or* deny temporal characteristics. In this case, the reality confounds the logical process we use in seeing things *either* within *or* outside time. Mystery is clear when we recognize that in some sense God is involved in time as well as beyond it.

The Mystery in Christology: Creation: My studies have convinced me that Jesus' nature was never the fundamental issue. The doctrinal data indeed focused on whether Jesus was divine and how his divinity could be reconciled with his humanity. But neither of these issues in themselves explained the tortuous path taken by the Christian movement in expressing its faith. What could not be resolved, no matter what, was what it meant to be human and what the status of the world itself was. The root mystery lay in the notion of creation itself, which focuses on the value of humans and the world, whether this-worldly human work makes any difference.

The clue that creation was the central mystery is that those thought of as heretics did not directly question Jesus' divinity. They all explicitly affirmed that Jesus was divine. The difficulty always lay at another level, namely the meaning of divinity. What divinity meant, however, was never resolved. Examining why they were unable to resolve what they meant by divinity leads to the mystery of creation.

What divinity means, ultimately, is a matter of how God relates to humans and to the world. How God relates to humans and the world, of course, is definitively known only by God. Humanly speaking, God represents whatever any person or culture regards as the ultimate source of value. This makes our statements about God serve as statements about how well-founded we think the realities we value really are. To the extent that we doubt our own value, we will be inclined to have a source of value, a divine reality, whose relationship to us is dubious. To the extent that we question the reality of our world, we will assign the world origins and/or goals which make the world expendable. A practical test of value is whether we think that our work, what we do with ourselves and our world makes any real difference.

Creator-God Makes Created Realities Intrinsically Valuable: The Hebrew conception of God as Creator of the world and humans implies something about both that is less clear or denied in other conceptions of God. The Creator God wills the existence of an "other," realities different from God and in some sense of independent and intrinsic value. Other conceptions of God in one way or another say that God expresses or manifests himself through creatures, so that creatures are divine media. In this scheme of things, the value of manifestations of God is *extrinsic*, from outside their own beings. On the other hand, creation says that God makes someone or something that was not there, not even in God. There are tasks to be done by these others that only they can do. The Creator God implies that humans and the world are of value in themselves, intrinsically.

Once humans and the world are seen to have intrinsic value, value independent of their mediating divine reality, then what they do or become is significant. History is not pointless nor is its outcome predetermined. It must be determined in the collaboration of creatures with the Creator. In essence, to say that Jesus brings this collaboration to a new climax reinforces the idea that what humans do is significant. Humans will partially determine the final outcome.

Piety tempts us to say something less, to say that humans are to be an image or symbol of divine activity, instead of saying that humans are in the divine image because they have some of the divine power of creating. In the Hellenistic world this flawed piety, which reserved all decisive action to God, was a presupposition. It was manifest in a consistent tendency to devalue everything human, historical, time-conditioned and worldly. The Christian discovery of the significance of Jesus always opposed this powerfully ingrained habit. But our capacity to express our discovery has always been limited by the prevailing understanding of divinity.

GOD AT WORK WITH HUMANS: THE CHRISTIAN MYSTERY — As the Christian movement lived out its life, it lived out an experience of God so concerned for the future of humans and the world to collaborate with them in common activity initiated by and sustained by Jesus. We learned various ways to express this, but none was quite adequate to the lived experience. That experience was that God was at work with humans, as with Jesus, to the point of and in death itself.

Christian experience revealed a meaning for human history that humans may discover, and thus believe, but cannot simply learn from the data. At each stage of the history of the Christian movement the discovery, being fresh and unique, had to be and was restated. So long as the process of discovering God's collaboration with humans continues, change in statements of belief about Jesus is the clearest and most inevitable evidence for this experience. We always tend to ask the question "who do we say that Christ is?" But the more fundamental question is "how does God relate to us and to the world?"

WORKS CITED

Avery Dulles
    1974 *Models of the Church*. Garden City, NY: Doubleday.
    1982 *The Survival of Dogma*. New York: Crossroad.
John H. Elliott
    1981 *A Home for the Homeless: A Sociological Exegesis of 1 Peter: Its Situation and Strategy*. Philadelphia: Fortress.

Bernard J.F. Lonergan
>   1958 *Insight: A Study of Human Understanding*. London:
>   Longmans.
James A. Sanders
>   1972 *Torah and Canon*. Philadelphia: Fortress.
Albert C. Sundberg, Jr.
>   1976 "Canon in the NT," in Keith Crim, ed., *The
>   Interpreters' Dictionary of the Bible: Supplementary
>   Volume*. Nashville: Abingdon. pp. 136-40.

CHAPTER TWO

ACROSS TIME: NEW TESTAMENT FRAMEWORKS

Questions to think about:

— *Why does the New Testament give Jesus various titles?*
— *Do these titles represent different understandings of Jesus?*
— *Do they show the early Christians growing in understanding?*
— *Are the later titles more definitive than the earlier ones?*
— *How does the passage of time change our perceptions of others?*

As today's lay person knows too well, New Testament research yields mixed results. Caution in forming judgments on New Testament teaching is the rule, not the exception. Can any conclusions based on contemporary New Testament research provide foundations for Christianity? Once we acknowledge the variety in content and perspective in this collection of twenty-seven books, will we able to answer the question: who was Jesus? Theologians today often share the lay person's perplexity. The issue is fundamental. Neither lay persons nor theologians can afford to wait for final answers from biblical experts.

RECOVERING JESUS FROM THE NEW TESTAMENT: The Christian rightly expects to find Jesus in the New Testa ment. Indeed, just as Christians believe Christ is present in the Eucharist, they also believe he is present when they hear the gospel. Recent liturgical reforms aimed at recovering awareness that the Eucharist is a communal meal. By entering into the spirit of a family feast Christians are more vitally nourished by Christ sharing his life. Today they hear another ancient idea, that in the homily the preacher "breaks the bread of the Word." To understand preaching in this way implies fresh appreciation of the biblical texts as both literary and religious treasures. The gospel text must be broken to be adequately absorbed. Discerning the layers of meaning in the text prepares contemporary Christians to hear Christ's voice with greater clarity. Learning to listen for different accents in the text, they have begun to recover some of the stereophonic richness of the biblical witness to Christ.

Each verse of the gospel witness to Christ is open to a wider range of meanings, and subject to more questions than was formerly suspected. For example, Mk 1:1, "This is the gospel of Jesus Christ, the Son of God," appears to be little more than a book title. Yet, this single verse presents a number of questions. Indeed, to see what it means and what it meant reveals different attitudes toward Christ taken by Christians in many different situations.

In two thousand years *gospel* has become at once a special type of writing and a liturgical proclamation. Because it is literature, it is studied critically. Because it proclaims faith, one stands when it is read in church. *Christ,* originally a title of honor, has come to be taken as though it were Jesus' surname. Neither *gospel* nor *Christ* connotes what it did originally. Moreover, some scholars argue that "Son of God" has been inserted in this text by someone after Mark's time. In any case, *Son of God* would have meant one thing to Mark, something else to later Christians. The questions raised about this apparently simple verse in Mark illustrate how much work is needed to determine the original meaning of many New Testament statements.

To clarify texts and their meanings, biblical experts are necessary. But non-experts need a more general critical framework to analyze the specialists' data. The text critic may tell whether "Son of God" was in the original composition. The philologist may advise about the meaning of *Son of God* in the year 100, in 325 or in 1900. But how such historical and philological details contribute to our understanding of the gospels is another matter. However much we need specialized help, the expert leaves us with new problems. How are we to understand language so remote? How, for example, do we grasp what Mark meant to say when we no longer live in his world?

Throughout the ages Christians, and especially preachers, have tried to imagine themselves walking in the footsteps of Jesus and his first disciples. Although entering into the world of the gospel writer is a worthwhile objective, these imaginary Christian pilgrimages have had limited critical success. A person of the fourteenth, nineteenth or twentieth century imagines what it would have been like to travel with Jesus. In their naivete, pious Christians often carry the baggage of preconceived notions of who Jesus was and how his contemporaries perceived him. Their imaginary pilgrimages are similar to visiting a historical place. They can not relive, as they would like, a historical event. To hear what the gospel writers wanted to say we must somehow appreciate what it was like to know Jesus before there were gospels.

Significance of Time: To hear the gospel message, we have to enter a time before there was a written gospel. Time frames the identity of every person, including Jesus. Moreover, time-frames condition how one person or generation of persons understands or misunderstands another. A sense of the time, sometimes called the "times" of a person's life, provides a unique basis for figuring out how the person thought, acted and placed value on everyday reality.

We measure time by the appearance or disappearance of certain persons or things. In marking off "time-before" from "time-after" we uncover what we or others value. Sometimes the length of time a belief prevailed reveals how much value it had. To chart the way the word *fact* begins to appear everywhere in the eighteenth century, or *progress* in the nineteenth gives us a window into the mind and values of those ages. Such clues help us date texts and put people in perspective. We sense what was truly valuable for those otherwise distant from us. Perhaps, we also begin to understand them as planners oriented to the future, or as fatalists tied to the past.

TIME-FRAMES IN THE NEW TESTAMENT: To enter into Jesus' time is one thing. To enter the times of those who wrote about him is another. Observing what topics were common for people before Jesus' ministry provides some insight into his world. Taking note of the ways the New Testament writings presented him, and in what contexts these portrayals appear, reveals the various worlds in which his disciples lived, moved and found their meanings. These observations establish the time-frames in which the writings interpreted Jesus.

Our task is to distinguish one layer of perception from another: to situate Jesus first in his own time, then in the successive times of his disciples and the early Christian writers. Finally, we gain a self-critical perspective. We perceive the difference between what we have brought to the text from our own tradition and what it said on its own.

In the New Testament Jesus is called by a variety of titles. With each title he is given a somewhat different identity. Notable among the titles are *Son of Man, Lord* and *Son of God.* Each of these identities fits logically within a particular time-frame. Thus, *Son of Man* is used during Jesus' public ministry. *Lord* most characteristically designates him as present to the early Christian community after Easter. The title *Son of God* signifies a relationship that moves him back indefinitely towards the time of the creation of the world.

To see Jesus in each of these three time-frames, during his public life, after his resurrection and from the time of creation, situates him in the typical perspectives in the New Testament. In this way we begin to assess the meaning of three distinct New Testament Christological options.

1. Time of the Son of Man: Jesus in his Public Ministry

One of the most enigmatic terms in the Bible, *Son of Man* is used in reference to Jesus seventy times in the synoptic gospels. It also appears twelve times in John, but only once outside the gospels (in Ac 7:56). With only one exception (Jn 12:34), the expression is invariably placed on Jesus' own lips. Thus, the New Testament writers consistently situate this designation within the span of Jesus' public ministry. They characteristically associate the title with an understanding of Jesus appropriate to those who followed him during his public ministry. For disciples during this period the crucified and resurrection are future and unknown events. Jesus, under the title *Son of Man,* is a person whose real significance remains to be disclosed in these momentous future events.

Figure 1: SON OF MAN

Mark	**************
Luke	*************************
Matthew	*******************************
Acts	*
Paul	
John	************

(Figure 1 shows the relative frequency with which the title *Son of Man* appears in the various New Testament writings.)

DID JESUS CALL HIMSELF SON OF MAN? This question is debated. In the gospels no one other than Jesus is depicted using this title. This supports the argument that he used the title. The one apparent exception to the rule by which the title is always placed on Jesus' lips proves how clearly it was taken to be his own term. In this one case, Jesus was asked, "How can you claim the Son of Man must be lifted up? Just who is this Son of Man?" (Jn 12:34). This instance indicated that others spoke of the *Son of Man* only when Jesus introduced the expression.

Nevertheless, questions about Jesus' understanding of *Son of Man* remain. Did he see himself as the *Son of Man*? Or was he speaking of someone to come after him? This question raises more debate. As we will show later, Jesus' *Son of Man* saying fall into five types. One of the five types is especially ambiguous. This type apparently depends on the only reference to a *Son of Man* in the Hebrew Scriptures, in Dn 7:13. Daniel had spoken of an eschatological figure, one to come in the future. Where Jesus speaks of the *Son of Man* in the spirit of Daniel, it often sounds as if he is referring to someone else, using the title in the third person.

The vast majority of *Son of Man* sayings, on the other hand, are clearly first-person references. In these it would be easy to substitute "I" for "Son of Man." Whether the historical Jesus spoke of the *Son of Man* in the first-person or the third-person, or even possibly in both, is not known. Whatever Jesus himself did, the evangelists clearly present *Son of Man* as a title by which Jesus designates himself.

Some argue that understanding has been hindered by a questionable translation. In Hebrew "son of" prefixed to a collective noun often indicates only an individual member of a species. If this use is applied here, the Greek and English equivalent should say only "man" rather than "son of man" (see McKenzie: p. 831). Possibly, Daniel meant to say only "a man." Likewise, Jesus may only have meant to say "I" in the colloquial pattern of subdialects of English where "the Man" or "this Man" represents "I."

Contexts of the Son of Man: We have already mentioned that *Son of Man* appears in five different types of sayings in the gospels. Each type fits within a somewhat different context. In the first three types of statements the immediate situation of Jesus' public ministry is central. In the fourth type he anticipates his passion and death, and in the last he speaks of a future coming of the Son of Man. Taken together, the five types of sayings plot a chronological path from his ministry to his second coming. They begin with the earthly human Jesus and move forward to his return as the Christ of judgment and glory.

1. *In human condition:* Modern Christians expect the title *Son of Man* to emphasize Jesus' humanity. Their expectation appears to be realized in the first group of sayings. Typically speaking of himself, Jesus declares:

The foxes have lairs, the birds in the sky have nests, but the Son of Man has nowhere to lay his head (Mt 8:20).

Again, he says, "The Son of Man appeared eating and drinking. . ." (Mt 11:19). Statements of this first type assume not only that Jesus was human, but more importantly that he lived humbly, without manifesting a more than human nature. Nothing beyond ordinary human power is attributed to the *Son of Man*. Those who see the *Son of Man* in this way see someone like themselves.

2. *With extraordinary power:* In the second group of sayings, modern Christians would see something beyond ordinary human power. But these sayings must be read with care. Supernatural power, at least in the stricter sense the term has today, is not necessarily at work in these sayings. For example, when he confronts a paralytic at Capernaum, Jesus says:

> "Which is less trouble to say, 'Your sins are forgiven' or 'stand up and walk'? To help you realize that the Son of Man has authority on earth to forgive sins" — he then said to the paralyzed man — "stand up!" (Mt 9:5-6).

On another occasion he speaks of the Son of Man as "Lord of the Sabbath" (Mk 2:28).

To interpret these passages accurately, first century beliefs have to be respected. At that time, sickness was believed to be the result of the presence of an evil spirit (or the absence of the good breath/spirit of God). In either case, the sick were alienated from God, sinners. Thus, eliminating sin or sickness was the same. To restore health was to forgive sin. In demonstration of this perspective, notice that no one challenged Jesus' assumption that healing implied forgiveness.

Secondly, it was widely assumed that human beings could be agents of God or Satan. They could be empowered to deal with these bodily spirits, i.e. to heal. The only real question was whether a healing came from co-operation with God or with Satan and the evil spirits. On this point Jesus answered a charge from Jewish authorities, "If I expel demons with Beelzebul's [the prince of demons'] help, by whose help do your people expel them?" (Mt 12:27). In statements such as these Jesus' hearers would have heard only that he was a human being who enjoyed a special relationship to God, that he could call on God to cure, to forgive. Beyond this popular understanding, the priestly class would have perceived a threat. For they asssumed that the power to heal belonged to the priestly class, or to those whom the divinely appointed channels approved (see Hollenbach, pp. 580-584).

3. *On mission*:   The third set of *Son of Man* sayings are closely related to the second. In them Jesus' mission becomes central. They focus on this public ministry. Jesus likens the work of the Son of Man to a "farmer sowing good seed" (Mt 13:37), which will grow along with the bad until harvest time. To Zacchaeus the tax collector, he brings reconciliation. He tells Zacchaeus "this is what it means to be a son of Abraham. The Son of Man has come to search and save what was lost" (Lk 19:10).

In these sayings Jesus often distinguishes his earthly work of preaching and reconciliation from events and deeds to come at the end of time. Notable is his statement, "Whoever says anything against the Son of Man will be forgiven, but whoever says anything against the Holy Spirit will not be forgiven" (Mt 12:32). During his public ministry, lacking guidance from the Holy Spirit, people will rightly weigh and re-weigh the evidence that Jesus represents God's will. Those who refuse him as he humanly presents God's will to reconcile can always change. The meaning of Jesus' public ministry could only be known after Easter and the outpouring of the Spirit. In each of the first three sets of sayings the

still-to-be-explained or future significance of the *Son of Man*
stands out. All these sayings about the *Son of Man* point
towards Jesus' future.

4. *In announcing his passion*: By far the largest
number of *Son of Man* sayings are those in which Jesus
announces the climactic phase of his future, his passion and
death. Characteristically, just before his final Passover, Jesus
declares to his disciples:

> You know that in two days' time it will be Passover, and
> that the Son of Man is to be handed over to be crucified
> (Mt 26:2).

Again, at the supper he elicits Judas' question when he
mentions the "man by whom the Son of Man is betrayed"
(Mt 26:24). But throughout the synoptic gospels, references
to impending suffering or death typically use *Son of Man* for
"I."

Suffering for the Son of Man provides shocking contrast to the glorified state associated with the Son of Man in
the fifth series of sayings. Even though the first three series
depict the Son of Man as truly human, Jesus had no precedent when he spoke of him suffering and dying. If they
made any connection with earlier use of the title, first
century hearers were undoubtedly shocked. For prior to the
time of Jesus, as we see when Daniel spoke of the *Son of Man*,
this title designated a special agent of God, who stood at
God's right hand. The *Son of Man* would always have been
seen in a state of glory.

To associate the *Son of Man* with suffering was novel.
For this reason, a number of modern scholars have argued
that Jesus did not directly speak of himself as a suffering Son
of Man. They agree that he may have made statements
about his own impending crisis. But they argue that his

statements have been edited to include the title. When they inserted this title, Jesus' disciples transformed descriptions of suffering into assertions of exaltation through suffering. Historical evidence is inconclusive. Nonetheless, the statements about the suffering to befall the Son of Man show one fundamental gospel conviction: Jesus' way to the Father, and the way by which he reconciled humanity to the Father, was the way of the cross.

5. *In a future coming*: Closest in spirit to first century expectations is a series of *Son of Man* sayings that refer to his coming in the future. The presumed model for this series is Dn 7:13-14:

> I saw one like a son of man coming on the clouds of heaven; when he reached the Ancient one and was presented before him, he received dominion, glory, and kingship; nations and peoples of every language serve him. His dominion is an everlasting dominion that shall not be taken away, his kingship shall not be destroyed.

The most typical gospel expression of this imagery comes in Jesus' trial scene. He says, "Soon you will see the Son of Man seated at the right hand of the Power and coming on the clouds of heaven" (Mt 26:64). Other statements associated with this imagery speak more generally of things that will happen before the Son of Man comes to judge.

Because these statements all conform to the pattern in Daniel, some scholars consider it more likely that this was Jesus' meaning. Others propose that Jesus' disciples may have been as puzzled by the term as modern readers. Mentioned only in Daniel and other more obscure writings, passed over by the first generation of disciples before the gospels were written, *Son of Man* may never have been self-explanatory. If true, perhaps the statements of glory were created when the precedent in Daniel was finally uncovered. However close a parallel is drawn between Daniel's *Son of Man* and the New Testament's, the meaning in either case remains difficult to determine.

More important than what *Son of Man* meant, or exactly who used it, is the time-frame in which it appears. These sayings portray Jesus on mission, living a human life, instructing his disciples and pointing them toward a future that was yet to be accomplished. The greatest proportions of these texts refer to the *Son of Man's* suffering and dying. The accent on suffering and death, a novel development of the earlier eschatological figure, tailors the *Son of Man* figure to the actual pattern of Jesus' historical existence. This retailoring confirms a fundamental pattern. This title belongs in the time-frame of Jesus' public ministry. This time-frame comes closest, however different it is, to the context modern Christians try to reconstruct in studies of the historical Jesus.

2. Time of the Lord: Jesus Present to Post-Easter Community

Outside the gospels, Jesus is called Lord (*Kyrios*) more frequently than he is given any other title. In the epistles of Paul, who did not know Jesus during Jesus' public ministry, *Lord* becomes almost a proper name. *Lord* is the name by which Paul and his communities addressed the risen Jesus. How appropriate in the light of Easter to designate Jesus by this title! For those who said "Lord," through faith Jesus was experienced in the Church's life as the exalted one. The Jesus addressed with this name was thought of in the time-frame of his own resurrected life, not his public ministry.

Figure 2: LORD

Mark	*
Luke	******
Matthew	*****
Acts	******
Paul	******************************
Hebrews	
John	******

(Figure 2 shows the relative frequency with which the title *Lord* appears in the various New Testament writings.)

Calling Jesus *Lord* certainly shows that he was now seen within a different context from his public ministry. Nonetheless, the title itself is open to a wide range of meanings. In both Greek (*Kyrios*) and Latin (*Dominus*), *Lord* was a title of courtesy like *Mr*. It was appropriate for any superior, elder or teacher. But it was also assigned to rulers, emperors and kings, who were frequently believed to be quasi-divine. Similarly, it was used for the deities themselves. Many have argued that Paul or the Hellenistic Christians adopted the title to assert the divinity of Jesus. Others argue for an earlier, more spontaneous choice of this word. Given its wide range of possible meanings, this title alone would scarcely settle the question of Jesus' nature.

AN AFFIRMATION OF JESUS' SAVING ROLE: As ambiguous as *Lord* may be, it clearly asserts Jesus' central and exalted role in human salvation. For Paul, confessing Jesus as Lord and believing that God raised him from the dead provides the basis of salvation (Rm 10:9). In this declaration, Paul asserts Jesus' relationship to human beings. Calling him *Lord* proclaims the significance of Jesus, as one raised from the dead, for the world. It attests the saving nature of Jesus' deeds without reflecting theologically on the nature of his person. *Functional* Christology describes what Jesus did, and *ontological* or *metaphysical* Christology defines who he is. Those, like Paul, who call Jesus "Lord," affirm *what Jesus does* for their salvation.

CONTEXT FOR CALLING JESUS LORD: This affirmation of faith fits a perception of Jesus framed in the time after his death and resurrection. Paul, who barely notices Jesus' public ministry in his epistles, does not attempt to reconstruct or even recall the Jesus of the immediate past. Jesus is perceived by Paul and other disciples as they experienced him in faith. They knew him as he appeared to them, spoke to them and provided the foundations for their new life as his disciples. Sometimes, the Risen Lord was experienced dramatically, in conversions like Paul's on the road to Damascus. More often, he was routinely felt to be present in community life and worship. Such religious experiences are not immediately scrutinized or analyzed. Religious experience does not produce a formal theological definition. Definitions come much later. But given an intense religious experience of Jesus living among them, believers must express themselves with whatever terminology is available.

The dynamics of faith which propelled early followers of the Risen Jesus offer better insight into what *Lord* meant than secular uses of *Kyrios* can provide. It is appropriate to examine religious tradition for insight into the dynamics of their faith. These early believers had one important precedent. The Greek translation of the Hebrew Bible, the Septuagint, had used *Kyrios* for both *Adonai* (Lord) and *Yahweh* (God). Thus, they would have been aware that *Kyrios* would suggest an identification of Jesus with God.

It is difficult to imagine a Jewish community *suggesting* absent-mindedly that a fellow human being was divine. For Jews the tradition of monotheism was too strong for that.

For this reason, scholars have long assumed that Jesus was first called *Lord* in the Gentile churches, rather than among Jewish believers. They have assumed that early Jewish converts would have hesitated to call anyone *Lord* because the name was too closely linked to the One God.

AMONG JEWISH DISCIPLES IN WORSHIP?:   Oscar Cullman (1959: pp. 195-237) has proposed an alternative theory about how the title came into use. He argues that Aramaic speaking Jewish converts made the identification of Jesus as *Lord*. Jesus, he notes, was already known as *Rabbi* (Teacher, Master) during his ministry. In Aramaic, the vernacular of Jesus' day, a Rabbi was commonly called *Mar* (Master, Lord). Cullman notes that *Mar* appears in 1 Cor 16:22 transliterated, not translated, into Greek. When Paul transliterated Mar-anatha, he apparently regarded this formula as already traditional. Mar-anatha means "Our Lord comes," or "Our Lord, come!" Cullman also believes the phrase is liturgical. If it is, early believers would have invoked the Rabbi Jesus as *Mar* in a eucharistic context. In the Eucharist when *Mar* Jesus was recalled, he was experienced as somehow present, and his future coming in glory anticipated. Closely bound to this setting in worship, Jesus as Mar/Lord would be increasingly identified with God.

When such an identification of Jesus as Lord took place, at a minimum Jesus would have been perceived as one through whom God worked. He was the agent or personal representative of God. Modern Christians need to be reminded that a defined understanding of Jesus as a divine person came about in stages. Had a definition been made abruptly it would have been misunderstood. For Gentile believers a divine person would have been a half-human, half-divine offspring of a god mating with a human. For Jews a divine Jesus contradicted God's oneness. Experienc-

ing Jesus' work as representative of the Father and reflecting on his exaltation to new life in the resurrection, the early
community moved in stages towards a functional identification of Jesus with God. What Jesus did was seen as the act of
God. The *Lord* was at work.

POST-EASTER PERSPECTIVE IN THE GOSPELS: The
gospels themselves provide evidence for insight developing
in stages. Composed after Paul's epistles, they were influenced by the Pauline post-Easter perspective. Comparison of parallel accounts shows how the gospels began to
apply the title *Lord* to incidents in Jesus' public ministry. In
some instances the synoptic gospels may well have used *Lord*
as no more than a courtesy title, in the way that Americans
from the South say "Sir." But in other passages, not only the
title, but the atmosphere closely approximates the spirit of
Paul's post-Easter perception of Jesus as the heavenly Lord.
In these instances the title is often accompanied by a definite
article "the."

For instance, in the account of the widow of Naim, Luke
writes: "when the *Lord* saw her" (7:13). More tellingly, compare Matthew's version of Jesus' cure of the epileptic boy
with Mark's presumably earlier account. We see post-Easter
glory gradually casting a halo-effect over events from the
public ministry. (See Appendix A for underlined texts of Mk
9:14-28; Mt 17:14-18.) Matthew creates a new tone from the
beginning. Mt 17:15 has the boy's father petition Jesus,
"*Lord,* take pity on my son," where Mk 9:17 says, "*Teacher,* I
have brought my son to you because he is possessed." But
his use of *Lord* is only part of a more impressive transformation. Matthew's version tells of an incident during Jesus'
public ministry in which Jesus acts as, and those around him
perceive him as, though he were already the glorified Lord
of later Christian experience.

Matthew's narrative style contributes to the transformation. A longer gospel than Mark, Matthew here compresses the narrative. In effect, the cure is simplified. The cure appears to take place in immediate response to Jesus' word rather than in the stages detailed in Mark. In Matthew, Jesus' power is further highlighted because the story is told as though there could never have been any question of Jesus' curing the boy. Details would distract from Matthew's purpose. Faith, which will later empower Jesus' disciples, is the point. The condensed narrative highlights this (see Held: pp. 165-71; 187-92). Jesus cures with the same assurance that Peter, after the resurrection, will say to the lame man, "In the name of Jesus of Nazareth, walk" (Ac 3:6). Implicitly in this passage Matthew sees Jesus more as he would be seen after Easter than as he appeared during his public life.

Calling Jesus *Lord* is a spontaneous response to the experience of his presence in risen form after Easter. Those who have this experience are overwhelmed with the reality of his presence and power in their midst. Reflecting upon his earlier ministry, they see it in terms of the glory he now has. At least while this experience is still most vital, they feel little need to define who Jesus is. Calling him *Lord* expresses the truth that their lives have a new center, a focus so vital that everything else is interpreted in terms of the Risen Jesus. In a sense the future is contained in this present, and thus it also is settled. The past is rather irrelevant. The need to interpret the Risen Lord is barely felt.

3. Time of the Son of God: Jesus in the Father's Work of Creation

Modern Christians call Jesus *Son of God* without a second thought. They are usually surprised to discover that this title is relatively rare in the New Testament. *Son of God* became common as time for reflection on Jesus' work passed. Thus, in later writings, the gospel and epistles attributed to John, *Son of God* appears three times more often than in earlier writings, the synoptics. Moreover, in the synoptics others call Jesus "Son of God." In the fourth gospel, Jesus speaks of himself as *Son of God*. Only in John is Jesus presented as the Son who openly acknowledges his sonship.

Later Christians gave this title both prominence and defined meaning. Thus, the image of Jesus as *Son of God* became the seed for significant theological growth. The path taken by this title illustrates how properly theological reflection about Jesus emerged from the faith of the early Church.

Figure 3:   SON OF GOD

Mark	****
Luke	*****
Matthew	********
Acts	**
Paul	**********
Hebrews	********
John	*****************************

(Figure 3 shows the relative frequency with which *Son of God* appears in the various New Testament writings.)

Figure 4:   SON OF GOD (Jesus' self-description)

Mark	
Luke	
Matthew	***
John	*****************************

(Figure 4 shows the frequency with which *Son of God* is placed on the lips of Jesus.)

SYNOPTICS: In the synoptics, Jesus is designated as God's Son by others. As we have noted, some doubt that Mk 1:1 originally included this title. But at Jesus' baptism (1:11), and at his transfiguration (9:7), both key points in his gospel, a voice in the cloud declares, "You are [This is] my son, my beloved." During his interrogation by the high priest, Jesus is challenged, "Tell us if you are the Christ, the Son of God" (Mt 26:63; Mk 14:61; Lk 22:70). Similarly, he is asked by the devils expelled at Gerasa, "Why meddle with me, Jesus, Son of God Most High?" (Mk 5:7). Finally, at the climactic point of Jesus' death, the centurion declares, "Clearly this man was the Son of God" (Mk 15:39). Mark's use of *Son of God* establishes a pattern for Matthew and Luke. It is a designation others give Jesus.

When the synoptic gospels quote those who call Jesus *Son of God* it often appears as though this title is presented as a revelation. In some cases, those who use it would not know all that they were saying. In others, the title comes from a more than natural source. Thus, the voice in the cloud and the devils are vehicles of not only a name but of revelation. The high priest and the centurion say more than they might have meant. Clearly, the evangelists intend the reader to hear a message that would have been incomprehensible to those who heard Jesus called *Son of God*. In effect, the title is shown to be somewhat obscurely revealed during Jesus' life. But the fuller meaning of *Son of God* emerged in the community of the evangelists rather than in the community among whom Jesus lived and worked. This meaning is the product of reflection in the early Church.

THE SON IN JOHN: In John, unlike the synoptics, Jesus often speaks of himself as "the Son." For example, the Jesus of the fourth gospel says, "God so loved the world that he gave his only son" (Jn 3:16). As a matter of fact, with only three exceptions, when Jesus is described as *the Son* or *Son of God* in John's gospel, Jesus himself is speaking (see Figure 4).

In the epistles attributed to John, Jesus is called *Son of God* (compare Figure 3 with Figure 4), but not *Lord*. The Johannine community apparently experienced the Risen Jesus speaking as *Son* about himself and his Father. This experience has superseded any memory of a Jesus who identified himself as *Son of Man*. Moreover, even in John's gospel *Lord* is far from prominent (see Figure 2). Jesus is *the Son* who enjoys intimacy with the Father and includes John's community in this intimate relationship.

John consistently recasts Jesus in terms of the conviction that his fellow Christians enjoy the living presence of Jesus. They have been born again through the gift of Jesus' Spirit. Scholars are divided over how directly John presents an interpretation of sacramental life (see Brown, 1966: pp. cxi-cxiv). Nevertheless, John contributes the idea that God begets his children through water and the Spirit (3:5-8). Likewise, in John, Jesus promises water which gives everlasting life (4:13-14). And Jesus speaks of himself in John 6 as the bread of life, saying:

> Just as the Father who has life sent me and I have life because of the Father, so the man who feeds on me will have life because of me (6:57).

As Raymond Brown (1979: p. 79) argues, John launched a distinctive Christian understanding of sacramental life as a means of communicating divine life. No image of God is more appropriate to this conception than the image of fatherhood. Perhaps this explains why the Johannine community sees Jesus as *Son of God*.

Context for Acknowledging Jesus as Son: More than anything else *Son of God* arose in early confessions of faith. As I Jn 4:15 says, "Whoever confesses that Jesus is the Son of God, God lives in him and he in God." This confession, an embryonic creed, is more a heartfelt affirmation of faith than a theological definition.

Subsequent tradition built on this confession, defining divine sonship in theologically precise language. The New Testament confession by itself could not settle the crucial theological issue of the early councils. *Son of God* is a metaphor; what theological truth does the metaphor imply? This question requires extended critical reflection. Nevertheless, the New Testament confession of faith in Jesus meant more than pagans meant when they described miracle workers as sons of god. It was more in line with Hebrew traditions. In the scriptures a person with a special mission, notably the king, was called *son of God,* as Israel was called the people of God. To confess Jesus as *Son of God* was to acknowledge that in him God had drawn close and become intimately associated with humans.

CHANGING TIME-FRAMES FOR SONSHIP IN PAUL: The confession so central in John has deep roots in earlier phases of New Testament reflection, especially in Paul. In Rm 1:3-4 he spoke of Jesus in terms of two sonships:

> This news is about the Son of God who, according to the flesh, was of the seed of David; it is about Jesus Christ who, in the order of the spirit, the Spirit of Holiness that was in him, was proclaimed Son of God in all his power through his resurrection from the dead. (Translation based on *The Jerusalem Bible*)

These two sonships have different foundations. They exist within different time-frames. One form of sonship will eventually have to define the meaning of the other. When later Church councils decided how to define Jesus' divine sonship, they had to determine where to place the emphasis in Paul's statement.

For Paul himself, the decisive sonship is the one that begins with the Resurrection, the sonship in the Spirit. The clue to Paul's interpretation is uncovered by noticing the time-frames in which the two sonships function. The sonship in the Spirit is placed in the time after Jesus' resurrection, consistent with Paul's focus on this time. The sonship in the flesh is situated in the time of Jesus' earthly life, but extended back through his family tree to David. Potentially, this lesser sonship could move reflection backwards through David to Adam and the origins of the human family, to creation.

Pursuing this possibility, Paul does describe Jesus as the link between creation and its final consummation. In I Cor 15:28:

> When, finally, all has been subjected to the Son, he will then subject himself to the One who made all things subject to him, so that God may be all in all.

Paul has described Jesus as "Son" in terms of Jesus' obedience or subjection to the Father. This subjection will bring about the subjection of all creation to God. Paul thinks of Jesus as the obedient Son, bringing about the Father's purpose in creating.

But for Paul the post-Easter time-frame is decisive. When he considers the future consummation, he opens up a question about Jesus' relationship to creation. Later Pauline tradition, represented in Col 1:15 would push Paul's thought backwards in time, calling Jesus the "firstborn of all creation." In the Epistle to the Hebrews, this idea is further developed when Jesus is described as the one "through whom he [the Father] made everything there is" (Heb 1:2-3). Once Paul and others saw Jesus as the One through whom the Father would establish his reign over creation, they increasingly saw him as intimately linked to the creating God, as in some sense always *the Son*. The foundations for the Johannine experience of Jesus as *Son of God* lie deep within the life of the whole New Testament community.

When Jesus is seen as *Son of God* in a deeper sense than the then conventional use of this designation for kings or semi-divine persons, it represents reflection on the new life the Christian community experienced. John and Paul have not only experienced Jesus as risen, but as empowering them with a new life, a new intimacy with God. Through Jesus a new family relationship with God has come into being. Their statements show deep appreciation of this, making it clear that their lives are built on this new reality. How this religious experience of Jesus was to be theologically defined was not their immediate concern.

4. New Testament Christologies Met the Challenge of Time

Christologies answer questions about who Jesus is and what his significance is. Obviously enough, the New Testament presents a variety of Christologies because over time the questions changed. Less obvious is the truth that in important ways time itself shaped the questions. In the New Testament we find steady movement toward a *theological* understanding of Jesus. This in time permitted his followers to part company with the Jewish community. This theological movement was greatly influenced by the passage of time because Jesus came to be understood in a steadily expanding temporal framework.

When Jesus was present on earth, the disciples might ask only: What is he about to do? Upon realizing that he had risen, they first asked: When will he return to complete the work? As time passed, experiencing his risen presence, they begin to ask: How does he exercise his power now? At the same time, they also began to wonder: Was this new life already at work when he was carrying out his earlier ministry? Finally, as Jesus' return appeared less and less imminent, his present power moved into focus. They began to ask: Does this work of Jesus extend back towards earlier deeds of God in calling Israel, in creating the world itself?

This scenario is oversimplified. Some moved to the later questions very quickly. Others hesitated to move at all. But we understand how Christological statements fit different temporal frameworks.

Progress or Distortion?: Should we regard the movement in time and theological understanding as "progress"? Modern people, especially Americans, tend to assume that change or movement is for the good, is progressive. For slightly different reasons Catholics and like-minded Christians presume that the movement that marks the New Testament, and subsequent development of the creeds, was guided by the Holy Spirit, and thus a good growth.

We need to scrutinize this movement to determine not only whether it was true growth, but also what was good about it. Otherwise, we might wonder if we should return to the earlier perceptions of Jesus, to follow him as he was during his preaching ministry.

More is at stake than a sentimental preference for the old over the new, or the more recent over the earlier forms of faith. One thing that resulted from developing Christian faith was a decisive break with Judaism. From that break came centuries of hatred and persecution of Jesus' own people by Christians (see Ruether: pp. 64-116). Could all this have been avoided? No one really knows. We can seek better understanding of the more comprehensive and developed expressions of faith in Jesus by seeing how one question led to the other. Understanding may restrain our impulse to draw conclusions harmful to ourselves and others.

FROM METAPHORS TO CONCLUSIONS: The Christological interpretations in the New Testament, Jesus as *Son of Man*, *Lord* and *Son of God,* are metaphors. Anytime we interpret anything we use metaphors. Metaphors apply a term usually associated with one person or thing to another. When we use metaphors, the Christological metaphors included, we reach a point where the metaphor fails or must be redefined. Knowing where the metaphor fails, or when to redefine its meaning, we gain fresh insight. We clarify the truth the metaphor expresses by recognizing the limits of the metaphorical framework.

For example, a map is a metaphorical replica of the earth, in whole or part. It provides a convenient way of assessing distances between places. But, because it is drawn on a smaller scale than the territory represented (for the sake of convenience), it fails to convey the sense of distance one would experience travelling on foot from, say, San Francisco to New Orleans. Likewise, drawn on flat surfaces, maps do not show that the earth is a sphere. From them we do not learn that one can reach the East by sailing West. Of course, once we recognize the limits and distortions inherent in the map and calculate what purpose it serves and where it fails, it becomes useful in a new way. It is redefined. A significant element in the redefinition is a judgment about what the map really describes. When any metaphor reaches its limit point, to continue to use the metaphor requires a judgment about what the metaphor describes.

The Christological metaphors required unprecedented

judgments. Christians had to decide what their images of Jesus really described. In the movie "The Parable," a circus clown is a metaphor for Christ. At its end, the circus parade begins again, followed by an enigmatic figure who looks like the clown. This last scene represents resurrection. But what does it describe? Is the clown at the end the same clown who was hung up on the high wire? Or has someone else put on his white suit and grease paints? The Christological implications are clear. Jesus of Nazareth lives again bodily. Or, the spirit and power of Jesus live on in those who follow his way. Either or both? The answer is fundamental for Christian life. When we apply the metaphor of "rising from the dead" to Jesus, we reach a point where we will draw different conclusions about our own lives if answers to these questions are different.

THE EXAMPLE OF PAUL: As we draw our own conclusions about the New Testament's meaning, Paul's struggle for fuller understanding is a good model. As a zealously observant Jew, Paul had to reflect on the meaning of the Law (Torah) in the light of Jesus. when he wrestled with this issue, Paul moved to the brink of a complete break with his Jewish past, to a total rejection of the Law. But he hesitated. His hesitation shows the realization that a fundamental theological question had arisen, and that no clear answer was present. Can God abandon his people?

From the opening sentence in his epistle to the Romans, Paul proclaimed that Jesus was the fulfillment of the Law, of all the promises made throughout Israelite history. The scriptures, the prophets, the Davidic anointment — all culminate in Jesus, the new Adam. Jesus as God's gift (grace) is so totally and exclusively sufficient for our salvation that we conclude that the Law really has no place. It is a positive assertion.

Paul does not have a negative counterpart to his assertion. He refuses to say that the Israel which observes the Law is corrupt or rejected. Fulfilled in Jesus, the Law stands not rejected, but displaced. Indeed, the fulfillment exceeds the original. Paul must describe and explain Abraham, Moses, David and the prophets in terms of Jesus, rather than Jesus in terms of his predecessors. Jesus has become the final expression of God's will, the Word of God (a term Paul never uses for Jesus). Jesus realized what the Law anticipated.

Reading history backwards from Jesus, Paul implicitly decides that humanity begins with Christ not Adam. Salvation begins with Jesus not Moses or Abraham. By shifting the time-frame, he has reinterpreted the whole Jewish tradition as a foretaste of Jesus. His present experience of the Risen Jesus has reshaped the past. Some in the New Testament do not go as far because they see the Risen Jesus primarily as a promise of Jesus' return as the Messiah of Israel. But even they now believe that what the Law promised, rather than the Law itself, is now decisive.

In subsequent Christian tradition others have abused the metaphor of old and new. They have spoken variously of Adam/Christ, Law/Gospel or two covenants, accenting the negative. They have typically seen the new covenant, the Gospel, Christ and the Church as implying rejection of the old. They have fitted all the elements into a framework of question and answer, or problem and solution. The old is the questionable, the problematic. Christ is the answer. The old is rejected as evil, corrupt and inherently problematic to create the ground for the new. Within such a framework Christianity is seen as built on a rejection of Judiasm 'rather than as a community of Jews and Gentiles blessed with a unique experience of God's nearness in Jesus.

Jesus' early followers experienced a genuine tension. For Paul, it was building on sand to rely on what God held out in Jesus, if God had abandoned and rejected Israel. If the promises to Israel could be revoked, why not the new promises also? (see Romans 11)? God is trustworthy.

Defining how the new relates to the old might be difficult. Paul had reached a point of decision. He trusted God's older deed because he trusted the new. What to do with the old, with Judaism and the Law? This unresolved issue, frequently prematurely eliminated by later Christian rejection and persecution of Jews, was probably best dealt with by those who moved out into the world to preach and live Christ's message. The early Church's movement through the Roman world (its missionary movement, which is the focus of the next chapter) would bring new tensions and further insight into Jesus' significance.

WORKS CITED

Raymond E. Brown
  1966 *The Gospel According to John I-XII*. Garden City, NY: Doubleday.
  1979 *The Community of the Beloved Disciple*. New York: Paulist.
Oscar Cullman
  1959 *The Christology of the New Testament*. London: SCM Press.
Heinz Joachim Held
  1963 "Matthew As Interpreter of the Miracle Stories," in G. Bornkamm, G. Barth and H.J. Held, *Tradition and Interpretation in Matthew*. Philadelphia: Westminster, pp. 165-299.
Paul W. Hollenbach
  1981 "Jesus, Demoniacs and Public Authorities: A Socio-Historical Study," *Journal of the American Academy of Religion* 49: pp. 567-588.

John L. McKenzie
   1965 *Dictionary of the Bible.* New York: Macmillan.
Rosemary Ruether
   1974 *Faith and Fratricide: The Theological Roots of Anti-Semitism.* New York: Seabury.

CHAPTER THREE

FROM THE LAND OF ISRAEL TO THE HELLENISTIC WORLD

Questions to think about:

— *Why ask where, when and why different Christologies first arose?*

— *How did marginal New Testament Christologies become central for later Christians?*

— *How does a future orientation shape Christian life and belief differently than a present or past orientation?*

— *How does Christology give the Church identity?*

— *Does Christian belief about Jesus lose or gain significance by showing development and even relativity?*

— *What does the New Testament Church have to teach contemporary Christians about change?*

By the mid-second century the Christian movement had taken root not in the Land of Israel, but in the Roman Empire among Gentiles. By this time the twenty-seven books later called the New Testament had been written. In life and worship these books were beginning to rank with the Torah and Prophets as authoritative guides. They interpreted Jesus as both the fulfillment of the Jewish scriptures and the teacher of salvation for Gentiles.

These contrasting interpretations enabled the Christian movement to meet different needs presented by the Jewish and the Gentiles worlds. It had to speak the language of each, all the while trying to clarify its own message about Jesus. In this double task, its own identity and existence were at stake. The various New Testament interpretations of Jesus are responses to missionary challenge. The challenge was to relate effectively to different communities while building up the Christian community.

As expressions of the mission movement, the epistles and gospels were addressed to specific communities. Their authors did not write for anyone anywhere, appealing to human reason in general, as philosophers presenting abstract ideas. As a rule, the epistles name their addressees. Analysis shows that the gospels focused on the needs of specific audiences. Both the writers and the editors of the New Testament tailored their message to meet the challenges of preaching in particular communities.

New Testament interpretations of Jesus have some of the characteristics of political platform statements. This is not to minimize their truthfulness. It rather underscores that God reveals a plan for the salvation of people, particular people. Reaching these people is not a matter of clever packaging, mere style or technique. Reaching people is the heart of the message itself. The political platform meets the needs of particular constituencies. It plays a part in party ritual. Likewise, the New Testament books were designed to rally people to the cause of Jesus, to deepen their commitment, and certainly to limit the chance of their turning away.

Moreover, these books had to be hand-copied. The copyists reproduced works that met the needs of their own communities. Responding to the same needs, they revised and supplemented texts, occasionally omitting anything offensive or unhelpful. In this process of adaptation and transmission they followed the example of the rabbis who passed down the Jewish Bible and traditions. To understand the final product of the lengthy process of writing, copying, editing, and collecting, we need to examine the communities in which all this effort took place.

Different communities, then, provide an explanation for dramatic shifts in the interpretation of Jesus. In the earliest New Testament traditions, Jesus is the fulfillment of Israelite history, good news for Jews in their occupied homeland. In the latest accounts, he is spoken of as the Word pre-existing before history. This Christ before time made the gospel meaningful in the thought patterns of Hellenistic culture where history had none of the salvific significance Jews had given it.

In this chapter, we will follow the missionary movement from Judaism in the Land of Israel, to Judaism in the Diaspora, and then to the Hellenistic Gentiles. For our purpose we will consider each of these three settings as though it were isolated from the others, in order to highlight contrasting perspectives behind the New Testament writings. This is, of course, somewhat artificial as there was in fact considerable overlap and sharing between Jews and Gentiles and between Jews in the Land of Israel and in the Diaspora.

Each time followers of Jesus moved into a new setting, new interpretations arose. These interpretations responded to questions arising within the successive missionary contexts. The cumulative effect of the questions was to create a fairly irreversible momentum crucial for understanding later Christianity. That momentum would be carried much further when the Christian movement became a central part of the cultural establishment in the fourth century. Thus, this chapter prepares us for later chapters presenting the

Christ known in the faith of Christendom, as presented in the creeds more than in the New Testament.

1. Missionary Movement in the Early Church

To understand movements, momentum or direction is crucial. Where is the movement coming from? Where is it going? But, more significantly, what drives or motivates it? More precisely, why this direction rather than some other? Answers to these questions explain the shape of the message and community that the movement produced. To understand the Christological options produced by the early Church's missionary movement we always have to ask where they first appeared and why?

How the Missionary Movements Shaped the Message: Modern laypersons think of the early missionary movement as a Church expansion program. Theologians and Church leaders interpret this work as a movement guided by the Spirit. But the analytical skill of historians is needed to explain the different effects of missionary expansion. Historians prefer to speak of not one but many movements. Each missionary movement had a particular motivation. What drove the Twelve out of hiding to proclaim Jesus' resurrection openly in Jerusalem was not the same motivation as led Paul to preach to Gentiles. A variety of movements, shaped by different social and personal needs, converged in the missionary expansion of the movement created by Jesus' life and ministry.

At the end of the Gospel of Matthew, Jesus commissioned his disciples to "make disciples of all the nations" (28:19; see also Mk 16:15; Lk 24:47). But this scene is not a literal historical reconstruction of a final meeting with the Risen Jesus. The gospels were written two generations after

Easter and reflect the more mature attitudes of their writers. This text, then, shows how the early Church understood its missionary responsibility about the year 80.

Even if the text were strictly historical, exactly what Jesus commanded would not be clear to us. For example, "nations" translates a Greek word which first century Jews would have used for "Gentiles." If Jesus clearly commanded a mission to the Gentiles, why did the early Church strenuously debate the propriety of admitting Gentiles? More to the point, when Jews said "nations," meaning "Gentiles," they usually did not include themselves. As it stands, what Matthew presents as Jesus' final commission to the disciples envisioned no mission to Jews. Yet the disciples went first to Jews and debated whether to move on to the Gentiles. While the disciples felt compelled to preach, and in time determined where and how to do so, they had no missionary blueprint for the expansion of their movement (see Brown 1975: pp. 52-55).

AMONG JEWS IN THE LAND OF ISRAEL: Instead of following a missionary plan, Jesus' disciples responded to their experience of Jesus in light of their situation at different times and places. As Jews, they experienced Jesus risen from the dead. For Jews, resurrection of the dead belonged to the new age in which God would restore Israel and provide a Messiah or Son of David. Resurrection was part of a two-act event. When the first act began, they expected the second to follow quickly. Following Jewish belief, they assumed that Jesus' resurrection was the beginning of a general resurrection of all the righteous, who were to enjoy the life of the kingdom. Thus, the initial announcement of the resurrection of Jesus by the disciples looked towards this immediately expected future. Especially in the Jewish homeland the Risen Jesus was initially expected to return as Messiah.

AMONG JEWS IN THE DIASPORA: Many Jews lived in the *Diaspora,* which means "dispersion" and refers to the parts of the Roman Empire in which many Jews had been settled for centuries before Jesus. Given the bonds between Jews in the Land of Israel and those in the Diaspora, as time passed a Christian mission to Jews throughout the Roman Empire was natural and relatively easy. Paul himself was from the Diaspora and returned there after his conversion. Tolerated but not fully assimilated into the wider society, Diaspora Jews were far less inclined than those in the homeland to think about national restoration or a Messiah. Jews like Philo of Alexandria, a contemporary of Jesus, reinterpreted Jewish tradition to make it acceptable and understandable to their Gentile neighbors.

Jews in the Diaspora would interpret Pharisaic teaching about resurrection in light of Greek hopes of a personal afterlife. Yet living ethically in the present was their central concern. For Diaspora Jews, Christians presented the Risen Jesus as a new foundation for their hopes, and as a model for a way of life leading to eternal fulfillment.

AMONG GENTILES: Hellenistic Gentiles, made up of diverse cultures and religious convictions, were bound together by Roman law and communications. But they also shared elements of the culture that had given them their common Greek language. And they were influenced by Greek philosophical assumptions, that the world was meaningful, that the source of its meaning was eternal and that the truly human life should be linked to this eternal foundation whether by ritual or ethical living. For them Christ was presented as the mediator, the link between the eternal world and this world, the point of contact with ultimate foundations.

2. Mission to Jews in the Land of Israel: Jesus the Messiah-Designate

Sermons in the early chapters of the Acts of the Apostles offer the best examples of the early Christological model that belongs to the mission to Jews in the Land of Israel (see Appendix B). The author of Acts, who in all probability also wrote Luke, promises to "trace the sequence of events from the beginning" (Lk 1:3), to provide a historical account of Jesus' movement. Classical historians, on whom he models his work, felt free to construct speeches for historical personalities that portrayed what they taught and did. These literary discourses were never meant to provide a word-for-word report. But they are all the more significant because they were designed to highlight what the writer thought was central in the speaker's ideas. Thus, Peter's speeches are meant to dramatize the meaning of the mission to Jews in Jerusalem.

Luke presented his own understanding of Jesus in Peter's speech in Acts 2. There, Peter speaks of Jesus' having been raised by God from the dead. Jesus had been exalted at the right hand of God, received the Holy Spirit from the Father and poured this Spirit out on us (Ac 2:32). Because of this outpouring of the Spirit, Peter declares, all Israel knows "that God has made both Lord and Messiah this Jesus whom you crucified" (Ac 2:36). The power of the Risen Jesus, God's Spirit, which is now transforming his disciples, shows that they are living a new life. In Jewish eyes they are already living in the messianic age. The Spirit has been poured out as the prophet Joel (2:28-32) had said would happen in the last days (cf Ac 2:17-21). Because the "last days" are the age of the Messiah, he proclaims that the crucified Jesus has been made Messiah.

In another speech in chapter 3, Luke retains a formula

which draws a more limited conclusion. There, Peter calls for repentance so that God will give them a time of refreshment by sending "Jesus already designated as your Messiah" (Ac 3:20). It appears that the "last days" have not yet arrived. Peter says that Jesus "must remain in heaven until the time of universal restoration" (Ac 3:21). Jesus seems to be understood as Messiah-Designate or Messiah-Elect, as we regard elected officials who have not yet been inaugurated.

Perhaps this understanding of Jesus preceded the interpretation in Acts 2. After an election, even before inauguration, power begins to be attributed to the future officeholder. Thus, we can see how Acts 3 might have led naturally to the interpretation in Acts 2.

In both traditions represented in Acts, Jesus is understood in terms of his future return as Messiah. His present status, Messiah-Designate, is based on this future power. His public ministry, especially his death, has been reinterpreted in terms of the future deeds he is to perform as Messiah. These deeds were inaugurated with his passage through death to new life. Jesus was understood in terms of a future which is presumed to be already beginning, now on the brink of a total fulfillment. The future is almost now, imminent. What remains of the present and the past has begun to lose its own significance.

Time-span of Mission to Jews in the Land of Israel: Jesus was interpreted as Messiah-Designate during the earliest mission. But even more significant, this Christological model is the product of the briefest reflection and lasts for the shortest moment in Christian experience. Those who proposed it were asking, what next? About Jesus, they were sure of one thing. He will be the decisive agent of the new era that God was about to bring into existence. This new era was rooted in all the tradition of Israel, finally settling all the accumulated problems. Thus, all the past had a purpose.

But equally, all the past had become only a promise shortly to be fulfilled.

A Transitional Stage: The mission to Jews in the homeland and its Christological model were transitional. They were overshadowed in the movement into the Diaspora and among the Gentiles. Both early Jewish Christianity and its interpretation of Jesus faded from the scene for a combination of reasons.

The most important reason was that an intense expectation of an imminent concluding event could not be sustained very long. The expectation would either die or be transformed. For the longer we live with a hope, the more likely we are to see it as long-range rather than immediate. When Jewish disciples of Jesus began to speak of Jesus as already Messiah, as we saw in Acts 2, they were already transforming their hope into a reality they felt they were currently experiencing. Those who could not reinterpret their expectations in this way probably abandoned the hope.

Undoubtedly, the limited success of the mission to Jews in the Land of Israel was another reason this Christological model faded. How successful it was is difficult to assess. It may never have been exactly clear who belonged to the Church in Jerusalem. Continuing the religious observances of their fellow Jews, they apparently came into conflict with converts of Hellenistic background represented by Stephen. After the Hellenistic party withdrew from Jerusalem, Jewish converts, other than being relatively poor, were not externally different from many other Jewish sectarian movements. When revolt against Roman rule broke out in the late sixties, two Jewish parties abandoned the city. The Pharisees went north into Galilee and the followers of Jesus east to Petra in modern Jordan. Some Palestinian Jewish Christians remained in Galilee and areas to the north in Syria, but the heart of this community, the Church in Jerusalem was gone.

Finally, Judaism in the homeland after the Jewish Wars was almost as new as the emerging Christianity. The upheaval changed the Jewish community perhaps more than it changed the Jewish believers in Jesus. Although outbursts of revolutionary action continued for seventy years, and a leading Rabbi, Akiba, hailed Bar Kochba as Messiah, the Pharisaic party effectively redefined Judaism in terms of domestic and synagogue life. Both national restoration and future hopes became very remote dreams (see Neusner). Thus, the appeal Peter made on Pentecost Sunday would have had less, if any, impact on the Judaism that survived the destruction of the Temple and City of Jerusalem.

3. Mission to Jews in the Diaspora: Christ the Lord of the Church

No one text characterizes the Christological model used in the missionary movement to Jews in the Diaspora. Most of the New Testament writings were prepared for or edited by converts in Jewish Diaspora communities. They left a permanent mark on both the thought and the structures of the Church that emerged from Judaism. No group contributed more to the Christian conviction that Jesus as Risen Lord not only reigned in heaven but was Lord of the community that shared his new life on earth. They reshaped all the earlier Jewish and Christian traditions to express this conviction.

SYNAGOGUE CONTEXT: Jewish communities, each known by the Greek word *synagogue,* which means "assembly," existed virtually everywhere in the Roman Empire before Christ. The synagogue provided a natural context for the work of missionaries like Paul. Synagogue Judaism, led by lay persons rather than priests, focused on prayer, study and mutual support of all its members. It presented a model for a community of faith under God's law. Not only was it officially tolerated within the Empire, it was an attractive religious option for many Gentiles. After the destruction of the Temple in Jerusalem, it has also been the most workable model for Jewish life until the present.

With special genius, Diaspora Judaism refocused the entire ancient tradition on community life in the present. The God revealed to Moses and Israel became present in the life of the community that lived according to the Torah. The past was seen less as a promise of the future than as the foundation for present life. This pattern of thinking, as well as the actual synagogue structure, was followed by Diaspora Jews who accepted the gospel and shaped the churches of the Empire. They refocused the tradition about Jesus, seeing him as the revelation of a new life shared by the community. In effect, Jesus became the foundation for present life. Or better, as the Christ reigning in heaven, he became Lord of the Church.

FROM TORAH TO CHRIST: To make Christ Lord of the actual Church, the Risen Jesus had to be seen not only as the way to new life but as teaching a way of life. In synagogue Judaism the Torah provided a religious interpretation of Jewish history plus concrete rules for its continuous realization. The Torah provided an *ethos,* a way of life, embedded in a *mythos,* a story of the people (see Sanders: pp. 535-537). The Diaspora or Hellenistic churches taught a new way of life embedded in the account of Jesus' life. Among Jewish converts in the homeland the Risen Christ as Messiah was the promise of future deliverance. Diaspora communities had to deal with life in the present. There Jesus himself had to be seen as the model for living. His earthly ministry had to reveal a way of life as Moses had in the Torah.

Certainly, Paul's epistles offered a way of life. For example, he drew ethical conclusions from baptismal incorporation into Christ. For the baptized, the Risen Christ was a guide for the present as well as one who promised salvation in the future.

However, Mark's gospel made a dramatic breakthrough. At Jesus' baptism by John, the beginning of the earthly ministry, Mark showed the heavens open and a voice declare: "You are my beloved Son. On you my favor rests" (1:11). For Mark, the exaltation of Jesus, associated with his resurrection by Paul, Peter and Palestinian Jewish disciples, was in effect shifted back to the earliest stage of his ministry. Jesus' ministry was revealed to be a guide for life in the present.

Jesus' Life as the Way to Live: In the infancy accounts in Matthew and Luke, the process of making Jesus' life a concrete model for Christian life was brought to completion. In Luke, Gabriel's announcement to Mary of Jesus' birth proclaims his exaltation as "Son of the Most High" (1:32). Thus from the earliest moment of his human existence, he was already seen as he would later be understood in the light of his resurrection. His entire human life, with all his teaching, had become a pattern for life under the reign of God.

THE BIRTH OF THE MESSIAH: Examination of details in Luke's announcement clarifies this Christological model. First, the central assertion of Lk 1:26-37 is that the child to be born is *Son of God*. This is a Davidic or royal title, indicating one anointed, i.e. given the power of the Spirit of God, to rule over Israel. He was thus called Messiah at birth. Mary is told:

You shall conceive and bear a son and give him the name Jesus. Great will be his dignity and he will be called Son of the Most High. The Lord God will give him the throne of David his father. He will rule over the house of Jacob forever and his reign will be without end (Lk 1:31-33).

Jesus' birth, secondly, is placed in the line of extraordinary births, such as Sarah's bearing Isaac in old age. This point is emphasized by the announcement of Elizabeth's conception of John at an advanced age. Yet, Jesus' birth deviates from the pattern because Mary is not old. Virginity is the sign for this extraordinary divine intervention. The people promised Abraham (through Isaac) and the everlasting rule promised David (through heirs) is realized in the life about to begin.

Having surrounded Jesus' first coming (birth) with the same glory as earlier Christians expected in his Second Coming, Christians in the Diaspora began to regard Jesus as having been *sent forth* from on high. They did not call him divine in an unqualified sense. Nor did they say that the Christ pre-exists before Jesus of Nazareth. But they no longer see Christ as *what he will become* but as what Jesus in fact already has been from the beginning of his human life.

At the end of his gospel, Matthew rounds out the picture by having Jesus commission his disciples to make disciples, saying, "Teach them to carry out everything I have commanded you" (28:20). In this command, Matthew effectively tied Christian teaching to what Jesus taught during the public ministry that he has narrated.

This Christological model gave the Christian community a basis for its own identity and life. The community was no longer oriented to an unfulfilled future as the Messiah-Designate model implied. It was able to focus its faith on the present and past activity of Jesus as its Christ. It would interpret Israel and the Torah in terms of Jesus, rather than vice versa. It now had a basis for a new code, cult and community life in this newly emerging creed: Jesus is Lord, Christ. At this point, the break that may have always been inevitable with the synagogue became clear. The Church had become a new synagogue with a new Torah or guide, Jesus Christ.

4. Mission to Gentiles: The Pre-Existing Word of God

Jesus as the Word of God pre-existing before creation is more than a Christological model. In Christian tradition it served as the paradigm, the systematic framework by which other models were interpreted and integrated. It provided the most meaningful Christology for the Church's movement into the Gentile world. In the light of Hellenistic ideas, it was uniquely open to development in response to questions Gentiles would raise. Its long-term success is evident in the way modern Christians assume that the doctrine of incarnation is central to the faith.

Proclaiming Jesus as the pre-existing Word made flesh was separated from the post-Easter proclamation of his future exaltation by miles, years and culture. Between the two positions was a gap as great as that between homeland Judaism and the philosophically sophisticated Hellenism of the Roman Empire. Appreciating how dramatic this development in interpretation really was may help the modern Christian understand an otherwise unsettling discovery. What has become central in Christian faith is marginal in the New Testament. Moreover, where the idea of pre-existence appears in the New Testament, it scarcely has the systematic meaning discovered by later Christians.

GREEK DESIRE FOR WISDOM: Paul understood the challenge of the mission to Gentiles. He spoke of Jesus crucified as "a stumbling block to Jews, and an *absurdity to Gentiles*" (1 Cor 1:22). He had already accurately depicted the Greeks as looking for wisdom (1:21). Centuries before, Greek philosophers, discovering the possibility of abstract thinking, laid the foundations for the Hellenistic conviction that reason was the key to the good life. The irrational, the absurd, occupied the place that moral evil had for the Jew.

To find ever more comprehensive reasons, wisdom that could stand any test in any time, was the cultural goal. It was avidly pursued by some and admired by virtually everyone. Philosophical reasoning had the place science holds in modern life. From this came the hope that the universe itself was wholly rational. It was sometimes claimed that it was founded on and governed by an eternal rationality, a Word or *Logos*.

The Greek mind wanted a basis for explaining everything. Its passion for ultimate rationality could be satisfied only by an eternal truth. Anything contingent, conditioned by time, requiring explanation in relationship to something else was imperfect. Whatever changed over time, whatever grew or declined was evidently less real than timeless being. The reality behind the universe was its pre-existing unchangeable source of meaning. Anything meaningful in this world was only an appearance of the eternal. For this reason, material being was only the manifestation of spiritual being, and the bodily person only the temporary state of the immortal soul.

HELLENISM: AN INTERNATIONAL STYLE: As the "international style" of its day, Hellenism contributed themes and issues for Judaism even in the Land of Israel. Especially for the upper class urban Jew, wisdom and truth became significant concerns. Impressed with Greek philosophy, Diaspora Jewish writers like Philo of Alexandria argued that the Greeks had learned this wisdom from their ambassadors in

Egypt who were taught by Moses' students. In the last centuries before Christ, the Wisdom books of the Hebrew scriptures provided rational maxims and guides for life.

But it is important to notice that in the Semitic mind, wisdom is revealed rather than intuited or figured out by reasoning humans. It is what is taught about the world rather than a hidden foundation for it. Moreover, it tends to be eminently practical and focused on action, not theoretical and the object of contemplation. Jewish thinkers used Hellenistic ideas to affirm the value of a God who transcended rationality. But in the process even they tended to push the divine wisdom, their revelation back before history and creation.

Reflection on divine wisdom also filled a religious need among Hellenistic Jews. When divine transcendence is emphasized, more religious people find God too remote. Some Jews used intermediary beings, angels, to fill the gap between the divine and the creaturely. More rational Hellenistic Jews made the Greek *Logos* serve a similar purpose. The *Logos* was an aspect of God, yet all rational beings participated in it, had as it were a spark of this divine fire. It was transcendent and yet immanent (see Sandmel: pp. 37-42). What the Jew was unwilling to do was to make wisdom or the *Logos* of human experience fully divine, for that would compromise God's unity. Nonetheless, the drive to experience God as wisdom or *Logos* within human reach, a drive Hellenistic Christianity was able to fulfill, was felt by Hellenistic Jews.

Jesus' Pre-existence in the New Testament: A tendency to push the gospel back before history and creation appears on the margins of the New Testament. This shows some concern to portray the message of Jesus as fundamental wisdom. Jesus revealed what had been true from the beginning. This affirmation is made especially in hymns, which were probably used by Christians before insertion in New Testament writings. Indeed, the hymns may be pre-Christian. Whatever their origin, they were edited for a new purpose. They were adopted to illustrate the conviction that Jesus' revelation surpasses all other wisdom.

THE HYMN IN PHILIPPIANS: Paul included the earliest example in Philippians 2:6-11. The vocabulary and metre in these six verses make it clear that Paul did not compose this poetry. It speaks of Jesus, saying

> Though he was in the form of God, he did not deem equality with God something to be grasped at. Rather, he emptied himself and took the form of a slave, being born in the likeness of men (Ph 2:6-7).

The hymn clearly depicts One who existed before the historic Jesus of Nazareth, in the *form* or *state* of God, equal to God. In the next verse, the pre-existent One is identified as Jesus of Nazareth, for "he humbled himself, obediently accepting even death, death on a cross" (2:8). The concluding verses affirm that God has exalted him because of his "emptying himself" even to death on the cross.

Note that the cross has become a replay of an "emptying out" that goes back to Jesus' birth. The truth of the cross remains the central element. Jesus is exalted because of the cross. But the mystery of the cross has been reinterpreted as a recurring reality, a fundamental wisdom revealed by Jesus. The truth of the cross has become a timeless, eternal truth.

THE PROLOGUE TO JOHN: The more familiar prologue to the Gospel of John pushed Jesus' pre-existence back to creation itself. This hymn begins with a clear allusion to the opening verse of the creation story in Genesis:

> In the beginning was the Word; the Word was in God's
> presence, and the Word was God. He was present to
> God in the beginning. Through him all things came
> into being, and apart from him nothing came to be (Jn
> 1:1-3).

Later, the Word is identified with Jesus in the affirmation
that "The Word became flesh and made his dwelling among
us and we have seen his glory: the glory of an only Son
coming from the Father, filled with enduring love" (1:14).

But, unlike Philippians, John's hymn does not speak of
the cross or exaltation. The Word (*Logos*) became incarnate.
But throughout the prologue he is spoken of as one already
exalted, manifest already in creation (1:3), a light in darkness (1:5), finally manifest in the flesh (1:14). God's Word
has now been uttered in its definitive form, but
what is now manifest has been present from the beginning.

In Paul the pattern of Jesus' life was extended backwards as a pre-existing reality. In John, the pre-existing
reality has become the starting point, setting the pattern for
interpreting Jesus' life as the incarnation of this eternal
Word. Thus, in his gospel, John had Jesus say such things as
"before Abraham came to be, I AM" (8:58). John never
again referred to Jesus as the Word. Yet throughout his
gospel Jesus speaks as a divine oracle. And his passion account depicts one who virtually reigns from, more than he
suffers on, the cross.

TIMELESS REVELATION FOR GENTILES: It may indeed
be debated whether the actual source of the imagery, espe-
cially *Logos* (Word) is Gentile. A strong case can be made for
Jewish sources. *Logos* may well come from Jewish efforts to
Hellenize *Torah* (Hebrew for *Law*) and *Hokma* (Hebrew for
Wisdom). But this debate is incidental to the main issue.
Whatever the source Christians used, the structure of the

argument is understandable in a Gentile world. That world has no expectation of a future kingdom or a privileged revelation. It is the timeless world of Hellenism into which Jesus has now been fitted.

In both hymns, Gentile questions are addressed. No longer is the future of Israel at issue. In fact, the past history of Israel's salvation is scarcely more than a manifestation that something more significant has taken place outside of history. Jesus' life itself has become the point of contact in history with a reality that is essentially beyond history.

5. Missionary Reinterpretations Met Successive Challenges

In the end a community of Jewish origins addressed the Gentile world as a whole. It met the challenge of translating its vision of Jesus into language Gentiles as well as Jews could understand. It had learned to speak the language of world and even cosmic history. Without repudiating its original gospel message, that the history of Israel was shortly to be fulfilled, it had begun to say that the gospel was present at creation. It took considerable courage, perhaps better faith, to make this journey.

By Becoming a Church: This journey of outreach and growth in understanding Jesus was not undertaken by solitary individuals. Individuals may have vision and creative ideas. But vision and creativity are dynamic realities. They commonly present two dangers. As we know from dynamite itself, it is difficult to open up new possibilities without destroying existing foundations. Many people tend to be almost as threatened by individuals with creative ideas as they are by explosives. The avoidance of these twin dangers requires an explanation.

Why did the new interpretations not lead to a break

with the old? Why were people willing to accept the new interpretations? Our primary response to both questions is that the reinterpretations were as much the product of the Church community as of any individual. But, secondarily, reinterpretation helped to deepen the sense of community and community identity.

A relatively stable identity is a basic requirement for any community. We do not feel that we belong to any group that is constantly and fundamentally changing its understanding of itself. Faced with fundamental change in a community to which we belong, we often react with a sense of betrayal. We wonder if the community has abandoned us or fallen apart.

We can contrast the early Church with contemporary Catholic experience in this area. In the last couple of decades some Catholics have reacted angrily to Church leaders who have de-emphasized the rosary or Latin. For some people these incidental items were central to their Catholic identity. And they were de-emphasized or abandoned by theologians and bishops without warning or consultation. Traditionalists might have changed more than the bishops had they spent four years in Rome at Vatican II coming to know all the different people contemporary Catholicism includes. In the missionary movement of the Church, the community assimilated new people and reshaped its ideas together. The new interpretations were not imposed from above.

EARLY CHRISTIAN STRATEGIES: It is satisfying to have someone tell us that they got an idea from us, or that we helped them come to it. We are also more comfortable with ideas that tell us we are part of something great or good. Utilizing these common human feelings, the early reinterpretations of Jesus proclaimed that his followers were part of a great and growing movement. Their proponents identified with the tradition of the community they addressed. They empathized with their anxieties, and they sensed their need to feel at home in the wider world of the Roman Empire.

When Peter addressed the crowd in Jerusalem as "Men of Israel" and spoke of events the prophets Joel had said would happen in "the last days," he spoke as a Jew to fellow Jews. Even though he confronted them with an entirely new vision of who Jesus of Nazareth was, he held out a future exceeding their expectations. He implied that everything new was consistent with the central tradition of the Torah and prophets.

Perhaps twenty years later Paul had to redirect the Thessalonians away from the future to attend to present obligations. Some had taken the promise of Jesus' return as a reason to abandon work. Some were discouraged because the promise was unfulfilled and they faced persecution by non-believers. The Thessalonian community had become restless, quarrelsome, uncertain about its mission and identity. Paul's response was to reassure them that those who had died or would die before the coming of Christ would rise with Christ. But the assurance was accompanied by detailed instructions to live up to the model of Christ's own life, both to hasten the fulfillment of the divine plan and to serve as an example to non-believing neighbors.

Paul demonstrated empathy for Thessalonians undergoing persecution and anxious about the future. He told them, as many preachers might today, that they were suffering like the churches in Judaea from those "who killed the Lord Jesus and the prophets and persecuted us" (1 Th 2:15).

But Paul also turned the suffering in a pastorally constructive direction. Insightfully he led them to understand that their suffering had a definite limit. This he suggested by arguing that their persecutors have "their quota of sins"

(1 Th 2:16), a certain limit. Evil is limited, finite. This insight was helpful and typical in a Church that had begun to focus on the present, on everyday life. Throughout Christian history, and for that matter in secular life, groups that accept nothing but a perfect future, a utopia, fall apart. If people recognize that good and evil alike among humans are limited, and decide to work out strategies to increase the good and decrease the evil, they enter the institutional phase that makes longer term survival possible. Moreover, they are able to organize their present efforts to "build up one another" (1 Th 5:11), to face the present together.

Facing the present together, as part of a new community, offers much satisfaction. But new communities, especially, must also deal with the surrounding world, which brings ambivalence. Followers of a new movement have not only their neighbors to contend with. They have their own past as part of that world. No matter how warm the new sense of brotherhood and sisterhood they achieve, no matter how strong the feeling of a new family, there is still a need to relate to the world from which they came. Countless couples have felt a similar need. However committed to each other, they still want their new family bond to receive some acceptance from parents and siblings.

Social groups as well as individuals must respond to this need. We see this even in the most revolutionary societies. After tearing down Czarist Russia to inaugurate a world revolution, the Soviets gradually reinstated the idea of Russian nationalism and an almost religious veneration of Mother Russia. This example is especially significant because more cynical observers explain the shift totally in terms of propaganda needs. That the old nationalism was needed to mobilize Russians is undoubtedly true. But this explanation misses the point. The propaganda worked because the people needed to relate their new society to the older and wider world that was still part of them.

So it was when the Christian movement related Christ and Jewish Wisdom to the Hellenistic *Logos*. After all, when Paul argued that Gentile converts were not bound to Jewish dietary laws or circumcision, his point was that Gentiles were invited into the Church as Gentiles. It was good propaganda, i.e. an effective missionary tool. But it also asserted that the new Israel, the Church, could benefit from Gentile diets and procedures, and ultimatley from Gentile ideas. Thus, the Church was able to go to the Gentiles not merely to save them, to give them something, but to receive what the Gentiles had to offer.

In traditional societies far more than in our own, a person or group achieves a sense of identity when recognized by others (see Malina: ch. 3). Purely private identity was at best fragile. Had the Christian community been unable to explain its conviction in terms that were comprehensible to Gentiles, had it not been identified by Gentiles as holding certain convictions Gentiles could talk about, its sense of identity would have remained insecure. The Gentiles claimed to have explanations for the whole cosmos. They would have asked Christians what explanations they had. Moreover, Gentile Christians felt this challenge within themselves: how did the new revelation about Jesus relate to the old questions about the world? To belong truly to a new community, they had to relate to the existing world.

By Changes in Christology: Modern Christians often focus on the question of Jesus' identity by asking: Who did Jesus think he was? Or did he know he was the Messiah? We seem to imply that Jesus' own self-concept is the only really valid one. We ignore his own example in the gospels, where he asked: "Who do the people say that I am?" (Lk 9:19). We even miss the point that he himself showed little interest in settling the question.

It would appear that Jesus accepted the fact that his followers and detractors would perceive him in a variety of ways. For different groups he would be called to play a variety of roles. He answered John's disciple,

> Go back and report to John what you hear and see: the blind recover their sight, cripples walk . . . the poor have the good news preached to them.Blest is the man who finds no stumbling block in me (Mt 11:4-6).

He would be a healer to one, a teacher to another, an offense to none.

Therefore, it is legitimate to interpret the dramatic changes in New Testament Christology as a series of reports from various observers about how the Risen Jesus appeared to them. Reginald Fuller has schematized the three major mission movements, correlating them with Christological models and the Church's sense of itself with extraordinary clarity (see Fuller: ch. IX). His diagrams show dramatically different accounts of Jesus' identity, role and origin in the three mission contexts. But however different the Diaspora Jewish Christian account may be from the earlier Jewish Christian account, clearly the second builds on the first and includes it. Likewise, the Gentile Christian Christology, which later chapters will develop more fully, includes the first two (see Figure 5). *There is continuity in the development.*

(Figure 5, at the end of this chapter, shows three Christological models in relationship to the three major mission movements of early Christianity. The present models are adapted from Fuller.)

Comparison of these Christological models with each other makes another crucial point. The life of Jesus as the

Christ is tied to the life of the community, the Church that awaits, follows and looks to him for meaning. What is present at each stage, and in each community is the conviction that Jesus lives, that he continues to relate to them. Whether the community looks to the future, focuses on its present or searches the remote past of all humanity, it experiences his presence. Thus, it spells out his role in each succeeding situation. *Jesus' living presence is central at each stage.*

There is genuine change in these Christological statements. The changes must be acknowledged to give credit to those who were ready to ask if Jesus could be a guide to life as the Torah had been, or was at the source of creation as the creating divine Word had functioned. We have to acknowledge that the changes were drastic enough that undoutedly some people were never quite able to accept them. All that conceded, however, the primary change lies in the fact that the band of disciples became a community. As a distinct community, the Church had moved out into an ever wider world. There it broke bread, gave thanks in Jesus' name, and recognized his presence, his life among the diverse people with whom it began to share his life. *How Jesus was experienced by each community was so vital that it was in some sense unique, sometimes even incommunicable to other earlier Church communities.*

Relativity has a negative meaning for many religious people, Christians included. The vast changes in Christology we have shown in the pages of the New Testament and the even greater ones to come in the post-New Testament Church suggest relativism about a fundamental belief. Perhaps we need to re-examine what relativity implies rather than deny that it is at work in our statements of faith. Relativity confirms a fundamental truth about God as Christians and Jews have known God. God is personal, and for Christians the primary revealer of God is the person Jesus.

To say that God and Jesus are personal is to say that they relate to humans as they uniquely happen to be in different times, places and circumstances. If the statements about those different relationships appear relative, it is because God draws near and Jesus is experienced by humans not absolutely, but in their own lives.

WORKS CITED

Raymond E. Brown
>   1975 *Biblical Reflections on Crises Facing the Church.* New York: Paulist.

Reginald H. Fuller
>   1965 *The Foundations of New Testament Christology.* New York: Scribner's.

Bruce J. Malina
>   1981 *The New Testament World: Insights from Cultural Anthropology.* Atlanta: John Knox.

Jacob Neusner
>   1984 "Mishnah and Messiah," *Biblical Theology Bulletin* 14:1.

James A. Sanders
>   1976 "Adaptable for Life: The Nature and Function of Canon," in F.M. Cross et al., *Magnalia Dei: The Mighty Acts of God.* Garden City, NY: Doubleday, 531-560.

Samuel Sandmel
>   1965 *We Jews and Jesus.* New York: Oxford University Press.

FIGURE 5. CHRISTOLOGICAL MODELS OF THREE MISSIONS

MISSION TO JEWS IN LAND OF ISRAEL

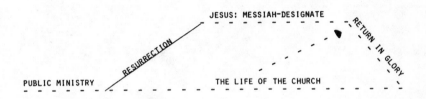

MISSION TO JEWS IN THE DIASPORA

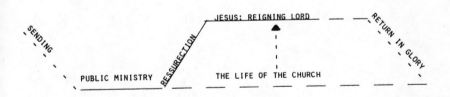

MISSION TO GENTILES

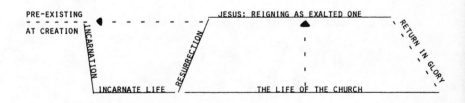

CHAPTER FOUR

INTO THE MAINSTREAM OF HELLENISTIC CULTURE

Questions to think about:

— *What did the Church need to take root in Hellenism?*
— *Why did Hellenistic Christians focus on Christ as the Word?*
— *Why did they focus on the divinity of the Word?*
— *How did the significance of Jesus' historical life change?*
— *Why did philosophical language subordinate Christ to God?*

How did Jesus the Jew come to be hailed by Gentiles as their Savior? How did Jesus whom Romans executed for treason become the center of the official religion of the Roman Empire? This chapter explains how post-New Testament Christians created a systematic statement of Christology suitable for Gentiles. It shows how the Christian movement became indigenous to the Greek culture of the Roman empire. In the next chapter, we shall see how the Church developed its creed while adjusting to its new political status.

Later New Testament writings document missionary response to the challenge presented by pagan audiences. Initially, the missionary works on the fringes of society, establishing a foothold. After gaining a foothold, a new religious movement can either remain on the fringes or enter the cultural mainstream. In the exceptional instance, such as early Christianity, it may come to dominate the culture. To enter the mainstream, the missionary Church had to become indigenous, take root within Hellenistic culture.

Early Christianity's success must be explained by its ability to answer the religious needs of Hellenistic citizens of the Empire. Christians had to wrestle with new questions, shaped by the needs of Hellenistic people. Gentile Christians had to shape a distinctive world view to answer these new questions and meet the religious aspirations of their fellow citizens in the Roman Empire.

What Hellenistic People Wanted Religiously: Divine revelation designates in religious terms an ultimate knowledge or wisdom, commonly seen as the gift of the gods and already central in Greco-Roman society. In this culture, oracles guided common people through a maze of life-threatening decisions. Likewise, inspiration in different forms was taken for granted by philosophers and more sophisticated people. Thus, for some divine knowledge assured salvation, and for others this ultimate knowledge enriched or divinized the good life. Revelation served two different needs, for salvation and for divinization. But revelation was central in reaching both objectives.

How Salvation Differs from Divinization: The need for salvation arises from a profound sensitivity to evil in the world or oneself. The desire for divine life, on the other hand, accords with a conviction that human fulfillment beyond this world is within reach. Though rooted in almost contradictory assessments of the world, these different objectives have often paradoxically coexisted in religious movements and individuals.

The need for salvation and the desire for immortal or

divine life, in fact, flow from different religious drives. More typically the need for salvation appears among dislocated or marginal people. For example, store front churches in the ghetto often have *saving, salvation, deliverance* on their hand-lettered signs. At the other end of the social scale, modern corporate executives, somewhat like the pharaohs who built Egypt's pyramids, often create foundations to perpetuate their name beyond death, the ultimate obstacle to personal power. These efforts are telling indications of the concern the powerful have for immortal or divine life. But however different these two religious drives may be, in the Hellenistic world salvation and immortality alike were typically brought within reach through the power of revelation. Thus, the Christian proclamation of Christ as the Incarnate Word met both objectives of Hellenistic people.

TERTULLIAN AND ORIGEN: Synthesizing what was authentically Christian and genuinely Hellenistic, creating a Christian view of the world, meant portraying Jesus as the Word who offered humans salvation and divine life. Among Hellenistic Christians, Tertullian (d. 230) and Origen (d. 254) provide striking but contrasting examples of how this was to be accomplished. Their creative but faulty formulations were first steps in the most significant era of doctrinal clarification in the Church's history. They demonstrated for the first time the promise and the limitations of using philosophical language to proclaim Christ and the Christian message. A century later, the Church would better appreciate the limits of philosophical language. Then, as a response to Arius' heresy, the synthesis between gospel and philosophical language would come to maturity in the creed of Nicaea.

Christological Adjustments to Hellenism: Tertullian and Origen are proof that the third century Christian movement was no longer merely physically present on the fringes of the Gentile world. It had begun to take root in the spiritual soil of Hellenism. As a culture, Hellenism was shaped by a vision of the world, the cosmos, rather than by a sense of history. As the Church developed within this culture, it had to explain philosophically how human beings fitted into the world instead of describing where history was leading. Its Christology, therefore, shed the historical orientation favored by Jewish Christians who saw Jesus as the answer to the question of where human events were headed, the future of God's people. Both Tertullian and Origen presented philosophically oriented Christologies, statements about Christ which also interpreted the universe.

For the Roman citizen the Empire represented a relatively finished and stable achievement. It included most of the known world and encouraged people to believe that whatever other needs they had would be fulfilled within this cultural and political framework, not by the creation or recreation of a new kingdom. Thus, history would reveal nothing essentially new. Accordingly, citizens of the Empire tended to focus on the state of the existing world. They wanted interpretations of the meaning of the world, not instruction about its future.

By contrast, Jews, the covenanted people of God, had seen themselves in historical perspective. Their history had been the medium for knowing who God was and who they as a people could become. For Jewish Christians, Jesus was God's anointed, the Messiah, ultimately the liberating King. For Hellenism, Christ became the ultimate foundation for the cosmic order.

MAKING DIVINITY THE CENTRAL ISSUE: When they spoke of explanations for the universe rather than directions for history, Gentile Christians gave Christology a new agenda. First of all Jesus' nature, his divinity, became the central issue. Who Jesus was came to overshadow the question of what he would do. Indeed, it was necessary to show that in a real sense Christ had always been the source of meaning for the universe and that Jesus was the revelation of this essentially unchangeable reality. Those who tried to understand the nature of the eternal Christ transformed Jesus' concrete historical deeds into revelations of his unchanging being, his divine nature.

GROWING NEED FOR ORTHODOXY: A second consequence of this Hellenistic concern for philosophical explanation can be epitomized in one word: orthodoxy. We do indeed speak of *Orthodox* Jews. But the term is less appropriate for them since their true concern is right *action, ortho-praxis;* not right *teaching, orthodoxy.* In John 3:19-20 Jesus is said to declare that we refuse the light, truth, because our deeds are evil. This implies that action guides understanding, hence the need for ortho-praxis. In contrast, Hellenistic Christianity increasingly asserted the priority of understanding, belief, and ideas over action. The Gentile Church would say that we do evil because our beliefs are false and our thinking wrong. Heresy trials dramatize how we have more often determined Church boundaries according to creeds professed rather than by deeds done or left undone. To believe that Jesus is the Christ, that the Christ is God, became the foundation for good life, for eternal life.

SUBORDINATIONISM IN TWO FORMS: Finally, somewhat ironically, the world and bodily existence had less value in Hellenistic Christianity than in biblical tradition. To a great extent the Hellenized Church acquiesced in this devaluation of created realities almost unconsciously. Christians like Tertullian saw the world of the senses as fundamentally flawed, while those like Origen saw it as a less than fully real symbol of the eternal. This world and life were subordinated to another world of eternal life. By contrast, in the Jewish tradition the physical universe and the human being were both simply gifts, creations of God, good in themselves, evil only if they lost their fundamental but practical orientation to the Creator.

Later Christians accused Tertullian and Origen as well as Arius of *subordinationism*, which treats the Son as a lesser being than the Father. Bernard Lonergan (p. 41) argues that it is anachronistic to charge anyone before the Council of Nicaea with subordinationism, because the issue only became clear in the controversy with Arius. Moreover, even Arius affirmed the Son's divinity. The basic flaw in these Christologies, not recognized even by orthodox Christians, lay in their assumption that the world, creation, and bodily existence had no intrinsic value.

Every time-conditioned reality in this world was subordinated in principle. They were taken to be pale reflections of the true being in the divine and eternal world. When Hellenistic thinkers looked at this world, they searched for its true reality not in the world, but behind it or beyond it in the other eternal world. Therefore, having blurred the distinction between God and creation, the meaning of the statement "Jesus is divine" could not be made clear. They subordinated the Son to the Father because they assumed that whatever took creaturely, this-worldly form was only a lesser expression of divinity. The Hellenistic Church tended toward subordinationism in two forms, assuming that whatever was human and historical, *whether Jesus or creation,* had to be judged against the backdrop of the divine and eternal.

Thus, in the Christologies of Tertullian and Origen we meet a conscious concern   (1) to define Jesus' nature in essential terms,   (2) to create an orthodox statement of faith as the guide for Christian life, and   (3) a largely unconscious tendency to subordinate the Son to the Father. The first two conscious concerns were probably required to give the gospel roots in Greek culture. The third posed a threat to Christian faith in Jesus as Son of the Creator who placed the highest value on this world by radical involvement in human history.

1. Saving Revelation: The Example of Tertullian

Tertullian's life is usually divided into two phases: one as an orthodox Christian, the other as a heterodox disciple of Montanus (d. 165). Montanus had claimed to have a "new prophecy." On the basis of this "new prophecy" his followers proclaimed that they lived in the age of direct guidance by the Spirit. In this new era everything was transformed; the authority of Christ and the Church were superseded because the higher, more spiritual truth was revealed. The secret of life was a truth, a revelation that offered salvation and freedom from the Law of Israel, the gospel of the Church. This doctrine of a "Third Age" has recurred throughout Christian history in charismatic movements. Its spirit is echoed in Hegelian thought, in the ideology of Nazi Germany's *Third Reich* as well in utopian Marxism. Even before he fully embraced Montanism, Tertullian's understanding of Christ followed this charismatic pattern.

Tertullian's Christology: Tertullian developed his Christology in conflict with the teaching of Praxeas. We know Praxeas' position only from Tertullian, an unsympathetic source. Apparently, Praxeas opposed the Montanist proclamation that the "New Age of the Spirit" superseded the preparatory forms of religion, namely Judaism and earlier Christianity. Before he embraced Montanism, but already attacking Praxeas' rejection of Montanus' claims, Tertullian presented his own Christology. A lawyer and a master of rhetoric, Tertullian was fond of distinctions. He was the first to designate the Hebrew Bible as the *Old Testament,* distinguishing it from the *New Testament.* He had distinguished between a God of Justice in the Old Testament and a God of Mercy in the New. The New Testament decisively superseded the Old because the Son revealed a new attribute of God that changed the human predicament, that offered salvation from God's wrath. He argued accordingly that Praxeas had eliminated the distinction between the Father and the Son.

Acccording to Tertullian, Praxeas had claimed that the Father, God, was manifest in the Son, Jesus. Praxeas stands as one of many bits of evidence of Christian concern to assert Jesus' divinity without contradicting God's oneness, maintaining monotheism. Where God's oneness is respected, real conflict between earlier and later divine actions is out of the question. Creating the world, gathering Israel, sending Christ and the Spirit, are deeds of one God. Emphasis on God's oneness calls into question some interpretations which make the Son a mediating being. In particular, monotheistic faith checks tendencies to see the Son as one who, by being himself partly divine, partly human, established a radically different relationship between God and humans. God's oneness, defended by Praxeas, counters any claim that the divine will in one age could contradict his will in an earlier age.

Wanting above all to dramatize both mediation and the new age, Tertullian insisted that if God manifests himself, or if he sends forth his Word, the Word is real, substantial. (We should notice for later reference that for him *real* and *substantial* are synonyms.) Moreover, if the Word is substantial, then he is distinct from the Father. The Father is one person; the Son is another, "another beside the Father" (*Against Praxeas,* 7; see Appendix C, #1). If this were all

Tertullian had to say, he would have effectively rejected monotheism and replaced it with a doctrine of more than one divine being. His actual position is much more complex. To understand it we have to examine his understanding of divinity and substance.

THE NAIVE UNDERSTANDING OF DIVINE SUB-- STANCE: The clear distinction Tertullian drew between the Father and the Son is easy to illustrate. In fact, he pictorialized it himself, saying that "God brought forth the Word ... as a root brings forth the ground shoot, and a spring the river, and the sun its beam" (*Against Praxeas*, 8; see Appendix C, #2). Lest anyone fail to see the picture clearly, he further asserted that the root and the shoot are "two things" (*ibid.*) When he drew the conclusion that there were "two persons," distinct as "two things," he had to face the question of whether the second was the equal of the first, fully divine. This is the crucial question in determining subordinationism. When he faced this crucial question, as examination of the whole of the cited text makes clear, Tertullian did more than pictorialize his ideas. He drew conclusions based on his pictures. Tertullian was a naive realist, one who was largely bound to picture-thinking.

His picture-thinking or naive realism led him to regard all substances, including spiritual substances, as being in some real sense corporeal or bodily. For philosophers, substance denotes "what" something is in the most fundamental way. For Tertullian and other naive realists, the "what" can be perceived, seen, pictured. It has physical, corporeal form. A plant is a plant if it grows from a root. To determine the substance of anything, its "what," we need only discover the stuff from which it was constituted.

THE SON'S DIVINE SUBSTANCE: The Son was divine because he was made out of the same divine stuff, substance, as the Father. However crude, this statement represents Tertullian's position. Individuals with the same substance have the same proper attributes, the same fundamental qualities (*Against Praxeas*, 8; see Appendix C, #2). Thus, the Son, having been made from the Father's substance, has the essential qualities of the Father. The Son, therefore, is divine.

Before we dismiss Tertullian's picture-thinking, we should take into account that he wrote a hundred years before the Church began to define the relationship of the Father to the Son at the Council of Nicaea. Acknowledging Jesus' divinity without denying God's oneness still poses difficulties today. Moreover, as an effort to show how God's gift of his Wisdom really reaches his people, Tertullian's language about the Word coming forth from God is similar to some of the descriptions of Wisdom in the Hebrew scriptures. Certainly, as religious imagery it is far better than the shamrock as an illustration of the Trinity. With this thinking Tertullian is able to defend his belief that the Son is divine.

WEAKNESSES OF NAIVE REALISM: Nonetheless, the weakness in his picture-thinking became manifest when he tried to draw further conclusions on the basis of his pictorialized account. There is no great harm in picturing God as like a wise old man, so long as we realize the limits of the picture and do not speculate on God's probable loss of hearing, vision or strength. Women today make us all aware that our picture of God has been more one-sidedly masculine than the Bible's, because we overextend male metaphors and ignore the biblical references to God's nurturing and maternal love of people.

Tertullian, however, drew almost fatal conclusions from the pictorial metaphors he employed. In particular, having pictured the Son as made from the divine substance, the Father's "stuff," he proceeded to say that while the Father had the whole substance, the Son was "an outflow [projection] and assignment [part] of the whole" (*Against Praxeas*, 9; see Appendix C, #3), and that the Son was not eternal (*Against Hermogenes*, 3; see Appendix C, #4). Tertullian, thus, concluded that both Father and Son were divine, but only the Father was eternal. In other words, both were divine, even though one was only partly divine.

Tertullian defended his conclusion that the Son was a "portion" or part of the divinity with Jesus' saying, "My Father is greater than I" (Jn 14:28). Later theologians interpret this saying as reflecting Jesus' understanding of his relationship to the Father as a human being rather than his status as a divine person. In Tertullian's logic, nevertheless, to have divine properties, the divine substance simply did not require the equality with God later Christian orthodoxy demanded. Thus, even though Tertullian wished to affirm that Jesus was really divine, his position is clearly subordinationist. His Son does not have the "Godness of God."

ETERNITY NOT ESSENTIAL FOR DIVINITY: Origen especially challenged Tertullian's conclusion that the Son was not eternal. If the Son was not eternal, then for Origen and other Christians he did not have an essential characteristic of God. Again, the contradiction escaped Tertullian because of his line of argument. God himself, according to Tertullian, had not been eternally "Lord," but became "Lord" from the moment when "things began to exist upon which the power of a lord could operate" (*Against Hermogenes*, 3; see Appendix C, #4). Likewise, God became "Judge" only after sin appeared. So also, God became "Father" only when the Son began to exist, and there was "a time when . . . there existed neither sin nor the Son" (*ibid*).

The Son had the substance of the eternal being, but the Son was clearly not eternal, but temporal.

There is paradox in Tertullian's willingness to see the Son as temporal. When he made the Son divine but temporal, we might suppose that he was attributing unique value to someone within the world of time and creation. But this is not the case. For him the time-conditioned, the creaturely, had value because it was derived from the eternal and non-temporal. He was unable to speak of temporal beings as valuable for themselves. Whatever existed in a time-conditioned manner had to be seen as part of the great chain of beings dependent on eternal being, subordinate to the timeless. All reality was finally one because the substance of the subordinate beings was to be found in their eternal source. If Tertullian had not been incorrigibly materialistic in his thinking, he might have been a pantheist. Only his materialism permitted him to see a plurality of subordinate beings.

A Defective Spirituality: On the basis of later Christian definitions, it is easy to criticize Tertullian's naive realism. It is perhaps more just to evaluate his Christology as a Christological spirituality rather than as theology. A spirituality offers a way of life, a method of interpreting the demands of faith, while theology attempts to explain theoretically who God is and how God relates to humans. Theological definition tries to satisfy the intellectual curiosity or aesthetic needs of the believing community. Spirituality tries to motivate the believing community to act. After all, Tertullian was a lawyer, a practical person, and his language is rhetorical not analytical. The persuasive language of rhetoric, common in spiritualities, achieves its purpose when its hearers are moved to do something rather than when they experience an insight.

Tertullian's Christological spirituality was designed to move Christians to act as though they really lived in a new age. They lived in the era of the *New* Testament, when God was manifest in Jesus as a God of mercy, who gave himself for others rather than exacting justice from them. Later, the more clearly heterodox Tertullian, under the spell of Montanism, would still try to persuade Christians that the Church's institutional compromise with the old age's way of life was unacceptable. The Spirit had been given and they were free to follow the lead of the Spirit. His pedagogical method, or should we say motivational technique, served his purpose of stimulating a new kind of moral action and enthusiasm. He wanted to draw people to newness of life by hammering home the newness of the situation in which they found themselves.

SECTARIAN: Nonetheless, spiritualities of this type are defective on at least two counts. First, they are divisive — as Tertullian proves by his own lapse into heresy and separation from the Church. A one-sided emphasis on the newness of one's experience of God or salvation leads to a repudiation of those who have gone before. In Christianity, this exphasis led to a contempt for Judaism, which Jesus never encouraged. It also justified persecution of Jews, pagans and even fellow Christians in clear contradiction to Jesus' teaching and example. Spiritualities that rely on clear black and white distinctions divide believers into opposed camps, the "observants" and the "non-observants." Those convinced that they represent the light of truth withdraw from the more open community, the Church. The "true believers" become a sect.

Admittedly, the earliest disciples of Jesus were perceived as a Jewish sect. On this basis, and because early Church history generally has been idealized, there is a persistent tendency in Christian history to see the sect as the most authentic form of Christian life. Without question, from Tertullian's Montanists to the peace churches today, sectarians have challenged more comfortable Christians to examine the depth of their commitment to the gospel. Yet other Christians may rightly pose their own question: Is the gospel inevitably opposed to all cultures, requiring that believers live apart from others? Or is the gospel to be preached universally? In Luke, for example, we find both views: "Any man who is not against you is on your side" (9:50) as well as "He who is not with me is against me" (11:23). The sectarian dismisses fellow believers who fail to separate radically from the non-believing world. They believe that Christ can be Lord only in another world.

ANTI-WORLD: Second, these spiritualities alienate human beings from their world. They see the world as fallen, evil, their own existence as corrupting. To recognize evil and try to right it is healthy. To see the world as evil and seek to escape it calls into question the good will of the God who created it, or it suggests that an Evil One as powerful as God created it. The motive behind such alienations is often a desire to place all one's hope in God, but it does this at the price of despairing for the world God made.

To a certain extent, sectarians do not reject the world God created as such. What they reject is the world as contaminated by evil, seen as under the power of Satan or organized as culture. For this reason, such people withdraw to form the ideal Godly community. They believe their sectarian community to be uncontaminated, ruled by the Spirit and capable of following totally and exclusively whatever they believe to be the Word of God. Tertullian's response to the Hellenistic culture, which his Christology expressed, required that he be sectarian. He broke with fellow Christians because he could not accept those who did not reject the world. He is the classic example of Christians who follow the "Christ Against Culture" model of thinking (see Niebuhr, ch. 2).

A Contextual Explanation for Tertullian: Why Tertullian spoke in black and white terms, why he dramatized distinctions and gaps in the history of salvation, may be explained by the state of the Church in North Africa where he lived. Though well educated, he was not an academic person like Origen in Alexandria. His Church in Carthage exhibited a tendency toward fanaticism for several centuries. The model Christian was the martyr, who like Christ died for the faith. Authentic faith had a clear criterion: it provoked opposition from the non-believing world.

In some ways Tertullian's spirituality is similar to the patterns of Islamic fundamentalists in our own day. Witnessing for faith is equated with martyrdom because the world at large is presumed to be hostile. In such situations, where martyrdom is a real possibility, those who avoid martyrdom whether by cleverness, compromise or apostasy have real problems. The North African churches erupted in controversies over readmission of apostates and the validity of sacraments administered by those who weakened before persecution. Even those who never had to face the choice saw death for the faith as the ideal, sometimes virtually volunteering for it. Finally, when martyrdom was no longer available because persecution stopped, these Christian communities were enthusiastic supporters of the most rigorous forms of monasticism, extreme bodily spiritualities providing a living death in the name of faith (see Clebsch, ch. 2).

2. Divinizing Revelation: The Example of Origen

If Tertullian confronted Hellenism and declared war on it in the name of Christ, Origen made the first systematic effort to relate the Christian message positively to Greek philosophical thought. Alexandria, second in size to Rome, but more than its equal in cultural influence, was his home. There, his Jewish predecessor, Philo, had planted the tradition of embracing wisdom from whatever source as God's gift. To Origen the gospel was the richest flowering of all the wisdom God had planted in humans. Christ was the Word clarifying all texts. Origen is a good example of those whose model for thinking is the "Christ of Culture" (see Niebuhr, ch. 3).

Before all else, Origen was a student of scripture and the first to systematically compare different versions of the text to determine the meaning of God's Word. He painstakingly collected and wrestled with biblical texts, treating them as a great treasure, but one somewhat buried and hidden. Again, following Alexandrian tradition, he favored the allegorical interpretation, which presumed that texts presented symbols whose spiritual meaning was far greater than their literal significance. If Tertullian personified the naive reader who sees everything in black and white, Origen insisted that there is always more than meets the eye. Beneath layers of textual material, he saw depths of spiritual meaning.

ORIGEN'S IDEALISM: In every way, for Origen, material beings were only the external sign of an underlying ideal or spiritual reality. What was real for Origen, the very opposite of Tertullian, was this spiritual reality, the idea behind the material form. As texts served as a medium for reaching spiritual depth, physical reality generally held a similar possibility. The Platonic understanding of the human person as a "soul imprisoned in a body" was a case in point. What was truly real in the human person was the spiritual reality of which the body was but a superficial expression. All reality followed this same idealist dynamic.

Moreover, the underlying reality was not only good,

but ultimately supremely good. Evil appeared on the surface, in the material world, which for Origen was less than fully real. Salvation was therefore not a problem. His fundamentally positive response to life is reflected in his doctrine of *apocatastasis,* the universal restoration of souls at the end of time to their primitive state of contemplation. So convinced was he of such ultimate goodness that, as his detractors charged, he probably did speculate on even Satan's finally being saved.

Origen's Christology: For Origen the Son is the "image of the Father's goodness." What did he mean by *image?* He was aware that Adam had been created in the image of God. In what way was the Son distinctive? Origen observed that *image* in ordinary speech "is applied to an object painted or carved on some material" (*First Principles,* 1, 2, 6: see Appendix D, #1). He asserted that we may use these material likenesses in reference to Adam. But this is not true of the Son.

"Sometimes a child is said to be the image of its parent, when the likeness of the parent's features is in every respect faithfully reproduced in the child" (*ibid.*) The Son is image of the Father in this second sense, in so far as "the Son does all things just as the Father does." Origen's careful analysis clarifies not only *what kind* of image the Son is, but also *how* the Image of the Father came into being: "His birth from the Father is, as it were, an act of his will proceeding from the mind" (*ibid.*). In other words, the Son as Image of the Father was produced as spiritual realities (ideas) are produced. Origen's interpretation, in striking contrast to Tertullian's, insisted upon elimination of all the materialistic elements in the concepts he used.

GOD AS SPIRIT: At the heart of his argument, therefore, Origen insists that God must be understood as pure spirit, because ultimately only spirit is real. His insistence on this point includes the corollary that *a true image of God must also be the image of spirit*. A material analogy for the spiritual is intrinsically inadequate. The divine image must really be non-material. Here the Platonic struggle against the flesh finds an ultimate challenge. Origen must describe an act of begetting in which pure spirit begets spirit. The primary point is that God is utterly incorporeal, so there can be no division of the divine being. "As an act of the will proceeds from the mind without either cutting off any part of the mind or being separated from it, in some similar fashion the Father has begotten the Son" (*First Principles*, 1, 2, 6; see Appendix D, #2). The Son is in no sense *a part* of the divinity, nor a reality *outside* of the divinity. In some real sense, just as ideas exist in the minds of those who have them, the Son is an instance of divine intellectual life at work.

Origen's contribution to the Christian understanding of God is immense. Yet, his intellectualist analogy, which had some precedent in Greek thought, required further refinement. Unfortunately, Origen did not avoid subordinationism himself. Nonetheless, it is hard to imagine how the orthodox doctrine of the Trinity could have emerged without this analogy. Otherwise, the conflict between God's oneness and the divinity of the Son would have presented a fundamental problem. As long as numbers are assigned as they are to physical objects, to say that Father and Son are God is to say that God is two, or that each is half-God, or perhaps that God is a committee! Only people who realized that thinking does not produce thought in the same additive sense as seeds produce roots could have come up with a way of thinking about God's oneness and the Son's divinity without contradiction.

Is the Image Truly God?: In modern common sense, images and symbols are pointers, representations of the real. Image and symbol were understood differently by Origen and Neo-Platonists. What moderns identify as the real world, the visible world, they judged to be at best a series of appearances of real being, which was spiritual being. An image or appearance of being was true to the extent that it participated in the inner nature of the spiritual world of real being, that the image re-presented. For anything to really "be" it had to have "being" as its necessary quality. *Being* had to be permanent, eternal. Ideas, because they were spiritual and incorruptible — not subject to division or decay — qualified as real being. Indeed, they were eternal, unchanging, and ultimately true and real. Images and symbols did not point to something less real, but to something more real, fundamentally real.

Is the Word, the Son, really real? Truly God? Eternal? Origen responded in two ways. First, he made a distinction. In relation to the Father, the Son is "the image of the invisible God, the Father, being *the truth*" (*First Principles*, 1, 2, 6; see Appendix D, #3). The Word is God's own innermost reality expressing itself. But considered in relation to us, within our physical world in which being appears, he is "the image" through which we know the Father (*ibid.*). For us the Word is the appearance, the image of what is more fundamentally real only to the Father. As image — in relation to us — the Son appears less fundamental a reality than the Father.

Yet, secondly, Origen asks if the Son can be seen as any less eternal — read *real* — than the Father. In contrast to Tertullian, his answer is no. "Can anyone . . . suppose or believe that God the Father ever existed, even for a single moment, without begetting this wisdom?" (*First Principles*, 1, 2, 2; see Appendix D, #4). He buttresses his argument by saying that God certainly would beget wisdom — the Word — at the first opportunity, and of course that this was from forever since God always had such power (*ibid.*). Thus, the Word is an aspect (not a part) of the very truth or reality of God. The Word is eternal.

Having succeeded where later Christians judged Tertullian a failure, Origen clearly considered the Son eternal. But this success rests on a wider and problematic premise. Moreover, it leaves us with a new problem. The premise is that all reality is eternal. The problem is: How does Jesus of Nazareth relate to this eternal Word?

PROBLEMATIC PREMISE: IS REALITY ETERNAL?: For Origen, reality is eternal. More precisely, the universe is eternal. Origen argued that wisdom is eternal, because wisdom is good and God is all powerful. God could have, and therefore must have begotten wisdom eternally. The same kind of argument forced Origen to affirm that the universe itself is eternal. The argument is: if it exists, it is good (since it comes from God). But again, God could never have failed to desire and think into being anything that is good. Therefore, the universe always was. The critical element, however, is that it is the *idea* of the universe (its essential and most real being) that is eternal. Specifically, this whole eternal world of being is created through the Divine Wisdom or Word, which "contains . . . the causes and species of the whole creation" (*First Principles*, 1, 2, 2; see Appendix D, #5).

Therefore, God always had the *idea* of creating the universe as we know it. Did it also mean that the actual physical world was eternal? Of course not. The appearance of being in physical form is time-conditioned and secondary. Did Origen mean, then, that the Word who became incarnate, the Word who took the human form of Jesus of Nazareth, was eternal? Logically, it would certainly not appear so. For this reason Origen, like Tertullian, presents the problem of subordinationism.

PROBLEM: IS THE INCARNATE WORD SUBOR°
DINATE?:   In fact, Origen's speculation on this point was so
vulnerable to attack that his translator-defender, Rufinus,
felt it necessary to "correct" Origen's text to save him from
charges of heresy. In the last portion of the crucial passage
(*First Principles*, 1, 2, 6; Appendix D, #3), Rufinus gives a
notably different text from Jerome (see Appendix D, #6 for
comparison). According to Rufinus' version, Origen says
"Our Savior," the Image, is "the truth, when considered in
relation to the Father himself." But Jerome's version of this
text reads, "The Son, who is the image of the invisible
Father, *is not the truth* when compared with the Father."

Jerome's version of Origen is the clearest evidence of
Origen's subordinationism. And Jerome's version certainly
conforms better to Origen's logic. For that reason, and
because it makes sense to assume that Rufinus wished to
protect Origen, Jerome may represent the authentic Origen. On the other hand, especially in theology, it is not
legitimate to force conclusions based on logic because the
mature theologian knows the subject matter, the mystery of
God, transcends any logic. Thus, we cannot really say
whether Origen drew the conclusion that appears in
Jerome's version. The conclusion, however, that the Son is
something less than the full expression of the Father's truth,
does fit Origen's argument. Accordingly, the Son would be
Wisdom only in relation to us, but in relation to the Father
subordinate, not fully God.

Another Defective Spirituality: Clearly, Origen proposed a systematic statement of Christian faith, theology in
the technical sense of the term. Nonetheless, especially for
Christian intellectuals of whom he is a prototype, theology is
in fact a mode of spirituality. The contemplation of God, the
vision of God is the goal and heart of their spiritual life.
Indeed, from this source more than any other, certainly not

from Jesus or the Bible, we received the tradition that the purpose of human life and the most fulfilling of human activities is precisely this contemplation. Thus, sympathetic appraisal of Origen requires consideration of the way of life his theology was meant to support.

Origen's overriding intention was to affirm the intimacy of the Father's relationship to the Son, indeed to make clear the intimate bond between God and all creation. In his vision of these relationships, it is no exaggeration to say that the Son and all creation were necessary for God. Without the Son, God is not Father and without the universe, God is not the Almighty.

Correspondingly, what is real, what is eternally significant in the Son is "wisdom," "the emanation 'of the clear glory of the Almighty' " (*First Principles*, 1, 2, 10; see Appendix D, #7). And what is really real in all creation is this same divine wisdom manifesting itself. This divine spiritual reality is in everyone and everything. This makes all creation meaningful. The person who would be fulfilled, perfect, must be in deepest touch with this inner reality. Nothing else has real significance.

VALUE FOR THE ETERNAL ALONE: The clue to Origen's thinking is in fact simple, perfectly logical. Origen is in the mainstream of Greek fascination with the *eternal* as the criterion of worth. Whatever changes, corrupts or passes away is to that extent unreal. Whatever is time-conditioned or historical, especially whatever is corporeal or fleshly, lacks value because it is not eternal.

By contrast, God is pre-eminently eternal and unchangeable. God, therefore, must always have had within his being both the Son and the universe, because otherwise the Son and the universe would have been somehow added to the divine. Origen asks, "Does it not seem anything but absurd that God should at first not possess something that is appropriate to him, and afterwards by a kind of progress should come to possess it?" (*First Principles,* 1, 2, 10; see Appendix D, #7). There could be no progress, no development, no growth or change in God, only eternal being. Therefore, at least the idea of everyone and everything, the Son and the whole universe included, always was because of God's own unchangeably eternal being.

Origen's was a beautiful idea. It appeals to many Christians and others. There is one great chain of being, by means of which we and everything else are essentially expressions of one eternal reality. This idea is logical. Moreover, it can inspire great detachment from self and availability to others. But, is reality as simple as this logic? Also, is this monistic vision of the world faithful to the biblical tradition of creation? To both questions, the answer is negative.

RATIONALITY IN SERVICE OF THE STATUS QUO: With regard to reality being logical and simple, consider only the imperial culture that both Tertullian and Origen faced. Origen integrated the gospel into the culture. He found points of contact which permitted the convert from Neo-Platonism to see the Word Incarnate in Jesus as the fulfillment of all his yearning for a rational universe. This vision would also confirm the Neo-Platonist conviction that this was the best of all possible worlds, that everything had a purpose, and that in the light of eternity all apparent difficulties, trials and evils had little if any significance.

This was a world held together by Roman legions. Slavery was a fundamental element of economic life. Those who questioned Roman power and those bound as slaves had no honor, and thus no rights within this world. Certainly, they lacked power. If disturbed by all this, would the Christian or the Church act to change it? Following Origen's logic, they might hope for betterment and even preach and teach an essential worth before God. But this spirituality led into the monastery rather than into apostolic service. This spirituality offered the wordly status quo an ultimate support because it insisted on seeing this world as an expression of an eternal idea.

NEGLECT OF GOD'S OTHERNESS: The Hebrews did not come upon the idea of a Creator God by contemplating the meaning of the world or its beauty. They deduced creation of the world from God's liberation of Israel from the slavery of the Egyptian pharaohs. The pharaohs had thought of themselves as manifestations of the divine. But for the Hebrew slaves, the world was not the best of all possible worlds. Moreover, for those slaves God seemed to agree that the world was real enough for him to decide to upset its status quo. God acted in world affairs. Thus, the descendants of the freed slaves understood creation in terms of God creating humans perfectly capable of standing against as well as alongside God. By creation, in biblical understanding, an "infinite qualitative distinction" (the phrase is Kierkegaard's, the idea biblical) was brought into being. The Creator and the creature are not part of each other; the Creator wills the existence of a reality utterly other than himself.

Thus, the world of this "other," creation, became significant. History is not the manifestation of divine ideas or decisions, but an undetermined course, producing good and evil. It was a field on which the human actors made a difference. Creation is from God, but to a certain degree the created was out of God's hands. On this basis, the spirituality of the biblical tradition became, especially in the prophets and in Jesus, a spirituality in which ethics had priority over contemplation, action over thought.

The Limits of Philosophy:

Tertullian and Origen represent two philosophical approaches to a common problem: how to make a systematic statement of Christian faith, especially faith about Jesus, understandable to Greco-Roman culture. Christ could be understood in opposition to the culture system or revealed as the culture's truest expression. Both approaches had many followers then and now. Their followers, perhaps because they were inevitably saturated with the culture in which they lived, found meaning for their faith in these expressions, indeed concrete guidance for their lives.

Philosophy's greatest failure as a tool for expressing the gospel was slow to be recognized. It lay in the reduction of the most fundamental theological issue of all to a simple and rational truth. This issue, who God is and what is God's relationship to the world and human history, transcends reason. Philosophers, who must work within the limits of reason, have helped believers to raise more or less appropriate questions. But, especially if Jesus is in some real sense the unique manifestation of the divine relationship to the human, rational propositions about who God is must be taken as working hypotheses, insightful, but radically subject to correction. Philosophers tend to think of Moses as one who taught monotheism. The larger truth Moses revealed, however, was that the One God uniquely loved Israel, a disclosure beyond reason. Likewise, to disclose that God had given his Son in Jesus to reconcile all the human family is a conclusion more concrete than the idea that our wisdom is from an eternal source.

Successors of Tertullian and Origen, especially Arius, made their philosophical propositions the foundation for further conclusions. In this they did the Church a service, because they exposed unacceptable conclusions, especially with reference to who Christ is. When they arrived at positions that unequivocally subordinated the Son to the Father, they seemed to deny Christ the divinity which Tertullian and Origen affirmed. Then, the Church as a whole was alerted to a fundamental defect in this line of thinking. That defect was experienced as an inadequate Christology.

But even then, the deeper defect, their faulty understanding of God's otherness and the value of the time-conditioned world of humans, went largely unnoticed. Ironically, they were trying to relate to a culture with a lower estimate of itself and of the created world than Jesus himself had. Their attempt to accord Jesus full recognition was faulty. They were not the first Christians to think that this was the only significant issue. Nonetheless, in spite of both the noticed and the unnoticed defect, Tertullian and Origen set the terms for an engagement between the gospel and Hellenistic culture. They laid foundations for a necessary clarification of what the gospel meant for participants in this culture.

WORKS CITED

William A. Clebsch
    1979 *Christianity in European History*. New York: Oxford Univ. Press.
Bernard Lonergan
    1976 *The Way to Nicaea*. Philadelphia: Fortress.
H. Richard Niebuhr
    1951 *Christ and Culture*. New York: Harper & Row.

CHAPTER FIVE

INTO THE WORLD OF IMPERIAL POLITICS: NICAEA'S ENDURING LEGACY

Questions to think about:

— *What kind of state needs religious unity?*
— *What does it mean to be created, to live as a creature?*
— *What is the link between images of Christ and political power?*
— *How do we reach consensus in faith when religious images divide us?*

At Nicaea in 325, as the Christian movement was in the process of becoming an officially recognized religion, it met the challenge of Hellenistic culture in the world of politics. In the midst of this political development it hammered out the statement of Christ's identity most commonly used by Christians. In the Nicene Creed it decided a major theological issue and created a model for resolving similar theological debates in the future. These three contributions of the Council of Nicaea have direct impact on contemporary Christian belief and life and merit careful attention.

First, no religious or theological reality is altogether lacking in political significance. Inevitably, our most fundamental values support, oppose or neutralize the exercise of power. The biblical tradition from the time of Moses clearly had directly political implications. Yet until Nicaea, the Christian relationship to power could have been described in terms of passive support or opposition. At Nicaea the Christian movement faced the challenge of actively exercising power within the Roman Empire.

Second, creeds shape the identity of religious traditions much as constitutions settle the identity of political systems. Creeds and constitutions are comparable in form and significance. Not every nation has a written constitution, and written constitutions do not have the same weight in every society. So also, some religious traditions do not put their creed in written form. Likewise, some of these traditions, notably Judaism, define themselves with little attention to formal doctrines. But the Church did not follow its Jewish parent in this area. At Nicaea the Christian movement formulated its most fundamental creed, defining Jesus as "the only begotten Son of God . . . of the same essence as the Father." It further made this statement the principal criterion for membership in the Church. For the first time, heresy was clearly marked off from orthodoxy.

Finally, mature religious traditions develop commentaries on their earlier tradition and scriptures. Theologies are necessary, if only to answer questions that arise at a later date. In some instances, commentaries do more than answer particular questions. They may achieve a fresh understanding of the tradition and create a pattern for meeting further challenges. It is one thing to generate new ideas, but it is far more productive to create a fresh model for theological thinking. A new method of theological inquiry has applications far beyond the range of issues implied in any particular concept. Again at Nicaea, the Christian movement produced just such a fundamental theological method. The council not only said something about how to talk about Jesus' nature, it said something about how to talk theologically.

1. The Arian Challenge in the New Political Context

Americans continue to be surprised when religion and politics combine to produce social unrest and even warfare in Ireland, the Midddle East or elsewhere. We do not expect theological controversies to move beyond the confines of the Church or the university. Even less do we appreciate the probability that some theological issues could not have been clarified, or would not have been clarified in the way they were, outside of a particular political context.

Our difficulty has a relatively simple explanation. In modern America, religion and politics still have considerable impact on each other. But they do not have the institutional relationship here that exists in most traditional societies. In a secular society such as ours, religion is an *autonomous* institution. The secular state takes no responsibility for religion. Secular societies do not, as many people suppose, abandon religion. Instead, they limit the state to purely political functions within society (see Murray: pp. 28-29). This provides room for a wide range of autonomous institutions like religion.

In typical traditional societies such as ancient Rome or contemporary Iran, by contrast, only the state and the family are institutionally autonomous. As an independent institution, religion does not exist in such societies. Instead, religious life takes place as an integral part of the activities of the state or the family. Those who perform religious functions within these two autonomous institutions act in the name of the state or the family, rather than on behalf of a religious institution.

Our admiration for early Christianity's family spirit is

therefore somewhat unmerited. The early Christian movement had less choice in this than we realize. It had to function as an extended family or, more often, as a private
association of persons who saw themselves as a fictional
family under Roman law. Christianity was embedded in
family or quasi-family life. In a society that was coextensive
with the sate, it had no public status or power, although it
did have the immunities enjoyed by families and private
associations. This partially explains why it did not occur to
the apostle Paul to suggest that slaves be emancipated (see
his letter to Philemon).

When Christianity gained recognition as the state religion in the fourth century, it became the religious expression of the Empire. Even then it was not an autonomous
institution, but rather part of the state. Enjoying civil power
meant that its leaders would be civil officials. At the same
time, civil officials, the Emperor included, would be recognized as leaders in this new expression of the Christian
movement.

The Political Challenge: In many respects the struggle
over Arianism was political. It lasted more than a half
century until 381, when the present form of the Nicene
Creed was adopted at Constantinople. The challenge was to
determine how the Christian movement would carry out its
new role as the official state religion of the Roman Empire.
This challenge explains why the semi-pagan catechumen,
Emperor Constantine I, became so involved in theological
debate. Meeting the challenge was essential to the unity of
his Empire.

In the face of the Arian conflict, Constantine's goal was
simple. In 313 he had given official toleration to the Church.
In 323 he had made Christianity the official state religion. In
so doing, he had conferred public responsibilities on the
Church. One by one the religious functions of the Empire

were placed in the hands of Christian bishops and authorities. Thus, for example, the Bishop of Rome became *Pontifex Maximus/Supreme Pontiff*. With these offices came civil responsibilities and state treasuries. Imperial funds were entrusted to religious leaders. Disputes over who legitimately was bishop became political as well as religious questions. In short, the affairs of the Christian movement were now matters to be decided within the imperial courts. Disunity within the Church was a threat to the unity of the Empire, to the authority of the Emperor. The goal of the Emperor was to eliminate disunity.

In the interest of unity, pagan and heretical worship would later be outlawed. Those found guilty of such worship would be subject to state penalties, including capital punishment. Being able to distinguish orthodox Christian practice and belief from heretical or pagan ways would be a matter for the law courts. A dispute over doctrine did not have the speculative status of a family dispute as it did in the days of Tertullian and Origen. It therefore had to be settled by something clearer than philosophically oriented expositions. There was a need for a fundamental norm, a binding statement of belief that could stand the test of fairness within the imperial courts. Thus, the Emperor's goal was unity, but being the patron of the new state religion, he had to press for a clear norm of faith.

In the ensuing conflict, the Christian movement met the simpler challenge. It created a norm of faith capable of serving its purpose within the new political context. A creed was produced that could be subscribed to, i.e. signed by, disputing parties as legal proof of orthodoxy. The more complex goal, unity, was not fully achieved. Debate over the meaning of the creed could and did continue. The creed itself laid out the ground rules for further debate rather than fully answering the question raised by Arius.

The Arian Challenge: Arius (d. 336), who had studied Origen's writings, was a priest in Alexandria. It is difficult to reconstruct his views because most of what we know of him comes from his chief antagonist, Athanasius (d. 373). In ancient times, anathematizing an opinion and excommunicating a thinker meant something more serious than post-mediaeval bookburning. It meant that pious scribes would not copy the condemned writings. The writings would be lost. Thus, our source for Arius' opinion on Christ's nature is seriously compromised.

The occasion that led to Arius' pronouncement is also not clear. Apparently, the Bishop of Alexandria, a man by the name of Alexander, had asked some of his priests to explain their opinions "about a certain passage in the divine law" (i.e., the Bible), which says about Wisdom, "The Lord begot me, the firstborn of his ways . . ." (Pr 8:22; see Pelikan 1971: p. 193). This passage had been popular in early descriptions of Christ as Wisdom. It appears that the issue was raised because of Christological opinions held by Arius and the other priests questioned.

EMPHASIS ON GOD'S ONENESS: At any rate, Arius' response, as reported by Athanasius, makes two points paramount. First, Arius emphasizes God's oneness. God's nature required oneness if it was spiritual. Arius speaks of "one God, alone Unbegotten, alone Everlasting, alone Unbegun . . . God of Law and Prophets and New Covenant" (Athanasius, *The Synods,* 16; see Appendix E, 1). Arius was insistent (following Origen) on the non-materiality of God. He rejected material images for the Son's relationship to the Father, such as the image of "one torch from another or as a lamp divided into two" (Athanasius, *The Synods,* 16; Appendix E, 1).

Likewise, he rejected the idea of the Son being "one in essence or as an issue" of the Father because then the Father is . . . compounded and divisible and alterable and material; . . . [*He*] *has the circumstances of a body, who is the incorporeal God* (emphasis added) (Athanasius, *The Synods*, 16; see Appendix E, 1).

In a nutshell, Arius saw any compromise of the unity of God as an attack on God's non-materiality and incorporeality. Only material beings could be numbered. Bodily realities alone could be divided in two or three or more. If God could be divided, God would be changeable. Thus, there was no possibility that God's substance or being could exist in more than one person.

Arius' difficulty is that his notion of oneness is purely arithmetical. When he says "one" or "two" he is always answering the question, "How many objects do we have?" Athanasius changed the question to, "What shall we call the person? Shall we say the same things about the Son that we say about the Father?" If yes, they are one in qualitites or attributes. Their being is one. This metaphysical or qualitative understanding of oneness was the fruit of the controversy with Arius.

THE SON AS PERFECT CREATURE: Arius' second point was that the Son was the "perfect creature of God, but not as one of the creatures; offspring, but not as one of things begotten" (Athanasius, *The Synods*, 16; Appendix E, 1). Later Christians, taken aback by the fact that Christ is described as a creature, probably overlook what it meant for Arius to say that he was "perfect." Arius himself leaves little doubt when he says that God *"begat* him, not in semblance [appearance], but *in truth* [reality] (emphasis added)" (*ibid.*) by *begat* he means that God made him as a Son.

Moreover, Arius underscores the point that he is the divine Son "in truth." For he adds that God made him "unalterable and unchangeable." Clearly, in the light of the importance Arius placed on immutability as a divine attribute, he wanted to attribute to the Son a radically incomparable status among all that God created. In creating him the Father "gave subsistence to his glories together with him," i.e., conferred his own glory on him (Athanasius, *The Synods,* 16, Appendix E, 1). The rest of creation had a temporary share of being from God. The Son was the fruit of the Father's irrevocable will, everlasting though not eternal. He was Son in reality because he was unchangeable, immortal.

THE SON IS NOT ETERNAL: Nonetheless, the Son's non-eternity was the heart of the matter. "He is not eternal, co-eternal with the Father." Arius repeats Tertullian's words, but with an entirely different meaning. He does not see the Word or eternity in Tertullian's material terms. Arius insists that the Word existed "before all time," and that it was through the Son that "the ages and the universe" were created. The Son, as "Perfect Creature" is not really temporal either.

Thus, the gap between the Son and the rest of creation is as great as the gap between the Son and God. When Arius said the Son is not eternal, he wished to establish the proper relationship between the Son and the Father, to say that God is without beginning. Calling him non-eternal was not meant to place the Son within the time-conditioned framework of the rest of creation. We might say that Arius declared that the Son was not eternal, but also that he was not temporal, part of history.

TIME-CONDITIONED CREATION DEVALUED: Here Arius follows the bias of Greek philosophy in devaluing this world, creation. Like Origen, and like his great antagonist Athanasius, Arius regarded the material world as inferior, unworthy because it was time-conditioned. Its reality was only apparent. True reality was spiritual, incorruptible, the idea behind the material appearance. Unlike Origen, who had spoken of the universe as eternal because the idea of the universe always was, he denied that the universe was eternal. Thus, for Arius, even the idea behind created reality was shown up as inferior. Real being, God, does not even have to "think" of time-conditioned beings. Creation, far less than even for Origen, serves as a murky reflection of what is real, valuable, eternal, divine.

Arius' pronouncement that the Son was "not in any way part of the Unbegotten; and that he does not derive his subsistence from any matter" (Theodoret, *Ecclesiastical History* 1, 4 (1. 71-72); see Appendix E, 2), established a double disjunction. The Son was not part of the divine being. Nor was he part of time-conditioned creation. Time-conditioned existence could only be apparently connected with the Word who existed before all ages. Arius implies that the historical Jesus of Nazareth can only be an outward appearance of the Word. He was the Word made flesh, *reduced* to a temporal form.

ALEXANDRIAN CHRISTOLOGY: Arian Christology is one expression of the *Logos/Sarx,* Word/Flesh, Christology of the Alexandrian Church. Arius shares this Christological model with Origen and Athanasius. Later, we will see how it contrasts with the *Logos/Anthropos,* Word become human, Christology of the Church at Antioch. The Alexandrians never succeeded in giving full value to human and historical existence even in Jesus. Arius carried their negative judgment on creation to its logical conclusion.

Athanasius himself saw only half of the Arian challenge. Because he and Arius were in agreement that God is "spiritual being," he did not dismiss Arius' denial of the Word's eternity, as Origen had once dismissed Tertullian. He recognized that Arius' understanding of "God" was not tied to material images. But because he and Arius shared the Alexandrian *Logos/Sarx* model, he tended to focus his own thought on the *Logos,* making Jesus' humanity little more than a "fleshy cover" for the Son's divinity. He recognized the importance of relating the Son to God, making him truly divine. He failed to recognize (as the Alexandrian school in general failed to) the importance of relating the world or humankind to God, and minimized the significance of Jesus' humanity.

2. Nicaea's Response to Arianism

The Nicene Creed: The Council of Nicaea forcefully countered the Arian challenge to the Son's relationship to the Father. But like Athanasius, who became its most important defender, the council was not sensitive enough to the Arian challenge to the significance of Jesus' humanity. The council's creed, so familiar to succeeding generations of Christians, asserts the Son's divinity unequivocally:

> And in one Lord Jesus Christ, the Son of God, begotten of the Father as only begotten, that is, from the essence of the Father, God from God, Light from Light, true God from true God, begotten not created, of the same essence (*homoousion*) as the Father . . .

The creed proceeds (see Appendix F) along two tracks in its response to Arius. It considers first how the Son came forth from the Father, and second the nature of the Son.

How the Son Came Forth: Arius had raised the question of how the Son "proceeded" or "came forth" from the Father when he called him the "Perfect Creature." To answer this first question, the creed asserted positively that the Son was "begotten" as "only begotten," and that he was "from the essence [the very reality] of the Father." This assertion prepared the ground for dealing with the second issue, the question of the Son's nature.

But, the creed further clarified how the Son proceeded from the Father. In a negative statement, it asserted that he was "not created." This ruled out any confusion between the way in which the finite universe came into being and the Son's begetting. Whereas creation implies making nothing into something, the begetting of the Son implies nothing of the kind. This begetting takes place within the eternal being of God himself. In other words, the begetting of the Son, of the "Only-begotten," is properly understood as a unique and unprecedented form of begetting, *sui generis*. "Not created," therefore stands as a warning that "begotten" is used in an unprecedented way.

THE SON'S NATURE: The second track of Nicaea's reply to Arius dealt with the nature of the Son, rather than with how the Word was brought forth. Arius had called the Word the "Perfect Creature," because he understood "created" in "The Lord created me as the beginning of his works (Pr 8:22)" as meaning "made something out of nothing." Following this conventional understanding of creation, the one created, however "divine," would nonetheless be a creature. We have already seen that this led the council to deny that the Son/Word was "created." It nonetheless felt impelled to clarify the Son's nature or essence.

Having affirmed that the Son's nature was divine, the creed had a formidable task in defining what that meant. To begin with, God's essence or nature is not strictly definable. Affirmations of "divinity" are often reduced to metaphors which say only "like God." The creed had already used a series of expressions, "God from God," "Light from Light," and "true God from true God." All these expressions, however, were acceptable to Arians, who interpreted them metaphorically. Thus, Arians interpreted the creed as "the God-like (the Son) from God (the Father)." The council's intention, however, was that the first term in each expression, "God," "Light" and "true God" be understood as strictly identical in nature with the second.

At the suggestion of Emperor Constantine, the council added the description "of the same essence [*homoousion, consubstantial*] as the Father." The meaning of this ambiguous phrase would be hammered out only after the council, especially in the works of Athanasius. It was inserted to describe the Son's nature, otherwise utterly mysterious, in a way that was compatible with the unprecedented way he was begotten. As Athanasius put it, Nicaea "wrote 'one in essence' that they might defeat the perverseness of the heretics, and show that the word was other than originated things" (Athanasius, *The Decrees of the Synod of Nicaea*, 20; see Appendix G, 1). For Athanasius, this difference might be summed up in the statement that in the Son the very "Godness" of God is present.

3. Athanasius' Interpretation of Nicaea

Teaching is always a two-way operation. Teachers communicate what they intend, and their students (hopefully) understand the intended message. Following Aristotle, Thomas Aquinas taught that whatever is received is received according to the manner of the receiver. At times, for various reasons, the Catholic hierarchy has been reluctant to accept the notion that Church teaching depends on the "consent of the faithful." Nonetheless, correctly understood, "consent of the faithful" means "what the faithful understand" (not *whether* the faithful agree).

Clearly, what the believing community understands finally qualifies what the Church authorities teach. In few cases is this clearer than in the creed of Nicaea. Shaping the understanding, the interpretation of the creed was at least as important as producing the creed itself. In this task, Athanasius, who became Patriarch of Alexandria in 328, played a major, and often lonely part.

Circumventing Ambiguity: The problem was that most of the Arian sympathizers were willing to subscribe to the creed, while interpreting its meaning in their own way. To his credit, Arius himself saw the contradiction and refused to subscribe. Athanasius' task was to interpret the creed so that the contradictions in the Arian position would be clear. Likewise, he had to make his controversial interpretation prevail in the face of compelling political reasons to acquiesce in ambiguous interpretations. In short, he had to circumvent ambiguity by getting at its roots. He perceived that the roots of ambiguity lay first, in the material imagery used from Tertullian onwards to describe the Son, and second, in the method of theological reflection on that imagery.

REINTERPRETING IMAGERY: Athanasius proposed a systematic reinterpretation of Tertullian's use of material imagery, especially of the relationship of the sun and its light, to describe the relationship of the Father to the Son. Where Tertullian saw separate bodies, Athanasius asserted identity. Athanasius began with the principle that because God is unlike both humans and nature, all analogies require purification. Of course, Origen had already partially covered this ground, attacking Tertullian's materialism. What distinguishes Athanasius' interpretation is that he perceived that the material nature of the images was not the only problem. Spiritual analogies were equally, though not as crudely, problematic. This insight was crucial because the Arians were disciples of Origen, and understood their imagery in non-material ways.

Of material images, Athanasius observed that though the "sun and [its] radiance [are] two, yet [they make but] one light from the sun" (*Discourses Against The Arians III*, 4; see Appendix G. 2). He argued against seeing the radiance of the sun as an accident of the sun's nature. Rather, its radiance is its "offspring," its way of being. We may distinguish mentally between the sun and its radiance, but each is nonetheless "one light." The Son's relationship to the Father is similar. Athanasius observed that "the Father's godhead being in the Son, . . . he that has seen the Son has seen the Father in him" (*The Synods*, 52; Appendix G, 4). Therefore, there is but one substance, one reality in Father and Son. On the basis of his fresh analysis of Tertullian's material images, Athanasius concludes that it is proper to speak of the Father and Son as *homoousios/consubtantial.*

Arius himself had insisted on non-material models for speaking about God. But his understanding of *oneness* was purely arithmetical. Even of spiritual realities or essences, he asked, "How many do we have?" On this basis, he concluded that the divinity of the Son was an "other" divinity beside that of the Father, or more accurately after that of the Father. He rightly insisted that spiritual realities are indivisible, but persisted in counting them as material objects.

Athanasius pointed out that the light of the sun and its radiance were but one light. In so doing, he transcended the arithmetical notion of oneness. He judged that the metaphysical being or essence of each was not a material object but rather an object known by those who assessed the nature of the material objects. We say we have one metaphysical reality when we answer the question, "Do we call this reality by the same name wherever it appears or occurs?" In other words, it is not enough to say that God is a spiritual being. It is also necessary to purify our conceptions of spiritual beings of attributes found in human and natural beings, notably arithmetical number.

THEOLOGICAL METHOD: Athanasius' breakthrough was the insight that theological language must dispense with the specific content of both ordinary (often materialist imagery) and philosophical (often non-material concepts) language. If the theologian is to speak properly about God, who radically transcends the physical world and human experience, the images *and* the concepts drawn from other sources must be transcended. Undoubtedly, others besides Athanasius perceived the need to reshape language to speak of the transcendent. Certainly, Arius recognized it, because he had stretched his own categories out of shape in speaking of a "perfect creature." What is unique about Athanasius was that he discovered a new way of using concepts in theology. He produced a revolution in theological *method.*

Athanasius discovered that theological concepts may be used as heuristic tools, as devices to find the truth of various statements rather than as statements of truth. A heuristic tool functions like "x" and "y" in an algebraic equation. It does not describe what the unknowns are, only the relationships that exist between two unknowns. Athanasius explains the meaning of the *homoousios/consubstantial* as though it were an algebraic function. His explanation of this term demonstrates his theological method.

Thus, according to Athanasius, to say that the Son was of the same substance as the Father is to insist that "the same things are said of the Son, which are said of the Father, except his being said to be Father" (*Discourses Against The Arians*, 4; Appendix G, 2). The formula functions as an equation. It does not say what the Father's nature is. There is no specific content ascribed to the concept "divinity." All that is said is that *however divinity is understood* it is to be affirmed without distinction except in name for both persons. This is a rule for theological thinking, or more properly for making theological judgments (and not an idea or a concept) about the nature of God or the nature of the Son.

Homoousios was itself an ambiguous term. It was opposed because it was clearly unbiblical and because it had been associated with heretical teachings. Athanasius bypassed its earlier conceptual meanings. He showed that while the concept was not in the scriptures, using the concept in his fashion permitted us to make proper interpretations of apparent contradictions in scripture. He made it into a tool for finding the truth in any number of statements that might be made about the relationship of Father and Son. In so doing, he laid the foundations for the development of theology as a science, a systematic study capable of producing and evaluating its own conclusions.

4. Political Implications of the Struggle after Nicaea

Athanasius explained and defended Nicaea in and out of exile until his death. Struggling for an unambiguously strict interpretation of Nicaea's "begotten . . . not made," he confronted Arians and semi-Arians who preferred ambiguity. Why did the conflict last more than half a century? What made the ambiguous interpretations of the Arians attractive? We have one important clue. The clue is that for the most part the Arians and semi-Arians enjoyed imperial favor.

Why? The simplest explanation is that it was easier to identify imperial power with divine power if the Son's relationship to the Father was ambiguous. If the Son was "somehow divine," the Emperor might also be "somehow divine." The Arian party inclined to ambiguity because it legitimated the hierarchical political and social structure which it took for granted. In turn, the political establishment recognized its natural allies. This was not so much a matter of a conscious conspiracy, as it was a matter of widely shared convictions about how heavenly hierarchies were reflected in earthly hierarchies.

A strict interpretation of the "begotten . . . not made" undercut those widely shared convictions. Athanasius read Nicaea so as to imply an infinite gap between God and the world, between the unbegotten God and all creation. He insisted that it meant that the Only-begotten of God has being in a radically different manner than created beings in the world. There is no third option, no intermediate form of being, between divinity and creaturehood. There is no quasi-divinity or share in divinity in any created entity or person. The notion of a quasi-divine Church, or more to the point, quasi-divine Emperor, is radically undercut by the strict interpretation. The created world in its entirety, is "made from nothing," radically "other" than the Creator. The universe is not an emanation of God, but is the "other" that God created. It is not divine, whether considered in its entirety or in a hierarchy of beings more or less sharing divine being.

NO HIERARCHY OF BEINGS: In a hierarchical society such as the Roman Empire, those in power are highly motivated to endorse and suppport the idea of a chain of being from God down to the lowest form of being. Within the society itself the powerful obviously are placed above others. Given this fact, to assert that beings exist in a hierarchy places them on a rung of the ladder between God and lesser mortals. Especially in the eastern world, this gave rise to the notion, in time adopted by the Roman Emperors, that the ruler was divine or a son of God. Minimally, it suggested that divine life flows through a hierarchy, with those in power somewhat more privileged.

To say that there is no third option between God and creation implies that the divine being is one reality and that created beings, however hierarchically stratified among themselves, are something altogether different. Earthly hierarchies of beings are not part of an infinite chain of being. The only link between the infinite and the finite is that the infinite created the finite. The finite world and its leaders have no share in divinity.

Ironically, if the created world is in no sense divine, then it is permitted and required to be simply "created," and it has value as "created." When we accept the radical distinction between Creator and universe implied in Nicaea's understanding of how the Only-begotten of the Unbegotten exists, we have to say that the world is not sacred, that none of its institutions are sacred. But we also leave room for non-sacred, secular realities to be considered valuable in and of themselves.

POLITICAL GOODNESS WITHOUT SACRALITY: If secular realities are considered valuable, but possessing no divine qualities, political power is not sacred power. Political institutions are valuable. But they have the value of created "goods," limited "goods." They are good for what they do, not for their status as part of a divine chain of being.

Often, the political "good" has been summed up as "the art of the possible." In the exercise of power, God is not directly at work, creatures are. What is achieved, even what is aimed at, is never an ultimate good, but rather the creaturely good. The Christian is encouraged to full participation in this-worldly life. But the Christian is also commanded by the First Commandment not to treat any feature of this life as identical with God's will or even nearly identical with it. The political arena provides an opportunity for goodness — but no opportunity for perfection, much less an arena that is sacred or divine.

In the Christendom inaugurated by Constantine, the principle that this-worldly power is good but not sacred would be violated as often as it was honored. Christian rulers, of both Church and state, would sacralize their power, identifying obedience to themselves with obedience to God. Anti-worldly ascetics would also ignore Nicaea's definition of the Son's relationship to the Father. For when ascetics denounce the world, they call into question Nicaea's implication that creatures, humans included, are called only to be creatures and not to renounce the world of creatures for that of the Creator. Thus, creation theology, implied in what Nicaea said of the Son's relationship to the Father, was the necessary foundation, however much it was neglected, for an ethic of authentic Christian life within the world of the Empire.

POLITICAL IMPACT OF NICAEA: The Christian imperial framework demanded of the Church theological and doctrinal clarity. Ironically, the Christian movement met this demand at Nicaea, but at the Empire's expense. For Nicaea provided a formula that served theological requirements far better than it provided the unity which political authorities desired. The immediate result of Nicaea was a half-century of strife.

In the longer run, the political requirement for a formula that would stand the test of fairness in discriminating between true and false positions in the law courts was even more disappointing. Nicaea introduced a style of dogmatic statements aimed at legal clarity. These statements have followed one another, being used in heresy trial after heresy trial. In each trial the contentious parties responded as the Arians and semi-Arians did to Nicaea's formula, convinced that the dogmatic statement supported their position. Thus, dogmatic decrees have more often justified disputes than settled them. Constantine's assumption that a divided Christian movement was politically disruptive was correct. He nonetheless set the stage, not for unity, but for Act One in a now centuries-long drama, when he called the bishops together at Nicaea to settle things once and for all.

5. Nicaea's Theololgical Achievement

The new theololgical clarity achieved at Nicaea served its properly theological purpose far better than its political objective. The growth in theological insight, specifically insight into how theological argument should be governed, was at odds with the imperial political need for order. It may be more compatible with the democratic political need for freedom, but this possibility would scarcely have occurred to Constantine or to other Christians for more than a thousand years.

A FORMULA FOR CHRISTOLOGICAL INQUIRY: Nicaea provided, especially in Athanasius' interpretation, an explanation and a legitimation for further inquiry about who Christ was. What was established at Nicaea was basic and elemental, something like Einstein's principle of relativity. Here was a formula for asking who Christ was, for talking about Jesus by later believers who might hold quite different understandings of what the words "divinity" and "human" meant. The formula equates the Son with the Father, and does no more. It authorizes Christians to devise any Christological statement that follows its simple equation that what is said of the Father is also said of the Son. The Nicene Creed provides, not a doctrine about Christ, but rather a logic — if you will, a theo-logic — for possible doctrines. As to content, it is open-ended, giving only the rules for the game.

A FORMULA FOR THEOLOGICAL OPENNESS: Theology, the study of God, was as radically affected by Nicaea as Christology. Nicaea radically reaffirmed the idea of God as Creator. But when the creed used a phrase that meant, "whatever is said of the Father," it acknowledged that the content of statements about God is also ultimately beyond definition. Theology is radically open-ended. No created analogy exists to adequately represent "what the Father is."

If we follow Athanasius' interpretation of Nicaea, here Christian thought probed *matter* (Tertullian) and *mind* (Origen) and delivered the verdict that what God is radically transcends both matter and spirit, as humanly known. God may be affirmed and acknowledged, but not described or defined. Except for one strangely overlooked possibility, the creed of Nicaea could be taken as the foundation for a general agnosticism, a fundamental unkowability, in reference to God.

The overlooked possibility is that the equation, "what must be said of the Father must be said of the Son" refers, in fact, to the historical figure of Jesus of Nazareth. This is the Jesus who suffered and died under Pontius Pilate. It is this Jesus who is clearly identified as the eternal Son. He is the subject of the discussion at Nicaea. This suffering and dying Jesus, then, is the one who is identified as being what God in essence is. Even while the creed remains apparently virtually agnostic as to what God might be, it asserts this identification of Jesus with whatever God is.

The creed knows only one thing to say with certainty about God: God is this man Jesus, this Jesus in the historical direction of his life, a life that led through suffering and death. Neither in mind nor matter is God revealed. God is revealed only in history, and specifically in this history. As we will see in the next chapter, this conclusion was largely overlooked at Nicaea and by Athanasius, even though they pointed in this direction.

Into the Imperial Arena: In the Nicene period the Christian movement entered the imperial arena. It moved out from the Hellenistic world of the academy even as it had once moved out from the synagogue. It required a theory for its activity and its newly given power. But it struggled at the surface level then and in succeeding centuries with questions from the Hellenistic schools: How do we make sense of Christian belief? How do we achieve logical consistency at the theoretical level? At Nicaea and in some of Athanasius' brilliant insights, it began to grasp the fact that the meaning of Christ was the meaning of history itself, of action aimed at recreating the world itself. Forces within both the Church and the Empire obstructed the vision of this mission, but this vision of who Christ was created openings for growth into the distant future. In our own age, these openings have become central concerns.

WORKS CITED

John Courtenay Murray
    1965 *The Problem of Religious Freedom*. London: Geoffrey Chapman.
Jaroslav Pelikan
    1971 *The Christian Tradition I: The Emergence of the Catholic Tradition (100-600)*. Chicago: Univ. of Chicago Press.

CHAPTER SIX

CREATING THE CHRISTIAN SOCIETY: CHRIST IN HUMAN HISTORY AT CHALCEDON

Questions to think about:

— *Why was it difficult for pious Christians in a Christian society to accept Jesus' humanity?*
— *Why is Christian identity at risk in a Christian society?*
— *How did conflicting schools of theology advance growth in faith?*
— *What are the links between Eucharist, politics and creed?*

At Nicaea the Christian movement faced an emergency situation. In its first foray into the world of imperial politics, it maintained its doctrinal integrity. Better, it clarified its theological methods. But this success capped the first engagement in a long campaign. Having become an integral part of the Roman Empire, the Christian movement had to either make the Empire Christian or accept its own eventual subordination to the imperial system. This Empire had condemned and executed Jesus. To properly assess its relationship to these political and social institutions, the Church had to come to terms with the human life of Jesus. The challenge after Nicaea was to grasp the meaning of Jesus' humanity while building a Christian society consistent with his involvement in human history.

Jesus' full humanity was clearly affirmed at the Council of Chalcedon in 451. This council arranged a truce between rival schools of theology centered respectively in Alexandria and Antioch. These schools fought for different interpretations of the relationship between Jesus' humanity and divinity. But they also differed over another fundamental issue. The second issue dividing them was whether the relationship of the world to God would follow lines set by pagan piety or by biblical faith. In the struggle over Jesus' humanity, this second issue was never fully addressed, though it did affect Chalcedon's resolution of the question of Jesus' humanity.

1. Understanding Jesus' Humanity to Christianize Society

Modern Christians rightly find part of the challenge that confronted Christians of the fourth and fifth centuries alien. We too want to know the meaning of Jesus' humanity to understand our own responsibilities in human history. But we no longer live in or wish to live in a Christian society. Indeed, to insure its own freedom, the Christian movement had increasingly found it necessary to insist on religiously neutral social and political systems. This is clear in the Church's confrontations with modern forms of totalitarianism. The Christian society is not the answer to the anti-Christian society. Rather, as we have learned, a limited and religiously neutral state is a better base for Christian freedom.

Nonetheless, throughout the Middle Ages, Christians lived in social and political systems in which religiously committed states were taken for granted. The Church could not be imagined as an autonomous institution. Society itself operated as an integrated system. Christians either took responsibility for the rest of society or withdrew. To function socially, the Church had to attempt a synthesis of the gospel and all of life. No better illustration of this attempt exists than the theology of Thomas Aquinas. No sadder examples of its limitations exist than the crusades and the Avignon papacy. Note that the best example is contained in a book, while the worst examples come from actual life. So practical a problem took centuries of experience to be worked out.

Christendom, Christ and Pious Christians: Three post-Nicaea developments need explanation. The Christian movement became an established Church; it attempted to build a Christian society; and in this process it tended to question Jesus' humanity. The link between these developments was a model of the God-world relationship shaped by the social and political relationships of the Roman Empire. The social cement that bound members of the Roman Empire to one another was their sense of *piety*. Almost without reflection the Church integrated this virtue into its own value system. Christians culturally disposed to be pious created the vast synthesis of faith and life, Church and society, which has come to be known as Christendom.

But, pious Christians also diminished Jesus' humanity in the interest of building Christendom. They preferred to see the Church as the embodiment of the heavenly kingdom, and to see Jesus as the heavenly human (an ultimately heavenly human). They focused on the presence of the divine in created and human forms, rather than on the human and created as God's always new work and gift. They did not deny Jesus' humanity, but they permitted it to recede into the background. They considered his humanity less significant than his divinity. They did not deny the human limitations of the Church and Christian society, but they preferred to focus on their divine or supernatural dimensions. Only when Jesus' humanity was explicitly denied could such pious Christians be forced to reaffirm it.

PIETY A PAGAN VIRTUE: It is difficult for us to use the terms *pagan* or *piety* as purely technical descriptions without making value judgments on them. We tend to see *pagan* as inferior and *piety* as good. I want to argue that *piety* is *pagan*. This requires a rather technical definition of *piety* in which we should abstain from value judgments for the sake of understanding its dynamics.

Piety is, first of all, devotion or loyalty to parents. Commonly, it is expressed by the son's wish to be like his father. In political and social life, piety requires honor to all one's superiors as to one's father. In its more specifically religious expression, it is devotion to God on the model of the son's responsibility to his father. Thus, piety finds in the human family and social order a model of the order of the universe. It sees a hierarchical model of social relationships with God at the apex.

Piety represents a value system at odds with the values inculcated by biblical faith in God as Creator. It tends to deny the "radical otherness" of God, because it fits God into the ordinary scheme of social and political relationships. For the pious, the world reflects God, while the idea of creation asserts that God made it freely, as other than himself. For the pious, God is "Supreme"; in creation, God is "Other."

WHY SACRIFICE?   Religious ritual, especially sacrifice, is a dramatic representation of the way people understand the divine to human relationship. Throughout the Hebrew scriptures, the prophets fairly constantly condemn sacrifices, while the people offered them and the sacred writings elsewhere command them. Why? It is too simple to say that the rituals were empty, that the people did not mean them. The problem was rather what they meant. Sacrifices may be offered for two rather different, opposed reasons. Sacrifices, on the one hand, may be offered to gain divine favor, typically at the beginning of the year. The fertility rituals of the ancient world employed "sympathetic magic." They were dramas representing God impregnating the earth at the beginning of the New Year, designed to gain a good harvest. God was ritually manipulated, induced to perform for those who carry out the ritual. The target of the prophets was sacrifice of this kind.

On the other hand, the Israelites were commanded to offer sacrifices of thanksgiving, tithes of their produce, *after* the harvest. What they had been given was to be returned, not to gain more but in recognition that it was God's gift. To further bring home the point that God was not to be manipulated, the sacrifice or tithe was to be given regardless of whether the harvest was abundant or not. What was given in sacrifice was given for the use of the Levites, who had no land, and for distribution to the needy. In other words, sacrificial offerings were meant to serve the cause of economic justice. If such sacrifice changed anything, it changed human beings not God. God was not to be manipulated by ritual. God did not follow the human rules of reciprocating gifts. God was "Other," "Holy."

JESUS IN PROPHETIC TRADITION: Throughout the gospels Jesus reiterates the prophetic view of God's relationship to humans in various ways. The parables of the kingdom of God emphasize its unpredictable character (see, e.g. Mk 4:26-29; Lk 12:16-21, 39-41, 13:18-19, 20-21; Mt 13:3-9, 24-30, 44-46). Those invited to the banquet are not the expected guests (Lk 14:15-24). The Father embraces both the prodigal and the elder son — neither of whom is especially "worthy" (Lk 15:11-32). But above all, Jesus attacks those who try to manipulate God by pious observances or hope to do so through sacrifice. In Jesus' spirit the New

Testament frequently describes Christian worship as "eucharist" (which means "giving thanks"), but never as "sacrifice."

Jesus' statement, "The Son of Man is Lord of the Sabbath" (Mk 2:28), may mean that Jesus is Lord of the Sabbath or, as he interprets it himself, "The Sabbath is made for man, not man for the Sabbath" (Mk 2:27). Either way, Jesus' God provides religious observances for humans, not for his own honor. Humans do not take on divine powers, but rather become their own better selves.

This is the core of the biblical understanding of creation. God is the unique Father, who decides to generate genuinely new life. He does not want to reproduce himself, but to create an "other," a collaborator. In contrast to pagan piety, which would require that God be the source of all knowledge, rabbinic Judaism even had the imagination to suggest that God studies his own Torah alongside humans. The course of human history is thought of as outside of the divine life itself, not a representation or replay of something divine. It is a new life given by God. The Creator is thanked for human life and history, not found within it. In this world there is something other than God that is good, worthy of celebration even though quite finite.

2. Conflicting Schools of theology

Theological reflection and development after Nicaea was dominated by two schools representing Alexandria and Antioch. These ancient Christian bishoprics competed for influence in the East with each other and with the emerging imperial city of Constantinople. In Alexandria, home of Origen and Athanasius, the more explicit statements of Nicaea, its more conscious positions, were affirmed and elaborated. In Antioch, Nicaea's implicit affirmation of faith in the biblical Creator God was better represented.

The Alexandrians and the Antiochenes are distinguished by their different philosophical perspectives, these being their "academic" trademarks. In the end, this academic divergence was significant only to the degree that it furthered the debate between them. For at Chalcedon, philosophically neutral "dogmatic realism" became the Christian norm. At that point, the religious positions of each school were accepted while their philosophical excesses were minimized. Nonetheless, both the emergent dogmatic norm and popular piety tended to give the final edge to the Alexandrians, without completely denying the counterposition of the Antiochenes. Such is the outline of the plot that follows in detail.

Alexandria: Logos/Sarx Christology: Christ as the Word-made-flesh, *Logos/Sarx,* dominated Alexandrian Christology. In the spirit of Neo-Platonist philosophy, the Alexandrians looked beyond the literal details of scripture for its underlying spiritual reality, its allegorical meaning. The text was a code to be deciphered, a shell encasing eternal divine wisdom. Likewise all the other details of human existence in history were to be similarly deciphered to get at their eternal meaning. Thus, Jesus was also seen as the fleshly appearance of the divine *Logos* or Word. He was the Word who had taken on flesh. The Word functioned as if it were the soul within a human body.

At home with inner eternal realities, the Alexandrians focused on Jesus' divinity, not his outward historical personality. The eternal Word was real, the historical person a somewhat shadowy reality. Given this approach, the Alexandrians had little difficulty in seeing Christ's person as a unified reality. The inner divine reality was pre-eminently real, and all else, historical or human, was explainable in terms of this divinity. In this they stood in rather sharp contrast to the Antiochenes, who had difficulty explaining how Jesus' human and divine natures constituted a single person.

ROOTS OF THE ALEXANDRIAN POSITION IN THE EUCHARIST: While the Alexandrians certainly read the gospels in the spirit of Plato, their position was also rooted in Christian worship, especially in the Eucharist. The Eucharist was no longer seen as a communal meal in which Jesus was present in the sharing (the breaking) of the bread among his disciples. It had come to be seen as a re-presentation of Calvary (now still understood itself as a sacrifice) and of the presence of the glorified and risen Lord in the bread and wine offered. Its deepest meaning, consistent with allegory, was now the appearance or presence of Christ in the bread and wine. The obvious response to the Eucharist understood in this way was to contemplate the inner divine reality. The Eucharist was the effective sign of God's nourishing presence in human life. So also was Christ, the sign of God's presence in fleshly form.

An attitude of awe, rather than a spirit of service and community, characterized this developing Eucharistic celebration. Ritual was elaborated and embellished to dramatize the point that on the altar divinity makes its appearance. Nothing borrowed from the Byzantine court of the Emperor was too fine. Gold-flecked icons, bejeweled vessels, and embroidered ceremonial robes provided scenery appropriate for a theophany, an appearance of God.

Leaders of the eucharistic community became clearly set apart from the members. Ritual development required both skill and clearly defined roles. But these liturgical roles were elaborated at the same time that bishops, priests and deacons assumed new roles within the Empire. In both settings, they were becoming a more clearly differentiated hierarchy (sacred order), ruling the laity. The clergy were not so much seizing new power as they were adjusting to changes in the way people understood the flow of grace from God to humans within the imperial setting. Indeed, had Church leaders not adopted specifically religious symbols for themselves, it is likely enough that their new political status would have transformed them into merely secular leaders. In any event, the clergy too became visible signs of divine power.

ALEXANDRIAN WEAKNESS: There is a logical progression from Athanasius' orthodoxy to the heresies later proposed by Apollinarius and Eutyches. The link is an inability to account for genuinely human experience in Jesus. The soul or human spirit, however it be defined, represents the human capacity to be self-conscious. Among other things, self-consciousness is what makes suffering more than mere sensation. But Athanasius spoke of Christ as though the Word replaced the human soul in his personality. Apollinarius denied that he had a human soul, and Eutyches held that the Word replaced the soul of Jesus at the moment of incarnation. In each case, how could one account for real human existence in a person without a human soul? Where was the basis for human self-consciousness?

ATHANASIUS AND THE ISSUE OF IMMORTALITY: To understand Athanasius properly, we must see that he made Christ the solution to the human defect that dominated much of Greek thought. What defect? Humans were mortal. Bodily corruption and death, the fact that humans were "wasting out of existence," framed his thinking about Christ (*On The Incarnation*, 8; see Appendix G, 3). The incorruptible and immortal Son became part of the human race to prevent the work of his Father, the creation of humans, from coming "to naught" (*ibid.*). Christ "assumed a body capable of death, in order that it, through belonging to the Word . . . might become in dying a sufficient exchange for all [bodies]" (*On The Incarnation*, 9; see Appendix G, 3.)

Thus, for Athanasius, to join "the incorruptible immortal Son with our human nature" was the crucial issue. By so doing, "the corruption that goes with death" would lose its power (*On The Incarnation*, 9, see Appendix G, 3). He spoke in terms of the Word "entering our world," "stooping to our level," "taking a body," "a pure body untainted by intercourse with men" (*On The Incarnation*, 8; Appendix G, 3). In Christ, two natures are joined so that a human being might experience a divine reality, namely immortality. The premise is that this human nature also undergoes the human fate of death, and triumphs because of his inner divine nature, death for humans is defeated.

Athanasius failed to show how Jesus' human nature could function as other humans. He has no room for a human soul. He did not provide for human self-consciousness. How, then, was this Christ to experience suffering and death in the way humans do?

To be sure, in the Arian controversy, Athanasius insisted that the Word "did not come into [a] man," as if he had "only appeared in a man." Rather, to avoid confusion, one had to say, "he became man" (*Discourses Against The Arians*, 30; see Appendix G, 5). Athanasius held that the Word was present in Jesus and in the Eucharist in quite a different sense from its presence in other human instruments. The body of Jesus was human and had its identity from the Word dwelling within itself. He intended to say that there was one person, truly human and truly divine. But without denying that Christ had a human soul, Athanasius had left little room for it. Apollinarius and others drew their own conclusions.

APOLLINARIANISM: Bishop Apollinarius of Laodicea (d. 390) moved a step beyond his friend Athanasius' position. Apollinarius did not totally exclude the possibility of a human soul for Christ. Instead, he held that the *Logos* or Divine Reason had replaced the intellectual soul and will, so that only the animal and vegetative functions of Jesus' humanity remained. Christ would thus be free from sin and physical passion. So also, his nature is one divine nature even though vested with a human body.

Even Athanasius recognized the problem in the Apollinarian position. It meant that Christ was not a real human, but only appeared like a human being. Against Apollinarianism, he had contended that rejection of a normal human psychology in Jesus clashed with the biblical portrait of Jesus living, suffering and dying as a human being.

Opposition to Apollinarius' teachings was best summed up in Gregory of Nazianzen's slogan, "What he has not assumed [human nature], he has not healed." This slogan epitomized anti-Apollinarian worry that a one-sided emphasis on Jesus' divinity would undercut the idea of human salvation itself. Local synods in Rome, Alexandria and Antioch condemned Apollinarius before an ecumenical council met at Constantinople in 381. Besides issuing a blanket condemnation of Apollinarianism, Constantinople also proclaimed, though it can scarely be said to have written, the final form of the Creed of Nicaea. This Creed of Nicaea-Constantinople is the version of the creed in use in today's liturgy.

Antioch: Logos/Anthropos: Apollinarius' efforts were directed against the rival theological school at Antioch. The Antiochene Christology model was *Logos/Anthropos*, Christ as the Word-become-human. In particular, Apollinarius had opposed Antioch's dualism, its tendency to make the two natures in Christ so distinct that the unity of his person was threatened. Dualism arose in Antioch because of Aristotle's definition of the human as a composite unity of body and soul. Following this definition, Antioch insisted on two human components, body and soul, even in Christ.

But emphasis on a human soul was not the only legacy of Aristotelian philosophy in Antioch. Aristotle's empirical approach to philosophy was reflected in the way the Antiochenes interpreted the scriptures. He had taught that knowledge arose from experience, from evidence that came through the senses. For example, when he questioned what justice was, he did so by observing the acts of just persons. Unlike the Platonists, Aristotle did not see justice as arising within the soul, from our having a share or participation in the divine idea of justice. Aristotelians appreciated the role of the senses in reaching truth. They did not look for inner meanings in eternal realms. The meaning of things was observable in the realities they experienced. So also, Aristotelians at Antioch studied the texts of scripture for their literal meaning, and where appropriate for their historical meaning.

Antiochene thologians were interested in the concrete historical details of the gospels' portrait of Jesus. His historical life was at the center. But their understanding of human life as involving body and soul was also helpful in distinguishing the human Jesus from the eternal Word.

THEODORE OF MOPSUESTIA'S SENSE OF HISTORY: No one better exhibits the Antiochene spirit than Theodore of Mopsuestia (d. 428). For example, attacking the allegorical interpretation of scripture, he made clear his concern for history. Allegorists had cited Paul's statement, "These things are said allegorically" (Gal 4:24). In rebuttal, Theodore commented that some people "make it their business to prevent the meaning of the divine scripture . . . They invent foolish tales of their own and give to their nonesense the name of 'allegory' " (*Commentary on Galatians;* see Appendix H, 1). Theodore argued that the apostle had used history "in support of his own purpose." Paul had begun with the historical sense and added an allegorical meaning without weakening the historical meaning. The important consideration is that "what happened" is the foundation for present belief.

ANTIOCHENE SPIRITUALITY: Indeed, a sense of history was foundational in Antiochene spirituality. Whereas, to put it simply, the Alexandrians taught that to see God was to be saved, the Antiochenes were moralists, doers. Salvation takes place where obedience to God's rule occurs.

Salvation, in Theodore's teaching, takes place in a historical process, what he referred to as an "economy." God progressively moves humans toward greater union with himself. First, the Hebrew scriptures presented the symbols for the life of the Church. Then, the life of the Church served as a pattern for life in heaven. In Christ, therefore, God showed humans the life of immortality prepared for the future, and in Baptism and the Eucharist humans are conjoined to Christ in anticipation of their future glory. Salvation was not a matter of gaining a share of a divine quality, immortality, as the Alexandrians taught. It was moral preparation for a new life in the future.

A striking contrast in sacramental perspective between the two schools is evident. Alexandrians made the sacramental experience serve as the appearance of the eternal, the discovery of what always and everywhere is the underlying reality. Theodore and the Antiochenes saw the sacramental experience as moving humans toward the future. The future had never yet existed. It could only be anticipated. Thus, Theodore saw the redeemed human just as he was in history, partly redeemed and partly not yet redeemed. Humans were not divinized, but were on the way to fulfillment.

ANTIOCHENE SENSE OF "OTHERNESS": Antiochene spirituality shows a profound respect for the empirical realities of history, but also a passionate sensitivity for the transcendence or otherness of God. God is not to be found in creation. God is not to be idolatrously identified with any historical human being. For Theodore the glorified Christ was visualized as a moral force drawing humanity into fully living the divine will. Christ joined heaven to earth by drawing earthly realities toward heaven. As Christ continued to act, so also Christians must act. This was a spirituality in which action for the good, rather than contemplation of it, was primary. The reason was that God was "Other," not within created reality.

The Spirit of God could be joined to the human spirit. But the human creaturely spirit could not be identified with God's. It was a *conjunction* of two beings, a moral union of two spirits. This took place in Baptism and the Eucharist. In the case of Jesus there is a perfect conjunction of the Divine Spirit/*Logos* with the spirit/soul of Jesus. But even this is a union at the moral level, a union of wills. Anything else for Theodore and the Antiochene school smacked of the Arian intermediate being, the Perfect Creature.

Whenever Alexandrians argued that the divine nature of the Word replaced the soul in Jesus, the Antiochene school suspected Apollinarianism. Theodore objected to the idea that Christ assumed "a body not a soul," saying, "if the godhead had replaced the soul he would not have been hungry or thirsty, nor would he have tired or been in need of food" (*Catechetical Homilies;* see Appendix H, 2). As he explained, the body suffers because the soul is unable to satisfy all its needs, but an infinite Spirit within would have more than satisfied all needs. Thus, without a fully human soul, Christ would have had no human experience. To say he had no human soul is to say that he had only the appearance of a human, as the Apollinarians erroneously taught.

DUALISM AND THE NESTORIAN CONTROVERSY: One of Theodore's students, Nestorius, pushed Antiochene dualistic tendencies to the breaking point. Having become Patriarch of Constantinople in 428, the year Theodore died, he set out to defend the existence of two complete natures in Christ. Unfortunately, he not only chose to battle Alexandrian theology, but to focus his attack on growing popular devotion to Mary. In Alexandria especially she was being called *Theotokos,* which means God-bearer or Mother of God. The Antiochenes feared that this made Mary a goddess. Nestorius argued that *Christotokos,* Christ-bearer, would be a more appropriate title. Even more appropriate would be *Anthropotokos,* human-bearer, to indicate clearly that Mary mothered only the human nature.

Advocating so sharp a distinction between the human and divine natures in Christ made Antiochene Christology appear almost schizophrenic. Worse still, Nestorius was on a collision course with popular piety and its overzealous defender Cyril, the Patriarch of Alexandria. Moreover, beneath the surface there lurked a struggle between Constantinople and Alexandria for ecclesiastical influence in the East.

Popular piety insured defeat of Nestorius. A council was held in 431 at Ephesus, a city where devotion to Mary had replaced, at least in name, devotion to the goddess Artemis. Satisfying devotional needs as well as the economic requirements of the vendors at what had once been the shrine of Artemis, popular demonstrations helped Cyril to secure Nestorius' condemnation, deposition and exile to Antioch. The new title, "Mother of God," was accepted.

After Nestorius' exile the Antiochene party charged that the Alexandrian Cyril was Apollinarian. To reconcile the contending parties a comprehensive "Symbol of Union" was drafted in 433. It acknowledged that Christ was "perfect God and perfect man composed of a rational soul and body." This "Symbol" or creed, which had been circulated at Ephesus, asserted that the two natures had been united. It added that statements appropriate to one nature should not be applied to the other nature as such, but to the person, Christ. For example, it would be inappropriate to say, "God died on the cross." More appropriately, "Christ died." For the moment this compromise met the major concerns of both schools.

3. Chalcedon and the Emergence of Dogmatic Realism

The Symbol of Union was a moment of sanity in two of the more contentious, if not bizarre decades in Christian history. At Ephesus, the Antiochene party had won the theological debate, that Christ's human nature was a completely human nature. The Alexandrians had won the quarrel over titles. But the Antiochene position was difficult to maintain, as Nestorius' errors had made clear. Moreover, it ran against the grain of popular piety, a fact dramatized by Nestorius' exile. Likewise, the Alexandrian position was easily exaggerated for piety's sake.

ALEXANDRIAN PARTY ASCENDANT: Hellenistic and imperial Christianity, as a matter of fact, would scarcely work and wait for God's appearance in the future, as the Antiochenes urged. So long as there were Alexandrian preachers to proclaim that God was immanently present, they had the upper hand. Delayed gratification is a mark of mature people and movements, and the Christian movement was still quite young. The issue of what titles were appropriate for Christ or Mary was a minor example of a more general situation. The piety that focused on Christ's divinity and identified God's work with particular persons and institutions in the present was ascendant.

Opposing philosophical positions had brought each school of theology to an impasse. Alexandrian Platonism was unable to give due recognition to Jesus' historical existence. Antiochene Aristotelianism was unable to maintain the unity of Christ's person. In the twenty year struggle from Ephesus to the final reconciliation at Chalcedon, the way was paved for a more fundamental settlement of the issues between the schools. That way was the emergence of dogmatic realism, which moved the Church beyond the limitations created by the philosophical commitments of each school.

THE COUNCIL AT CHALCEDON: Although clearly ascendant as a popular piety, the Alexandrians moved after Ephesus to snatch defeat from the jaws of victory. An elderly monk, Eutyches, who lived in Constantinople, criticized Flavian, the new Patriarch of Constantinople. Eutyches considered the Alexandrian teaching, that there was one nature in Christ, normative. He attacked Flavian for teaching that Christ was consubstantial with humans. Eutyches argued that the human nature of Christ was human only until Christ assumed it. He was willing to say that Christ was "consubstantial according to the flesh," meaning that Christ's body was a human body (Carmody and Clark: 113; see Appendix I). In this, he was expressing the traditional Alexandrian *Logos/Sarx* teaching.

But Eutyches' inept presentation of traditional Alexandrianism contradicted the compromise agreed to in the Symbol of Union. There it had been decided that Christ had a fully human nature. Eutyches tried to get around this by acknowledging "that our Lord was of two natures before the union [of the Word with the flesh], but after the union one nature" (*ibid.*). The Word made the human nature divine. He appealed to the teaching of Athanasius and Cyril as justification.

Constantinople's Patriarch, Flavian, condemned Eutyches, who appealed unsuccessfully to Pope Leo I (d. 461) in Rome. The dispute would have remained a local problem in Constantinople except for the intrigue of Cyril's successsor as Patriarch of Alexandria, Dioscorus. Dioscorus prodded Emperor Theodosius II to call another council at Ephesus in 450. Presided over by Dioscorus, who prevented the papal legates from reading Pope Leo's Tome or opinion on the question, this council upheld Eutyches. But it went further to depose Flavian and all the bishops who supported him, earning from Pope Leo himself the designation of "Robber Council."

Theodosius II died the same year and a new council was called at Chalcedon in 451. The new council was guided by Pope Leo's Tome. In scarcely diplomatic language, Leo said of Eutyches that "he knew not what he ought to think about the incarnation," and "he was not willing, for the sake of obtaining the light of intelligence, to make [a] laborious search through . . . holy scripture." Worse still, in Leo's judgment, Eutyches failed to receive "with heedful attention" the "general confession common to all" the Church (Appendix J). This last point was the heart of Leo's position. Leo was asserting that what Christians had always believed and taught was the dogmatic norm. This is the foundation of dogmatic realism.

DOGMATIC REALISM: Leo's Tome is characterized by the assertion of what he takes to be the facts or data of faith. He simply asserts that one fact, Jesus' divinity, not be compromised by another, Jesus' humanity, or vice versa. He also insists that neither fact be confused by the way they are thought to relate to one another. The explanation given for the facts or data of faith is one thing. This is often drawn from philosophy. The facts or data of faith are another matter and the primary one.

On the question in dispute, Leo asserts that the Son "was born as 'God from God,' Almighty from Almighty, Co-eternal from Eternal . . ." Likewise, "the same only-begotten . . . was 'born of the Holy Spirit and the Virgin Mary.' This birth in time in no way detracted from, in no way added to, that divine and everlasting birth." Moreover, however miraculous the virgin birth, "the newness of the mode of production" may not be understood to have done "away with the proper character of the species" (humanity). In summary, "therefore in the entire and perfect nature of a true man was born the true God, whole in what was his, whole in what was ours" (Appendix J).

Leo's Tome is a clear example of Roman practicality. The Roman church was neither as sophisticated nor as speculatively inclined as the churches of the East. The Tome is in fact Rome's first major contribution to the wider Church. Its originality lies in its ability to assert the elements of the developed tradition and leave the role of speculation to others.

But the Tome does more than dismiss speculation. While it may have been accepted at Chalcedon partly because people were weary with the debate, it also exemplified a shrewd method for setting doctrinal disputes. The Tome represents a method of theologizing, of understanding belief, that had matured after Nicaea, which may be called *dogmatic realism*. Dogmatic realism restates the belief expressed in scripture in new language, justifying the new language as a response to issues not explicitly raised by the biblical authors. Athanasius had set the style of dogmatic realism when he interpreted *homoousios* as a heuristic term, meant to govern affirmations made about the Father and the Son. He had implied that the new question, of Christ's nature, could not be answered with philosophical data, but that an interpretation of the scriptural data could receive greater precision by using a philosophical method for drawing conclusions. Leo's Tome represents such a procedure.

Bernard Lonergan has defined dogmatic realism as "realism" in the sense that it takes the biblical word as a word to be believed and not to be contradicted. The biblical word, then, is taken as relating a fact that is simply true. It is dogmatic, however, in the sense that it does not depend on philosophical reflection but on the fact that it is revealed to be known. The dogmatic realist wishes to affirm what is "implicit" in the biblical word, not what is explicitly stated, for he attempts to answer a new question to which the biblical word does not address itself. At the same time, the dogmatic realist assumes that he may not contradict anything revealed (Lonergan 1976: pp. 128-33).

In dogmatic realism the Church found a tool that served a double purpose. First, it provided the clear statements of belief that the Church needed to function within the legal structure of the Roman Empire. For a statement of dogmatic fact implies just the kind of judicial instrument that came to be attached to all statements of faith: "If anyone says such and such, let him be anathema." Second, it provided the Christian movement with a means of responding to speculative and philosophical problems presented by Greco-Roman culture. At the same time, it proclaimed the transcendence of faith over philosophy and allowed the Church to retain its identity by asserting the priority of its own revelation.

THE CHALCEDONIAN SETTLEMENT: Following Nicaea's example, but in the spirit of dogmatic realism, Chalcedon proclaimed a series of affirmations. These affirmations may be read as a series of open-ended statements: *(a) whatever it* means to be God, Jesus is; (b) whatever it means to be human, Jesus is; (c) whatever is necessary to maintain that there is only one person, this is true of Jesus. In language far from the language of scripture itself, the definition of faith at Chalcedon shows a clear intention to state what its authors believe is clearly implied and cannot be denied in the scriptures.

At the outset, the definition asserts that Jesus Christ "is perfect both in deity and also in humanity . . . actually God and actually man, with a rational soul and a body." He is "like us in all respects, sin only excepted." On this foundation they asserted that they acknowledged "two natures, without transmuting one nature into another, without dividing them into separate categories, without contrasting them according to area or function." Moreover, "both natures concur in one person" (Appendix K).

Chalcedon, thus, broke no new ground at the level of ideas. Its most important, even innovative, feature was to solidify a method. As after Nicaea, philosophical speculation about the faith would continue. But from Chalcedon onward, the basic dogmatic elements of Christology were firmly in place, indeed isolated from speculative activity.

One way to understand the method promoted by Leo's Tome and by Chalcedon is to compare it with the method of mime. Mime presents isolated scenes from everyday life and leaves the synthesizing process to the audience. Chalcedon isolated the elements necessary for a Christology that would justify the Christian movement's entrance into the world of the Roman Empire while keeping its own identity as Jesus' movement. The isolated elements look, as mime always does, very different from the everyday scenes of the New Testament proclamation of Jesus. The Chalcedonian settlement left the process of synthesizing to future audiences, to the continuing reflection of the Christian movement. In precisely this respect, it was very much in the spirit of the New Testament itself. The New Testament represents notes for those who would preach Christ rather than a fully descriptive account of who Christ is.

The Christ of Dogma: An Assessment: The Christ of dogma, one divine person with two distinct natures, appears light years removed from the Jesus of the New Testament. Dogmatic Christology speaks of the nature of an eternal divine person, and sees the world and humanity as vehicles for his appearance in history. New Testament Christologies speak of the life and work of a person in the world of time who brought history to fulfillment. To properly assess the validity and value of this rather radical shift in Christology, we must see it as an expression of the Christian movement, parallel to the gospel expression rather than merely in contrast to it.

DOGMATIC CHRISTOLOGY AND COMMITMENT: The creeds must be seen as prayer, as the response of the Christian community at worship expressing its relationships to Christ and among its own members. From Tertullian through Nicaea to Chaldecon, statements about Christ were closely linked to beliefs about the Eucharist. The terms in the creeds may be rather abstract, but they point back to the Christ experienced concretely in the bread and wine, in the preached word of the gospel and above all in the assembled community of believers.

In the period in question and for a thousand years afterward, this community of believers faced a unique challenge. For all practical purposes, the whole world they knew had declared itself Christian. This meant that the Christian movement was in serious jeopardy of losing its identity. Although he was given to ironic exaggeration, Soren Kierkegaard expressed the problems well when he said that if everybody is Christian, then Christianity cannot exist, because the New Testament shows a movement opposed by everybody significant. To proclaim the faith in a Christian society, Kierkegaard said, "first of all the illusion [that all are Christian] must be disposed of." Moreover, Kierkegaard observed that this will be done in part by "clarifying men's concepts" (Lowrie: p. 97).

Kierkegaard was speaking about nineteenth century Denmark, but he certainly saw the problem as a longstanding one. From the vantage point of twentieth century America, where one is Christian by personal choice, and where being Christian or not no longer has clear social sanctions, clarifying concepts may be less crucial. But the need for religious boundaries, even for clearly defined religious hierarchies and statements of belief, was intense when an entire culture claimed a single religious identity. There one had to ask where the faith ended and where the culture began. To ask this question was to be serious about the possibility of conflict between cultural presumptions and religious commitments.

Thus, the dogmatic statements must be read as efforts to identify who really belonged to the Christian movement when virtually everybody claimed to belong. The creeds were a needed line of demarcation between the Church and society at a point where few such lines existed. As late as the twentieth century, a Catholic writer, Hilaire Belloc, became identified with the slogan, "The Church is Europe and Europe is the Church." Were this true, then how would the gospel ever reach America or Asia except as a form of colonialism? One of the few defenses the Christian movement had against this identification of itself with society were the creeds that could be used to distinguish authentic from pretended faith. Christians have not recognized this often enough, but each time they proclaim the creed they assert that they belong to a communion of believers that is not the same as the community in which they live. The dogmatic Christ required that Christian loyalty to family, society and state always remain qualified by a broader, more universal commitment.

DOGMATIC CHRIST AND THE SENSE OF HISTORY: History is action, and indeed meaningful action. To have a sense of history is to agree with the proposition that the world is not finished, that its future is still to be decided. This sense is at the heart of the religious belief in God as Creator and it is opposed by the idea that everything happens in conformity with eternal ideas or plans. The most serious objection that is raised against the dogmatic picture of Christ is that it envisions Christ as an eternal idea revealed in the human nature of Jesus to restore or fulfill the eternal plan. Were the objection true, or substantially true, human beings do not do anything, do not really contribute anything to the making of the world. They are spectators in life.

Although many of those who contributed to the development of dogmatic Christology had little if any sense of history, the dogmatic statements themselves at least provide room for both the Creator God and history. They are open-ended formulas, which allow for and invite elaboration. Even more, they are statements which attest to their authors' recognition that the philosophical positions of their own day had definite limits, at least in defining God and Christ. They are proof that the Antiochene witness to biblical belief in the God of Creation qualified the pagan piety Christianized by the Alexandrians.

More remarkably, as much as the councils expressed a desire to restate the scriptures, the creeds themselves are evidence that they found the scriptural statements insufficient. In this there is a clear recognition that the divinely inspired word is seen to be historically limited.

It is one thing to repeat the formulas of dogmatic Christology, quite another to arrive at these formulas in the first place. The concepts in the formulas may be static, and lack the full dynamism of a historical perspective. Those who merely repeat them in the twentieth century, and perhaps others through preceding centuries as well, may convey a Christ and a faith that appear remote from the arena of human action. But the statements themselves came out of the dynamics of the Christian movement. They reflect a series of struggles so intense that the whole effort witnesses a deep, if often unconscious, awareness of the active involvement of both Christ and Christians in history and in all the currents of social and political life. Subconsciously at least, pagan piety had been opened to the dynamic possibilities of a faith that began with God in history creating new things through Christ.

WORKS CITED

James M. Carmody and Thomas E. Clarke, eds.
　　1966 *Christ and His Mission: Christology and Soteriology.*
　　　　 Westminster, MD: Newman.
Soren Kierkegaard
　　1956 *Attack upon Christendom.* Walter Lowrie, trans.
　　　　 Boston: Beacon.
Bernard Lonergan
　　1976 *The Way to Nicaea.* Philadelphia: Fortress.

CHAPTER SEVEN

INTO THE MODERN WORLD:
CHRIST AND THE CRISIS OF CHANGE

Questions to think about:

— *Why are modern people so keenly aware of change?*
— *What is new in the modern concept of personality?*
— *How has technology changed our understanding of Christ?*
— *How have modern needs changed our understanding of Christ?*
— *How does faith in Christ challenge modernity itself?*

1. Modernity, Christians and Christ

It may seem strange to jump from the year 451 to modern times. To make this jump is, however, typically modern. When the modern world began and when Christians moved into it is an open question. Typical modern people, of the nineteenth century for example, believed they were vastly unlike people of the fourteenth century. By way of contrast, people of the fourteenth century perceived little difference between themselves and people of the fourth century. Nothing is more typically modern than consciousness of change. Sensitivity to change and to the differences that arise from change greatly influence how modern Christians think of themselves and of Christ.

Many aspects of modern life help explain how we changed and how our views of Christ changed. Copernicus made humans see the sun, not the earth as the center of the universe. Columbus introduced Europeans to a new world. The steam engine freed workers from back-breaking labor. Important as other discoveries were, to get an overview of the transformation, we will focus on the impact of one invention, the printing press, to stand for the rest. Print created a practical basis for what it means to be modern. Thus, it was a significant condition for modern understandings of Christ. Books are not a modern invention. But books readily available to the ordinary person are very modern. Books made mass literacy possible. Mass literacy changed the way people saw themselves, others and their relationships to others. Inevitably, books changed the Christian reader's understanding of Christ.

The understanding of Christ that developed in the modern period corresponds to the modern person's self-concept, a concept nurtured in mass literacy. Modern Christologies are rooted in modern anthropologies, modern conceptions of the person. The person is (a) the product of a biography or history, who (b) must grow and develop in response to fundamental challenges and personal destiny, and (c) in this growth process will rely primarily on an inner strength derived from a conversion or orientation to an ultimately transcendent reality. The roles or offices represented by the New Testament titles of Jesus in such a context will be symbolic of inner identity. Definitions from the Hellenistic world will be transformed into ways of affirming a uniquely dynamic personal life. In this anthropological transformation of Christology none of the past tradition will need to be discarded. Virtually all of it will be remodeled.

Modern Christologies follow three typical models.

First, efforts to reconstruct the life of Jesus answer the modern need to know historical facts. Second, interpretations of Jesus' personality provide modern individuals with a role model. Finally, devotional portraits enable modern Christians to relate to Christ personally and immediately in religious experience. Although most Christians see these approaches today as more or less traditional, all three represent profound innovations, movements by the Christian community into a new world, the world of modern people with questions no earlier Christians asked.

2. The Modern Search for the Historical Jesus

From the eighteenth century onward, Christians have increasingly been driven by a need to know the history of Jesus. Certainly, earlier Christians saw Jesus as a person in history. But for them, despite the need to explain minor discrepancies in the gospel accounts, Jesus' life story was taken for granted. When the modern reader asks who the Jesus of history was, little is taken for granted.

A reading public asks critical historical questions for a number of reasons. First, printed books made it easy to compare one account with another, making discrepancies more noticeable. Second, print put the same materials in the hands of priests and lay people, experts and non-experts, leading ordinary people to ask questions theologians once would have kept to themselves. Third, printing gave people — as the computer does today — a marvelous new memory bank. What was known about the past for most people had been what the oldest person in the community remembered. What could be stored in print was virtually unlimited. In effect, books made the available past expand to an unprecedented degree and made everybody more conscious of the past and its significance. Literate Christians moved into a world of historical consciousness.

To understand why modern theologians typically speak of "the historical Jesus," it is necessary to understand what "history" has come to mean. Unquestionably, it is virtually universal for people to tell their stories. But to write scientific history is nonetheless peculiarly recent and western.

The gospels are indeed storied accounts of Jesus, and in all probability based on still earlier stories. In the Middle Ages, notably in the preaching and example of the mendicant friars, the stories of Jesus became increasingly elaborated. A middle class merchant's son, Francis of Assisi, initiated this movement potentially so much in tune with later individualist piety. The Christmas crib sets, the detailed stations of the cross and increasingly dramatic and human pictures and statues of Christ all show an interest in adding psychological depth to the rather stark gospel portraits and the statements in the creeds. But this is only the first stage, and not the decisive one in the modern search for the historical Jesus.

Modern Life of Jesus Movement: The earliest "Life of Jesus" known was probably written by the nephew of the great missionary Francis Xavier in the sixteenth century to impress a Hindustan ruler. But such "lives of Jesus" came into their own in the late eighteenth century. For two hundred years a steady stream of books has poured out, presenting reconstructions of the events of Jesus' life. Characteristic of this "Life of Jesus" movement is the effort to clear up the discrepancies among the gospel accounts, to present a chronologically clear interpretation of Jesus' personal development and of those immediately associated with him. At the popular level such books continue today. Notable examples are Fulton Oursler's *The Greatest Story Ever Told* and Jim Bishop's *The Day Christ Was Born* and *The*

Day Christ Died. They provide easy scripts for Hollywood productions.

Two challenges to the "Life of Jesus" movement have virtually removed such books from serious consideration. Theologians and historians have refocused their attention on a "quest for the historical Jesus," which is a more limited yet more intensive research project. The earlier challenge was theological, coming from the Lutheran Martin Kahler in the late nineteenth century. Kahler argued that the Jesus of history was essentially irrelevant to Christian faith. In part, Kahler was expressing a growing frustration with the task of writing a fully acceptable life of Jesus. But more importantly, he wanted to affirm that Christians believed in the living Christ. They should focus on the risen Christ of faith present and speaking in the word and sacramental life of the Church. Faith comes from hearing Christ, not from historical investigations carried out by scholars.

Growing conflict over what was historical in the gospel portrait of Jesus and frustration in reconstructing a complete life reached its culminating point in the work of Albert Schweitzer (d. 1965). In the early twentieth century Schweitzer examined all the lives of Jesus up to his time. He came to the somber conclusion that their portraits of Jesus had been "designed by rationalism, endowed with life by liberalism and clothed by modern theology with historical garb" (1968: p. 398). In other words, the best historians and theologians had remade Jesus in their own image. Subsequent lives and histories have been judged as harshly as those examined by Schweitzer.

Contemporary Historical Approaches to the Gospels: Historical investigation of the New Testament has not been eliminated. But it has become better focused. Much of the research of the earlier would-be biographers has been refined. In more mature form, the research of the historical

Jesus movement has provided the basis for (among other things) the official Catholic teaching on interpretation of the gospels. Thus, in 1964 the Pontifical Biblical Commission issued an instruction on the historical truth of the gospels. In strikingly clear points, the instruction transforms critical insights into expressions of faith.

STAGE ONE: JESUS' MINISTRY: Insisting that in the gospels "the doctrine and life of Jesus were not simply reported . . . but preached so as to offer the Church a basis of faith" (Instruction, X ; see Fitzmyer: p. 406), three stages in the development of the gospels were outlined. First, during Jesus' ministry disciples, seeing and hearing him, were equipped to be witnesses of his life and teaching (Instruction, VII; see Fitzmyer: p. 404). This recognition that Jesus' ministry of preaching and healing lies behind the subsequent preaching of the Church is central in modern historical understanding of Jesus.

In earlier more negative historical studies, the discontinuity between Jesus' ministry and that of the early Church was often emphasized. A typical slogan of that period: Jesus preached the kingdom and the Church preached Christ. Today scholars would insist that Jesus' own message includes more than the verbal content of his preaching. He proclaimed a kingdom that was to be enacted, inaugurated in the whole course of his life work, and most notably in the culminating events of his death and resurrection.

Christology of Representation: This view of the ministry and life of Jesus implies a Christology of representation. Jesus is the representative of the kingdom, or better the *rule* of God which he announced. He is taken, however, as more than a mere example or role model for people in the new age (world). His words and deeds, and especially the latter serve to create the new world in which God rules.

Thus, there is a new concentration on the work of Jesus. In the past his work had been seen as a sacrifice bringing about human reconciliation with God, making restitution to the Father for human sin. In the more recent model, Jesus more typically is seen as God's representative before humans, permitting himself to be sacrificed to bring about reconciliation among humans.

Modern historical studies frequently focus on the most distinctive features of Jesus' ministry. These features are thought to be at play in his condemnation by his contemporaries. They are also judged too original for later disciples to have invented. Most distinctive of all is his association with sinners, to the point of table fellowship, and his assertion of radical dependence on God, epitomized in his use of the familiar term "Abba." If the disciples later moved haltingly to reach out to the Gentiles, their step was foreshadowed in Jesus' far more radical breaking of the barriers between the observant righteous and the shameful sinners in Israel. Indeed, missionary outreach to Gentiles was common among Jews during the Second Temple period. But association with sinners was acceptable neither on the grounds of religious tradition nor the more general cultural tradition of the Mediterranean world. If the modern scholar found nothing else in the New Testament unequivocally associated with Jesus, this work of reconciling the unreconcilable in the human family to one another would be enough to set him apart.

STAGE TWO: JESUS' EXALTATION: Second, according to the Biblical Commission, after Jesus' resurrection, having newly perceived who Jesus was, the disciples orally "passed on to their listeners what was really said and done." This was done "with that fuller understanding" coming from Easter, and "according to the needs of their listeners" (Instruction, VIII; see Fitzmyer p. 404). Strangely enough, when primary traditions about Jesus' resurrection are sorted out from later accretions, the difference Easter made in the disciples' understanding of Jesus is highlighted.

For example, the accounts of Jesus' appearances to disciples are generally judged more ancient than the accounts of the empty tomb. Likewise, Luke's portrayal of Jesus' ascension to the Father after forty days, and the coming of the Spirit of Jesus after fifty are more recent understandings of the full Easter event. In the earlier tradition, when Jesus was seen by his disciples, he was seen to be exalted (taken up) to God's right hand, and to empower (anoint) his disciples with his own Spirit.

These conclusions permit a less problematic account of the process that Jesus' disciples followed in grasping the meaning of what happened. Older presentations rely on an implied assumption that the disciples had to follow clues to the point of conviction or conversion. Beginning with prophecies in the Hebrew scriptures, seeing their step-by-step fulfillment during Jesus' ministry and finally the cross and empty tomb, the disciples went to Galilee to wait for Jesus to appear. Then, presumably they returned to Jerusalem for the coming of the Holy Spirit. Far easier, we now see how the New Testament writers expanded a single reality into a drama of several separate acts. The Easter appearances radically reoriented Peter and the disciples (as they would later reorient Paul). Much later, they might have looked back on the clues.

From the experience of seeing Jesus alive, they knew him to be uniquely *with God*. All the past was now open to reinterpretation. In particular, Jesus' own public ministry would be inevitably colored by the Easter breakthrough of understanding. Easter meant that the disciples would believe themselves to be in direct contact with Jesus risen, to hear him directly, to focus on his present message to them.

It is thus difficult to distinguish between the words of Jesus uttered and heard during his pre-Easter ministry from those belonging to this post-Easter ministry.

Chistology of Presence: Implied in this historical insight is a Christology of presence. When the resurrection was seen as simply a sequel to the crucifixion and as an apologetic for Jesus' divinity, the vital connection between resurrection and the doctrine of the presence of Christ in the Church and Eucharist was often overlooked. It is more in line with the gospels to say that the resurrection proclaims that Jesus lives. Thus, what the first generation of Christians affirmed has begun to move back into focus. They witnessed Jesus' immediate presence to them, notably in the Eucharist. This provided a basis for believing him to be risen.

In the past Jesus' resurrection was frequently seen as a proof that his sacrificial death was accepted by the Father. Contemporary theologians have argued that the resurrection is an integral part of Christ's saving work on behalf of humanity. In particular, they have focused on the resurrection belief that Jesus is exalted bodily, that his bodily humanity is triumphant beyond death. Francis X. Durwell speaks of "the bodily humanity of the Savior [as] the point from which the divinizing spirit gushes out for us" (1960: p. 106). The bodily resurrection of Jesus reveals fundamental Christian convictions about human nature and the way God relates to humans.

Decisively, bodily resurrection asserts the ongoing significance of human bodies. Human beings are not "souls imprisoned in bodies." The earlier Church had found it necessary to state that Christ had a human soul, a center of human experience. Twentieth century theologians have found it necessary to insist that Christ exalted in his corporeal nature underscores two points. First, Jesus' humanity is not a phase or episode in an otherwise divine life, but rather a continuing reality. The Word became flesh not for a time, but remains among us as one of us. Second, the human body must be taken into account when we describe God's relationship to us.

Human beings relate to one another and to God (and thus are saved) in and through their bodies. As Edward Schillebeeckx has written,

> Mutual human availability is possible only in and through man's bodiliness. Therefore men who are dead and not yet risen again can exercise no direct influence upon us by mutual human contact... It is the resurrection that makes it possible for him precisely *as man* to influence us by grace. (1963: p. 42)

SACRAMENTAL PRESENCE: Christ' bodily influence is experienced above all in eucharistic life. Once again, our growing awareness of how human beings communicate and are present to one another has given new meaning to earlier theological expressions of the reality of Christ's presence in the Eucharist.

In part, our modern understanding of Schillebeeckx's "mutual human contact" reflects technological advances in communications. For the modern person, hearing a voice transmitted over wires or over air waves is no longer magic. Seeing persons through such media is now commonplace. Before modern media became commonplace, photography had brought images, first in concentrations of black and white dots and later in all the colors of the spectrum, of those in distant times and places within our reach. In each of these developments we confront modes of presence and communication that are first of all physical in themselves, and secondly transcend time and space limitations as we formerly understood them. Besides this, our knowledge of biology and cell life makes us aware that while we are never without our bodies, the physical elements that constitute our bodies are in constant flux.

Contemporary understanding of human communication and contact does not make us affirm the presence of Christ in the eucharistic celebration any more fully than it was in the past. But it does provides a model for understanding a physically communicated presence of someone beyond the reach of our immediate situation in time and space. Christ's eucharistic presence remains a mystery, but we understand some of its human dynamics somewhat better.

Thus, we see the connection between the Risen Jesus' new form of corporeality and his presence in sacramental life. In the physical forms of spoken words, broken and eaten bread and poured water or oil, Christ now reaches out to those who by sharing these elements become sharers of his life. The oneness achieved between persons who communicate and express themselves through common symbols — think for example of the oneness lovers achieve in symbolic actions — makes all who share these symbolic expressions of Christ's new life reach such a level of union with Christ that we speak of the Church as the Body of Christ.

The renewed sense of Christ's presence in the Eucharist and in the Church after his resurrection comes to a focus in theologies of sacramentality (developed among Catholics) which correspond in many ways to theologies of encounter (first developed by Protestants). In both theologies, the outpouring of the Holy Spirit, which John dramatizes on Easter and Luke dramatizes on Pentecost, is seen as an integral facet of the Easter event. In however many different ways the New Testament witnesses shift their focus from Christ's exaltation to the anointing of his disciples with his Spirit, the two realities are inseparable. In Christ's exaltation the triumphal presence of the Spirit of God within him is evident. This same Spirit becomes available to all with whom Jesus is able to have human contact through his own exalted human body. Schillebeeckx contends that at Pentecost a new people is "christened," or anointed, to be the sacramental extension of Jesus' mission and presence in the world (1963: p. 35).

Modern recognition of the link between the presence of Christ in and through the Church's life and his resurrection thus brings the contemporary Church closer to the perspective of the New Testament witnesses of the Risen Jesus. Instead of presenting the resurrection as a mere historical fact from which conclusions could be drawn, the earliest witnesses affirmed it because they experienced his ongoing life in a great variety of ways. They experienced the power of his presence, and thus affirmed the outpouring of his Spirit on their own community.

STAGE THREE: THE CHURCH'S MISSIONARY PROCLAMATION: Finally, the Biblical Commission says, "this primitive instruction" was   (1) put into the written form of the gospels by authors who   (2) "selected some things, reduced others to a synthesis" and   (3) "explained these now in one context, now in another, depending on their usefulness to their readers" (Instruction, IX; see Fitzmyer: p. 405). Thus, first, the contemporary Church knows that it probes for history in faith statements crafted to meet the needs of ancient people and movements. Secondly, it recognizes that the faith of those who contributed to the gospels was expressed in historically conditioned ways. These two points help account for the vast changes that have taken place in Christology from the New Testament to modern times.

Christology of Faith Experience: Recognition that the gospels provides historical evidence within statements of faith has made us both distinguish faith from history and affirm the priority of faith. The gospels are not "histories of Jesus" on which we build faith. The historian's approach to Jesus is objective, disinterested, aimed at describing a phenomenon with as little evaluation of its significance or commitment to it as possible. Of course, we realize that this objectivity is more an ideal than an achievement. Nonetheless, the historian would outline and account for events in the past and beyond our experience. None of the evangelists can be thought to have assumed such a task.

Clearly, the gospels are professions of faith in Jesus. They expressed what particular Christian communities believed, and were meant to arouse faith in particular situations. Faith statements are meant to draw others into an experience that corresponds to our own experience of Christ in our lives.

Statements of faith invite others to share a very personal, or better inter-personal knowledge. They conform more to the language of love than to the language of science. They state what someone, in this case Christ, *means to us,* using stories, sayings and descriptions to convey this meaning. But just as details about a person do not add up to what he (or she) means to those who really know and love 'him (or her), so also statements of faith are always incomplete. Moreover, because they are efforts to share an experiential appreciation of God's presence in our lives, they focus on the aspects of our experience that we think we are most likely to communicate to a given person or community. They are, therefore, both partial and historically conditioned statements.

Biblical scholars led the way in coming to a recognition that Christological statements are primarily theological, and that they are historically conditioned statements. For a variety of reasons, especially among Catholics, the partial and historically conditioned character of doctrinal statements has been grasped more slowly.

However, in 1973, the Vatican's Congregation for Doctrine applied principles very similar to earlier principles of biblical criticism to later Church doctrines. It acknowledged that: (1) "the meaning of the pronouncements of the faith depends partly on the expressive power of the language used at a certain point in time"; (2) "dogmatic truth is first explained incompletely"; (3) "when the Church makes new pronouncements . . . she usually has the intention of solving certain questions or removing certain errors. All these things have to be taken into account . . ." (Brown 1975: pp. 116-17). This pronouncement signals a general recognition that all Christological statements, whether in the New Testament or in the creeds, serve the same purpose. They are all part of the Christian movement's witness to its continuing experience of the Risen Christ, a witness springing from and accommodating to various cultural and historical circumstances.

Just as the gospel portrait of Jesus emerged in three stages, the modern search for the historical Jesus has taken three steps. First, the gospels were read as though they were histories of Jesus. Second, the historians attempted to separate the historical from the religious or theological statements within the gospels. Finally, it became clear that all that is historical in the gospels has been expressed from a theological or religious perspective. In this long development, the Christian movement has come to understand that it must understand itself, and therefore Jesus himself, historically, as part of history. But it has also come to understand that history is not its primary concern, at least not a disinterested history. Rather, its focus is on the manifold ways that Christ through the Christian movement has interacted with history not merely in the first century but in all succeeding centuries.

3. Jesus: Role Model for the Modern Person

Modern Christians likewise tend to see Jesus as a role model. Christians have always tried to follow Jesus. Yet, more typically, pre-modern Christians saw themselves as part of the community of disciples, the followers. Moderns see themselves as individuals more than as members of groups. They therefore see Jesus as a personal model to be imitated. Increasingly, some modern theologians have reinterpreted past statements about Christ to draw attention to Jesus' personality as the model for Christian or human anthropology. Others have speculated on ideal forms of humanity and imposed these qualities on their "Christs." Interestingly, the most typical example of *devotio moderna,* Thomas a Kempis' *Imitation of Christ,* is said to be the most reprinted book after the Bible.

Books in the hands of individuals contribute to their sense of individuality in important ways. Without books, people must come together in communities to listen to one another, but even more to listen to the community authorities to discover the meaning of life or how to live. Who Christ is was transmitted to earlier generations of Christians in the publicly read gospel, or even more likely in the sacramental celebrations of the Church. With printed books, the Christian could go off alone to study Christ. In such solitude the pious could measure themselves against the example of Jesus.

At the same time, with books in print authors could make a living writing by holding an exclusive right to their work. Copyrights made authors conscious of themselves as individual authors, and bolstered the growing sense of other people who saw themselves as individuals. Against this background poets and artists increasingly attributed their work to an individual and unique genius. Similarly, philosphers focused their attention on how the human mind functioned as well as on whether and how human beings reached some form of transcendent meaning or fulfillment. What does it mean to be a person? To answer this increasingly central question, modern Christians pointed to the model humanity they saw in Jesus.

Incarnation and Anthropology: The belief that Jesus is the Word become flesh, become human, incarnate, is the foundation for increasingly rich reflection on what it means to be human. Particularly in the writings of Karl Rahner (d. 1984), a challenging Christian anthropology has emerged from philosophical analysis of the humanity of Jesus. This anthropology maintains that Jesus' humanity reveals transcendent potentialities within the human person. These potentialities come to full realization only in Jesus' humanity. But if they are realized in this one person who is truly human, then they are genuinely human potentialities. Jesus, then, is the human being in its fullest realization. As such, he is a challenge to other humans to transcend their own limited realizations of humanity.

Can humans transcend their finite condition? Do humans have a real capacity to relate to the infinite? In practical terms the issue is: Do human beings contribute anything to their salvation or relationship to God? Catholic theology has always affirmed some co-operation between God and humans. Protestant theology has tended to insist that humans are saved by God's free grace, and thus has denied or minimized the human contribution. Some modern thinkers have denied the existence or relevance of anything really transcendent. Many modern religious philosophers have argued that God is infinite, humans finite, and have spoken of an "infinite qualitative distinction" between the infinite and the finite. Those who accept such a distinction have generally had to assert that this infinite gap has been bridged solely by God's decision to relate to humans, if they wanted to affirm the personal relationship that Christian faith envisions between God and humans.

In a creative way, Rahner's incarnational Christology responds to this problem of Christian anthropology. As a point of departure, he says that we should not speak, of *God becoming human*, but of *the Son or the Word becoming human.* He is not in any way challenging the Son's divinity. Instead, he wants to make a crucial point: the Christian doctrine of the Trinity affirms that there are real distinctions in God. The Word is God's self-expression, God is so far as God has given his own self. As Rahner says,

> He brings about that which is distinct from himself, in the act of retaining it as his own, and vice versa, because he truly wills to retain the other as his own, he constitutes it as his own reality. God goes out of himself, God in his quality of the fullness which gives away itself. . . Scripture defines him as love — whose prodigal freedom is the indefinable itself. (1966: p. 115)

Thus, the Word is the Infinite reaching out, first within its own being, but then through this outreach to others, whom the Infinite must create.

For Rahner, creation comes from God through this Word. The "Other" that is in God is the ultimate foundation for "others," creation. God in his inmost being is disposed to create and co-exist with "others." In this, Rahner is in agreement with the tendency to say that created beings are related to God solely because God created them. Humans are simply dependent on God, the finite on the Infinite.

However, the Word, even though he is "Other," is also fully and truly God, Infinite. If the Word has gone one step beyond being the "Other in God" to becoming one of the "others" created, then God's disposition to reach out includes becoming part of the history of finite beings. In other words, the Infinite is not only able to create the finite, but to exist within the finite. In some real sense a finite being, Jesus, is truly the human expression of God's own being.

"This man is, as such, the self-utterance of God in its self-emptying, because God expresses *himself* when he empties himself. He proclaims *himself* as love when he hides the majesty of this love and shows himself in the ordinary way of men" (Rahner 1966: p. 116). Therefore, finite beings are not incapable of truly expressing God's own will. They must be capable, because Jesus is finite and did it. No other finite being may do it adequately, but it is not their creatureliness as such that impedes them. The fact that the Infinite has become human reveals that humans have a potentiality for infinite being.

Simply put, a finite expression of God's love can nonetheless really be an expression of God's infinite love. Human love does not become infinite, but it really expresses the infinite. We can indeed love unselfishly, transcend egotism, in finite, historically conditioned steps. The human Jesus, whose self-giving love was absolute, makes this clear. Thus, Jesus, God's Self-Utterance or Self-Giving Incarnate, reveals the possibility that humans have for transcending themselves. Because God has related this concretely to us, we can respond with actions that are truly our own.

CRISIS CHRISTOLOGY: Many theologians find Rahner's theology abstract, i.e. divorced from concrete life. Karl Barth (d. 1968), perhaps the greatest Protestant theologian in the modern era, regarded this kind of theology as premature. He, too, finally capped volumes of theological exploration with a book entitled *The Humanity of God*. But Barth began and focused his work on the theme that God's Otherness is revealed in Christ. All history and creation must be seen in a new light because Christ stands in contradiction of ordinary human expectations and understanding. This emphasis on a divine otherness beyond human expectation came from Barth's reflection on the breakdown of Christian Europe which he saw first in World War I and then again in Nazi Germany. It was also a direct response to the optimistic nineteenth century theology that had seen human development in terms rather similar to Rahner. Barth did not repudiate this hopeful vision, but he did say that the humanity of which it spoke did not yet exist. If it was ever to exist, then theology had to address the present crisis situation, and speak of human salvation as the pure gift of God, not as a human project in itself.

The Man-for-Others: Barth's perspective was particularly shared by a Lutheran pastor who was martyred in the struggle against Nazism, Dietrich Bonhoeffer (d. 1945). His Christology is summed up in the phrase "Christ is the Man-for-Others." Bonhoeffer was far more interested in what Christ required his disciples to do and make with their lives than in what humans were capable of. Although he, too, began with the Incarnation, his Christology led first to ethics, and from Christology and ethics to a new vision of human life.

When Bonhoeffer framed the issue of human transcendence, he did so in terms of the crisis confronting modern human beings. *How can we live wholly for others and yet free from their control?* (Phillips 1967: p. 101). As a young theologian of great promise, he had been urged by American friends to remain in the safety of the United States. But

Bonhoeffer returned to Nazi Germany to give his life for his people, eager to be one of them without succumbing to their national idolatry. Shortly before his execution he outlined a chapter of a book, noting:

> What is God? ... Encounter with Jesus. The experience that here there is a reversal of all human existence, in that Jesus is there solely 'for others'. This 'being-there-for-others' to the point of death is the experience of transcendence! Out of freedom from self, out of 'being-there-for-others' to the point of death, emerges omnipotence, omniscience, omnipresence. Faith is participation in this being of Jesus (incarnation, cross, resurrection (Phillips: p. 197).

Being-there-for-others was the only form of human transcendence Bonhoeffer thought consistent with following Christ, and he thought it possible because of Christ.

Bonhoeffer insisted that the only legitimate question about Christ was "Who is Christ?" never "How could such a person be?" (1966: p. 27-33). His point is that Jesus is the God-Man, an utterly unique person. Human experience gives us no basis for asking the second question. However, if we accept the proposition that Jesus is the God-Man, we do so not by defining the terms, but only by following him. Bonhoeffer concluded, "The only true relation we can have with him [if he is the God-Man] is to follow him." Indeed, "Christianity without discipleship is Christianity without Christ" (1963: p. 64). Clearly, Bonhoeffer follows the long tradition of making Christ the exemplar for a new life, the life of the Christian.

But Bonhoeffer insisted that discipleship, following Christ, is not a matter of imitation. We are not "called to do the things that he does" (1966: p. 38). Rather we are called to be as he is, being-there-for-others. Bonhoeffer saw Christ as an incognito revelation of God, God present in weakness and suffering rather than in omnipotence and glory. God in Christ is in the finite created world (incarnation), God in Christ is under the sentence of death (cross), God in Christ is in a new form of humanity beyond the power of death (resurrection). The point is not so much that Christ suffered for us, but that he is there for us even though being-there-for-us required death. From this standpoint, his death becomes a context in which a truly transcendent possibility is revealed. Even in death God is present. Thus, for Bonhoeffer God is present even in creation and in the most mundane affairs of finite life. To follow Christ is being-there-for-others, a real transcendence of finite existence, in whatever any human being does.

In some ways Bonhoeffer continued Lutheran traditions that emphasized the following of Christ and a theology of the cross. But in significant ways, by focusing attention on the incarnation and also on the resurrection, he was led to see a meaning to all human actions within the world that was unprecedented in Lutheranism — and in the way he formulated it, even within the rest of the Christian movement. To an extraordinary degree he insisted that Christ is present, and that his being-there-for-others may be experienced throughout creation, in all kinds of people and situations. Consequently, the follower of Christ must be as immersed in the whole life of the world, in all kinds of activities and communities, as Christ himself. Bonhoeffer's phrase "religionless Christianity" needs to be interpreted in the light of his emphasis on the importance of the Church's task of preaching and celebrating the Eucharist. Nevertheless, he clearly saw Christ as a reality often experienced far beyond the bounds of what people regard as "religious experience."

Christ: The Model Human: Rahner, Bonhoeffer and many others have refocused the Christological question, "Who is the Christ?" around the issue of how Jesus relates to humans without in any sense calling into question his divinity. They have shifted the modern theological world more in the direction of the School of Antioch than of Alexandria. They made this shift in different ways. Rahner said that Christ reveals the transcendent possibilities in human nature. Bonhoeffer said that Christ remains present within the human community, revealing a way of being and calling humans to follow him in living it out. In both cases a new form of humanity is understood to be the principal effect of Christ's life. But each theologian drew not only a Christological and anthropological conclusion, but a properly theological conclusion as well: a fresh understanding of who God is in relation to humans, an understanding for the modern individual to reflect on as he or she comes to terms with what they are and what they have to become.

4. The Jesus of Personal Religious Experience

Frequently, modern Christians have understood Christ in terms of personal religious experience. Earlier Christians certainly knew Christ in religious experience. But more typically their experiences were communal, part of the sacramental life of the whole Church, not self-consciously individual. More often in the modern period, the experience itself is highly personal and the understanding of Christ is claimed to be unique and incommunicable. Those who "know Jesus as their personal Savior" bypass not only intellectual approaches, but social life.

Individualized Religiosity in Modern Life: Two rather different trends in modern life, both related to print, explain the preference for individualized religious experience. First, print created the potential for a world of information overload, more data than most people could process readily. Once Christians might have heard one gospel read with vague recollections of other gospels in mind. With print the rather diverse biblical collection could be immediately at hand, to say nothing of the endless commentaries and interpretations equally accessible. Especially for those who confronted such growing complexity in more and more areas of everyday life, the desire to escape complexity — to have a simple and immediate understanding of God — could be strong.

The other modern trend supporting personalized religious experience over communal definitions of religious faith was the half-conscious, half-instinctive cultural decision to *privatize* religion. *Privatization* was the process by which religion was increasingly removed from the arena of public life, from direct influence on economic, social and political affairs, and restricted to the domestic and interior life of the individual.

Often perceived as an attack on religion, sometimes interpreted as a cowardly retreat by the Church, privatization responded to the need to distinguish one area of life from another. In modern life no one person could master all the professions, just as no one person could read all available literature. Cataloguing books and segmenting life went hand in hand. If religion did not have a public role, then its ultimate justification lay in the satisfaction it gave the private individual. If it was inappropriate to bring religion into the marketplace or courthouse, then it was only necessary to know Christ within one's own heart.

THE THERAPEUTIC NEED: Information overload divides modern societies into those in the know and those in the dark, experts and non-experts. Specialization and clear lines demarcating one area of activity from another (e.g., politics from religion) also divide these societies into those who are in control in one area from those who are controlled. When we put just these two trends together (and many similar ones could be added) the effect is that modern individuals experience a lack of control in increasing areas of their lives.

In the past individuals did not generally control all the areas of their lives, but they probably did not experience the lack. Why? Because the individual person in a more traditional society presumed that each of the persons or powers in control of, for example, political life were put there by God to do what they did.

Today the characteristically modern political leader does not claim such a divine sanction. Politicians, as well as the professionals in education, business, medicine and even the Church, claim a right to do what they do based on their specialized skills and understanding. The problem with this is that the individual, who lacks such a background, does not know whether such a claim is true. Even more, competing claims among the specialists and experts leave people bewildered and frustrated. Their life experience is fragmented, broken. They need healing, some way of curing the brokenness. This therapeutic need is pervasive.

Jesus as Personal Savior: Given the modern therapeutic need, it is understandable that religious life would also take a therapeutic form. This has happened in ever so many ways. For example, pastors of all religious traditions are routinely expected to function as counselors, the rites of forgiveness have been restructured to provide more opportunity for personal catharsis, and vocation is increasingly defined more in terms of personal fulfillment than social responsibility. But the triumph of the therapeutic is nowhere better attested than in the new focus on Jesus as Personal Savior. Unquestionably, Jesus was always seen as Savior. Yet the central place this Christology has for some people, and the qualification of "Savior" with the adjective "Personal" shows a distinctly new therapeutic orientation.

All the terms associated with this approach to Jesus are traditional, open to a wide range of concrete meanings, but nonetheless modified as "Savior" was modified. This cluster of terms includes *born again, charismatic, baptized in the Spirit, pentecostal, evangelical,* even indeed *Christian.* Most of these terms are rooted in the New Testament. Moreover, we must be careful not to assume that everyone who is described in such terms has the same sort of religious life or commitment. Thus, to be a "born again" Southern Baptist is in many instances no more of an emotional experience than being a confirmed Episcopalian.

On the other hand, among those who stress the model of Jesus as Personal Savior each of these terms has been infused with a sense of a highly charged emotional experience by which the person is radically converted to Christ. This conversion is seldom seen as a step-by-step process of growth. It is rather an instantaneous transformation, in which the whole person for all practical purposes changes identity. It is this total transformation of the person, this healing experience of conversion to Christ, that modifies all the traditional categories of Christian faith and life.

Not surprisingly, theologies and Christologies are not characteristic expressions of this approach. Indeed, those who know charismatics will recall that they enthusiatically describe their religious feelings, make sometimes streneous efforts to recruit others, and place a great deal of emphasis on prayer. For the most part critical or philosophical analysis of their religious life and belief is avoided. For this reason it is difficult to name a representative theologian for this point of view. We can point to preachers, especially revivalist evangelists such as Billy Graham, and to healers such as Oral Roberts and Fr. DiOrio. Their books are sermons in print, and emotionally charged sermons at that.

The rhetorical style of the revivalist sermon illustrates, without making us fully appreciate, the dynamic of this approach. The preacher testifies to the power the Spirit of Christ has given in his own life, reinforcing this theme frequently by vivid contrast with his former wretchedness and sin. Everything leads to a call to decide to step forth into a new life, to receive Christ's Spirit, "to make a decision for Christ." Put off the old, take on the new. Become a new person with completely new powers given by the Spirit. More traditional Catholics will recognize here the psychology of the "Missions" that used to be preached in Catholic parishes.

Thus, the person who accepts Jesus as Personal Savior relates to Christ as the source of a new understanding of himself and even more of a transformed sense of his own power. His prayer becomes enthusiastic conversation with a close friend, rather than a formal ritual or a more meditative moment of reflection. His reading of the Bible becomes a means of gaining direct guidance from God on the details of everyday life. No problem of everyday life is faced outside of the context of this immediate relationship to Jesus. Even the outcome of historical events is often seen as immediately responsive to prayer, even though he knows that much of the world does not have the same relationship to Jesus. This is the pattern of the life of the "born again," though we must note that it is lived out with varying degrees of intensity.

FORMS OF HEALING: Although all who accept Jesus as Personal Savior do not emphasize charismatic gifts, and some stress one or another, we can see the healing power of their conversion by looking at the most dramatic gifts they attribute to the Holy Spirit. These are healing, prophecy and speaking in tongues. People need a reasonable sense of physical and mental well being, a sense of what the future holds and the ability to express themselves to others. To ground our confidence that we have these needs fulfilled in an immediate relationship to Christ through the power of the Holy Spirit does indeed impart a sense of being ultimately saved from all possible evils, and thus to have a source of control over our lives.

When the charismatic affirms that prayer will bring healing (even when he accepts the use of medicine), he affirms that Christ provides health. When the charismatic reads the Bible for "prophecies" being fulfilled in the contemporary world, or understands his own or others' pronouncements as predictions given by the Holy Spirit, he is enabled to deal with whatever threatens in the world as having both a purpose and, in the case of evil, an end. Even speaking in tongues, which is perhaps less emphasized than the others, serves a discernible purpose. As one observer noted, "what a blessed release the gift of tongues must be to people frustrated and defenseless because they are slow of speech" (Taylor 1972: pp. 217-18). Anyone who has dreaded the necessity of getting up to speak in public will recognize that to be convinced that what one says will come from the Holy Spirit might make all the difference.

The experience of Jesus, and the Holy Spirit he communicates, does indeed serve a healing function for these people. They call Jesus their Personal Savior because in a real way their experience leads them into a new life free from the frustration of their former lives. Jesus is indeed an anchor for their personal existence.

5. Modern Christs/Modern Christians: A Preliminary Assessment

Modernity confronts the Christian movement with the reality of change. Christology in the last couple of centuries has increasingly dealt with this great fact of modernity. The search for the historical Jesus documented and accounted for the changes Christians observed, for their growing sense of distance from the events of Jesus' own ministry. The effort to understand human existence and responsibility by analyzing the human Christ gave the Christian movement a deepened sense of its own relationship to the changing world, how it should or could respond to a constantly changing human family. The attempt to anchor personal life in an immediate experience of Jesus as the healing, transforming center of one's life reflects the Christian movement's conviction that change need not threaten the victory won by Christ. Each of these modern Christian movements, enrich our understanding of Christ.

On the other hand, modernity burdens the Christian movement, as did the Hellenistic world, with its own peculiar limitations. We are not yet in a position to fully appreciate these because they are our own limitations. Perhaps the most noticeable limitation is that while the Christian movement understands that it has changed, that we are different from earlier Christians, it still fails to fully understand that we are also different from many other people. We have come to understand Christ in terms of history, anthropology and personal identity. We have barely recognized that all of these are either Western, indeed European concerns, or are interpreted according to Western patterns. The Christian movement has been better at meeting Western needs than moving Western Christians beyond their fascination with themselves to encounter other peoples. Indeed, the greatest weakness is that we have tended to narrow our focus to the concerns of private Western life, downplaying the social and political implications of Christ's mission in the world.

WORKS CITED

Karl Barth
   1960 *The Humanity of God*. Richmond: John Knox.
Dietrich Bonhoeffer
   1963 *The Cost of Discipleship*. New York: Macmillan.
   1966 *Christ the Center*. New York: Harper & Row.
Raymond E. Brown
   1975 *Biblical Reflections on Crises Facing the Church*. New York: Paulist.
Francis X. Durwell
   1960 *The Resurrection*. New York: Sheed and Ward.
Joseph A. Fitzmyer
   1964 "The Biblical Commission's Instruction on the Historical Truth of the Gospels," *Theological Studies 25:* pp. 386-408.
John A. Phillips
   1967 *Christ for Us in the Theology of Dietrich Bonhoeffer*. New York: Harper & Row.
Karl Rahner
   1966 *Theological Investigations: Vol. IV*. Baltimore: Helicon.
Edward Schillebeeckx
   1963 *Christ the Sacrament of Encounter with God*. New York: Sheed and Ward.
Albert Schweitzer
   1968 *The Quest of the Historical Jesus: A Critical Study of its Progress from Reimarus to Wrede*. New York: Macmillan.
John V. Taylor
   1972 *The Go-Between God: The Holy Spirit and the Christian Mission*. New York: Oxford Univ. Press.

CHAPTER EIGHT

CHRIST AND THE CHRISTIAN MOVEMENT IN THE GLOBAL VILLAGE: PLURALISM, DIALOG AND COLLABORATION

Questions to think about:

— *What accounts for the broader vision of Christians today?*
— *How have new voices helped Christians become self-critical?*
— *How do dialog and collaboration reshape Christology?*
— *How has concern for the future focused attention on the Jesus of history?*

Although there had been a Jewish community in Rome long before Christ, they had their first truly warmhearted meeting with a Bishop of Rome in 1958. Pope John XXIII greeted a delegation from this community, "I am Joseph, your brother."

Pope John's greeting symbolized and to a certain degree helped establish a new relationship between the Christian movement and other groups within the human family. In the last half of the twentieth century the Christian movement has come to acknowledge and to accept cultural and religious pluralism within the human family. It sees the rest of the world differently. It has begun to employ dialog and collaboration instead of power and control to further the work of Christ in this pluralistic world.

As Pope John reached back to the account of the patriarch Joseph greeting the other sons of Jacob (Gn 45:4) for his own greeting, the contemporary Christian movement has searched its tradition for elements that promote dialog. As Angelo Giuseppe Roncalli identified himself by his baptismal name, Giuseppe or Joseph, rather than by his official name, John XXIII, so also the contemporary Church has tried to affirm that humans have a common task. Transcending institutional commitments, the Church must collaborate with others. Likewise, by meeting others as brothers and sisters, the late twentieth century Church community implies that it now shares responsibility in the world instead of ruling the world in Christ's name.

To be sure, popes and representative Jews had met before. But from the time of Constantine, popes met Jews (and the Church confronted other communities) on an unequal footing. It was assumed that the world, in principle, should be Christian, and in practice, that it should be Christian in a European sense. The faith and the European cultural embodiment of that faith would be brought to the ends of the earth. Missionaries from Rome, Constantinople and various Protestant centers might disagree over many details, but they all followed a missionary strategy that saw other religious and cultural traditions in colonialist terms.

Dialog and collaboration presuppose that both sides have something to give and something to learn, that neither side seeks to eliminate the other. So fundamental a shift in the Christian movement's understanding of its relationship to the rest of the world inevitably changes its answer to the question, "Who do you say that Christ is?"

Theology has been increasingly subjected to a political and cultural critique. This critique has demonstrated how the Christian movement has given legitimacy to both good and bad features of Western political and cultural institutions. In response, movements for liberation within the Western world and within the Third world have begun to create theologies that answer their own questions. Simultaneously, scholars have become increasingly sensitive to the Jewish Jesus. Jesus cannot be understood apart from his times and culture. To read the gospels and to understand early Christianity, this ancient milieu vastly different from our own must be studied. This realization may provide Western Christians with a basis for accepting genuine pluralism within the contemporary Christian movement.

1. Christianity in the Age of the Holocaust

Why, late in the twentieth century, have people around the world become so aware of their interdependence? Why do people so frequently speak of living on a small planet or in a global village? No single answer explains so great a change. But one powerful explanation exists. Today all humans, but Christians especially, live in the Age of the Holocaust. Holocaust refers to a sacrifice in which the victim is burnt up, totally consumed. Today, it applies to the actual Holocaust carried out by Nazi Germany in which European Jewry was virtually extinguished. The nuclear bombs dropped on Hiroshima and Nagasaki also signaled the possibility of a final Holocaust in which humanity could be extinguished. Because of this common threat we must consider the human race to be composed of interdependent, mutually vulnerable people.

Both forms of Holocaust, moreover, have forced Christians to make an agonizing reappraisal because of our own complicity in these nightmares. A nominally Christian Germany planned and executed the final solution to the "Jewish Problem." A nation in which the overwhelming majority of the population were active Christians developed and delivered the first atomic weapons. In the first case, the Nazis exploited centuries of popular anti-Semitism. This anti-Semitism had been nourished by Christian preaching that blamed Jews, if not always for the death of Christ, then at least for not accepting Jesus as the Christ (see Klein; Ruether). In the second case, Americans reflected a tendency to overidentify their cause with divine justice itself, a tendency even more pronounced in its later confrontation with Communism, making it difficult to set limits to its use of power.

If people genuinely think they are fighting "godless forces" or an "empire of evil," a call for compromise, dialog and co-operation is out of the question. On the other hand, more sober minded people have recognized that we have prepared a conflict in which at best the victors will envy the vanquished. Has the pursuit of victory finally become counterproductive?

In this new context people have to think the unthinkable, to raise fresh questions. For example, Christians have asked whether and in what circumstances it is permissible to seek the conversion of Jews (see Osborn). In one meeting between Jewish leaders and a Jesuit theologian in the mid-sixties, the Jesuit began by saying that Jews have to accept the fact that belief in Christ requires us to seek converts from all people including Jews. A Jewish theologian replied, "Then, Father, I take it that in the long run the Christians must wish that there be a world in which there are *no Jews.*" He added, "Judenrein," German for "uncontaminated by Jews," Hitler's slogan. His Catholic partner had to repudiate this conclusion, but the issue of how Christ was to be proclaimed in a genuinely pluralistic world remained.

2. Critique of Western Establishment Christianity

Modern Christians often complain that the Church is blamed for evils beyond its control. Were not the Nazis neo-pagans, or at least heretics from Christianity? Are churchmen today really part of the establishment? What power do they have over public affairs, issues of war and peace or social, economic and political life? Are they not limited to providing a moral background for socially conscious private individuals? The Church was responsible for injustices and persecutions of past ages when churchmen often directly intervened in public affairs by preaching crusades, trying heretics and even leading their own armies in battle. But that, some contemporary Christians say, is past history.

Political Theology: Nonetheless, a new theological specialty has appeared since World War II, political theology. Borrowing insights from sociology, political theology provides a critique of the political implications of theological statements. Political theologians argue that every statement about how God relates to human beings implies, at least, something about the use of power in society.

Earlier theologies often told Christians explicitly that the ruler was divinely appointed; that the existing social hierarchy was divinely intended. Modern theologies rarely draw direct political conclusions. But their silence lends support to the existing establishment. The modern Church also generally asserts that it is politically neutral. But political theologians contend that if one is neutral when one group effectively controls another, one acquiesces in the pattern of domination. Political theologians contend that the Church must take responsibility for its actual, though unintended, political involvment.

PRIVATIZED CHRISTIANITY: In modern times religion
has been increasingly removed from the arena of public life
and restricted to domestic and interior life. We have already
called attention to this process of privatization. Political
theologians, such as Johannes Baptist Metz, believe modern
theologians have collaborated in this privatization. Trying
to find new meaning for faith in the secularized world, they
have focused all their attention on "the intimate, the private,
the apolitical sphere. . . It is true that these theologians
strongly emphasize charity and all that belongs to the sphere
of interpersonal relations; yet, from the beginning and as
though there were no questions, they regard charity as a
private virtue with no political relevance" (1969: p. 109).

Metz asks: if the gospels were not meant to be
biographies of Jesus, are they not the *kerygma,* the public
proclamation of his message and work? How is this to be
appreciated if Christian life is described as though it could
be lived in private?

Political theologians observe that preaching the gospel
almost exclusively to private individuals distorts the gospel
and fails the individuals themselves. Why? Because the private individual is a modern though potent illusion, cut off
from his own real situation. Politics includes all activities by
which power is exercised, economic life as well as government. Certainly, economics touches even the most private
individual at the core of moral life.

Yet our understanding of ourselves as private individuals leads the modern person, especially Americans, to ignore
the political dimension of our economic affairs. But Frederick Herzog has observed, "Adam Smith's image of man
as economic man still dominates our political and economic
relationships, in fact, our entire existence" (1970: p. 1381).
Smith had argued that society is best served if each individual seeks only his own interests, that the good of society

will emerge if all individuals are left free to maximize their own wealth. Economic man is not merely an individual, but a competitor with fellow humans. If this describes the concrete person of twentieth century Western society, theologians have to help Western people to face their true selves, to see the individual's power over or powerlessness before fellow human beings.

The individual does not take power relationships seriously because moral teaching has given one-sided emphasis to private or interpersonal issues. Church leaders, especially Catholic leaders, have made frequent pronouncements on economic and political issues for almost a century. Yet private sin dominates the Christian conception of evil. Adultery and anger, for example, are far more likely to be seen as sin than the failure to provide a family wage or cooperating in racial discrimination. Even when social, cultural or economic evils are recognized, Christians frequently assume that these are problems to be addressed by each individual doing what lies within his own immediate powers. But if these evils are structural, supported by the norms and institutions of the larger social structure, an individual is relatively powerless. In such situations only organized groups taking politically meaningful action are adequate to do the good.

Individualist Christology: Because it has been privatized, Christianity preaches an individualist Christology. This began when Christians moved from the Jewish world into the Hellenistic establishment. Theologians began to ask questions about Jesus' nature rather than his work. The questions are revealing: Did Jesus have a human soul, a will? Was he born of human intercourse? Did he have freedom to sin or know who he was? All these questions refer largely to Jesus' individuality as a human person. The long-term effect has been to present Christ as a unique individual, one who stands out from all other human beings.

In other words, theologians described Christ as Western thinkers describe other persons. He is a true individual to the extent that he is free from others, surpasses others, or has success that others lack. When a recent Broadway production proclaimed "Jesus Christ Superstar," it borrowed a Western ideal of the person and epitomized this individualized Christology (see White: pp. 55-57).

Christ's humanity has been defined without reference to his relationship to other humans. The classical Christological text has been "The Word became flesh." Little emphasis falls on the rest of the text, "and dwelt (*literally* pitched his tent) in our midst." His uniqueness, rather than his embeddedness in the human situation, has been focal.

To be a human being is to be a member of the human community. This is the corporate definition of humanity. It stands in contrast to the definition that focuses on individual characteristics and achievements. Within the ancient Jewish context, the corporate understanding would have been self-evident. In less individualistic phases of Western culture, the communal foundation of personality would have been taken for granted. A person is part of a people, not an isolated individual. Personal identity, worth and achievements are shared realities.

Jesus' Humanity: When Jesus' humanity is defined corporately rather than individually, his relationship to human sin becomes more complex and meaningful. It is true that Jesus is "like us in all things except sin" (Heb 4:15). Likewise, Christians will always see his death as a sacrifice because of sin. However, both Jesus' sinlessness and his sacrifice have been presented in ways that create distance between him and the rest of the human race. Properly interpreted, these doctrines proclaim his identity with others.

Once human beings are understood corporately, the existential truth contained in the doctrine of original sin becomes clear. This truth is that all human beings share the good and evil of their brothers and sisters of all times. The moral options available to any individual have been somewhat predetermined by others. To act morally is to calculate the effect of our moral decision in terms of probable reaction and response from others. For example, to avert greater probable violence, we may decide to use limited forms of violence. Likewise, we know that even our best deeds may set in place a chain of actions producing incalculable evil. Therefore, the subjective question, whether the individual intends evil, obscures a major consideration. The objective fact that human deeds inevitably fit within partly evil patterns and structures, often turns a private good into a public evil. Not to take this structure into account is clearly unrealistic, if not immoral.

Given this human predicament, what does Jesus' sinlessness means? If Jesus' deeds took place within a partly evil human social structure, he is involved in human sin. Within his own ministry, for example, he chose Judas — a disciple who would not only betray him but also end his own life in despair. In choosing the other disciples from whom the Church devleloped, personal flaws were unavoidable. Throughout the long history of the Church the flawed personalities have proliferated. The history of Jesus' movement is a history that includes intolerance of others, Church-sponsored persecution, crusades and much else besides a growth in brotherhood and holiness.

It is superficial to say that the evil came in spite of Jesus' intentions. Clearly, in all too many instances people have been guilty of these evils precisely because of their faith, their concern for the righteousness Jesus taught, and to which he calls them. It is superficial to believe that evil comes only, or even primarily, from evil individuals. With the best intentions, genuinely following Jesus, good people sin. Jesus is implicated.

Since Jesus and all humans share responsibility for human history and its structural sin, how they have responded is the significant question, not whether they were involved. Typically, people isolate themselves from their fellow human beings, claiming that they have done their best, and are responsible only for their own private decisions and intentions. They focus on the issue of individual involvement to avoid responsibility. Evil comes from other individuals, or perhaps the devil, some will say. Others acknowledge a limited private evil and make some satisfaction for it. Their responsibility is limited, as though they could opt out of the human family. For this reason, the objective structural evil continues, unacknowledged because no one is responsible for it.

The only way to break the power of structural evil is to break the pattern of claiming limited, merely individualist, involvement in the human family. Only when people are willing to acknowledge their responsibility for all the evil their fellow humans suffer, and pay the price for this, is the pattern broken. Jesus took this responsiblity and paid this price. This is what his death means when seen as a sacrifice.

JESUS' SACRIFICE: Indeed, the whole point of Jesus' sacrifice is that he accepted his implication in and responsibility for human sin. Interpretation of the cross in sacrificial terms often gets off on the wrong foot. Is Jesus perceived as the priest offering the sacrifice? Or as the victim sacrificed? The gospels relate Jesus to the Passover Lamb slaughtered, not to the High Priest doing the offering. Only in the Epistle to the Hebrews is Jesus described as Priest. Primarily, Jesus is the victim, the "Lamb." Moreover, he is the "Lamb, who bears the sin of the world," who is marked for slaughter because he is the scapegoated representative of the sinful people. In this sense, he dies instead of them, or better he accepts his death instead of permitting others to give their lives to prevent it.

Jesus' death contradicts common understandings of sacrifice. How do sacrifices work? How is sacrificial activity commonly understood?

Commonly, we make sacrifice a ritual of appeasement in which the life of a human or animal victim is offered to hold off the threat that one's own life will be taken. Personal or community blame is placed on an animal or someone else. The scapegoated victim is cast out of the community to die, or is directly slaughtered. This victim's life is less important than the life of the priest or the community the priest represents. This common understanding of sacrifice implies that all are not parts of a single family or common creation before God. When a human being tries to defer or exempt himself from death by claiming to be less sinful than others, he denies co-responsibility in order to preserve his individual life and possessions. He sacrifices someone or something else.

Jesus completed a long process of redefinition of sacrifice in Israelite tradition. The story of Abraham's interrupted sacrifice of Isaac is generally thought to represent a rejection of human sacrifice in ancient Israel. The prophets challenged the conventional approach to sacrifice with more lasting effect than is generally recognized. By the time of Jesus, many Jews had come to see sacrifice in symbolic and ethical terms as signifying obedience to God. And "once the value of sacrifice was seen precisely as an act of obedient piety, it was not difficult to see other acts of obedient piety as being able to achieve what was previously thought to be achievable only by ritual sacrifice" (Daly: p. 137).

Thus, Jesus lived this life of obedient service, which contradicted the notion that one life should be substituted for another. He did not sacrifice himself; that would be suicide. He was the victim, not the offerer, not the priest. What he did was to obey his Father by acting in solidarity with his fellow humans. In going to his death placing blame on no one else, Jesus placed his life in his Father's hands and stood united with, unwilling to sacrifice any of, the human family. In so acting, he was the kind of Son the Father wishes all to be, one who is truly brother to his fellow humans.

Corporate Christology: Traditionally, the image of the Body of Christ has signified both the unity of Christians with Christ and the complementary roles that various members of the Church fulfill. Too little attention has been given to its Christological significance. The image expresses a truth about Jesus' person. It affirms a corporate understanding of Jesus. In the Church, Christ is embodied in space and time, not merely figuratively or in some mystical sense, but rather historically, politically and socially. Jesus' relationship to both kingdom and Church takes on a different character when his personhood is seen corporately instead of individualistically.

Individualist presuppositions have led scholars to ask whether the kingdom Jesus proclaimed was present or future and whether the Church is the kingdom. The central theme of Jesus' preaching, the kingdom or rule of God, has to be seen as the announcement of a future reality if it refers to God's actual rule over the lives of human beings. To date the announced kingdom has not arrived. To conclude that it would take place only in another life is natural enough.

How does this square with the New Testament? The gospels affirm that the kingdom is present, "among you" (see Lk 17:21), even though they also speak of a future kingdom (see Mk 14:25). On balance, the arrival of the kingdom is both present and future, but how to bring the two together has never been clear. And this issue casts shadows over the important question: Does Jesus announce the kingdom or does he create it?

If Christ is understood corporately, Jesus embodies the kingdom by beginning a movement of people who, over the course of history, submit as he did to God's rule in the world. Specifically, Jesus is the Son the Father wishes all humans to be. He was truly brother to all the other sons and daughters of the Father. The kingdom itself is the realization of the divine family, all humans truly in solidarity with each other. It is begun where barriers between the members of the family are removed. It is realized when no such barriers exist. To set in place the movement for the elimination of all such barriers is to create the way to, and the beginning of, the rule of God. But it is crucial to understand that Jesus' own task is incomplete without the collaboration of the rest of the human race. The divine family at peace is not the work of one or many individuals. It is embodied in all those with whom Jesus identifies as fellow humans.

From this perspective, theologians will have to reassess Jesus' relationship to the Church. In an effort to acknowledge the limitations of the Church and to prevent it from self-glorification, many contemporary theologians have insisted that the Church is not the kingdom of God. Some have also emphasized the gap between Jesus and the Church which comes after him. Although their motives are good, this thinking is still quite individualistic. It creates an unnecessary chasm between Jesus and the Church.

Such a chasm contradicts the intimate association between Jesus and his disciples during his public ministry. Jesus' gathering of a band of disciples appears to be an integral part of his work, not merely an accidental activity that insured that his teachings would be carried on. Indeed, Jesus did not compose teachings to be passed down. But he clearly did assemble a community of disciples. This community embodies, gives visible form to the work he carried out, because it lives the common life he began with them before God. The Church is the means to, and the beginning of the rule Jesus began and announced. As a community, it is the corporate extension of Jesus' own sonship in the world.

Corporate Christology implies that the Christian does not relate to God or Christ as a mere individual, but by relating to the whole human family. Specifically, it implies that this universal family bond is acknowledged by membership in the movement to bring it about, by accepting and developing the social responsibilities of being a member of Christ embodied, the Church. Thus, Christian identity and worth are not determined individualistically, but corporately and socially. A presentation of Christian faith which one-sidedly speaks of individual and private relationships between God and humans is revealed as the deformed reflection of Western individualistic culture. To recover the gospel portrayal of the embodied kingdom of God is to present a critique both of that culture, and of the Church that has over-adapted to its values.

3. Challenge from the Underside of History

History and theology have usually been written by the victors of human conflicts. In a limited number of instances survivors, for example Jews in exile in Babylon, have been able to write their own accounts of their tradition. But until fairly recently history recorded the deeds of the ancestors of those in power. Theology, likewise, tended to see most issues from the perspective of those who held power in the Church or in society. Thus, a major characteristic of social movements for liberation among blacks and women in America, and among Third world peoples in Latin America, Africa and Asia is that they all try to recover their own histories. They also attempt to rethink theological issues from the standpoint of their history and experience.

Black Theology: As the Civil Rights Movement of the early sixties became the Black Power Movement of the late sixties and early seventies in the United States, black theologians asked: What is the meaning of Christ's "existence in relation to the slave ships that appeared on the American shores?" (Cone: p. 198). Black theology made the political critique of Western theology concrete by demonstrating that theology has not only served the interests of the political and economic establishment, but that it has transformed Christ into a White Christ. But it took a further step to draw on the spiritual resources of the black Church to show what a Black Christ might be. Finally, it redefined salvation as liberation to make the point that the primary sin over which Christ is to triumph is the denial of dignity and freedom to any of God's people.

Black theology is proposed by black theologians for black people. James Cone is "suspicious of so-called white revolutionary theologians . . . [who] have the audacity to speak for black people" (p. 119). More self-consciously than other theologies, it is an emergency or crisis theology. It arose to meet a very particular challenge. It does not pretend to present a timeless, universal message. Indeed, its premise is that theology goes astray when it speaks *"sub specie aeternitatis"* (in the light of eternity) rather than in terms of God's concrete relationship to history. How God reveals himself in the struggle for black liberation is the unavoidable issue our concrete history presents.

WHITE THEOLOGY UNMASKED: When black theologians speak of "white theology" or a "white Christ," they are not merely pointing out the skin color of the images of God and Christ that adorn Church walls and religious books. Their aim is more than giving persons of color religious images with which they can identify. No, their point is that theology has presented a description of God and Christ that serves the interests of white people in a racist society.

One of the more telling examples of this distortion is the way theologians and Christians in general have related love to righteousness in God. Cone points out that the early Church condemned Marcion for drawing a dichotomy between the Hebrew God of wrath and righteousness and the New Testament God of love. But he contends that white theology failed to integrate love and righteousness, and in particular it failed to speak of God's wrath toward those who are unrighteous (unjust). Theology made God neutral in the name of a pretended universal and eternal perspective. Black theologians hold that in a racially divided society, a God who does not take sides permits the white power structure to continue. Without wrath against the oppressors, God's love is mere sentimentality (pp. 120-138).

Concretely, does the theological portrait of a universal God of love tell black people they have a right to oppose those who deny their rights? Deotis Roberts argues that all people must be confronted by the Black Christ, who is engaged in the struggle against oppression. Only then can Christ become Lord of all. We cannot know Jesus as reconciler, as revealer of a God of universal love, until we have permitted him to reveal God as liberator of black people (p. 138).

THE BLACK CHRIST: Although some black preachers have argued that Jesus was literally black, for black theology blackness is primarily a symbol. But it is a symbol that must be interpreted concretely, in reference to the condition of black people in American life. Cone asks, "What is the form of humanity that accounts for human suffering in our society? What is it, except blackness?" (p. 218). In the gospels Jesus is presented as an oppressed person, as the Suffering Servant, telling oppressed Jews that their ultimate everyday obedience must be to the rule of God rather than to the oppressive imperial system. Jesus' resurrection is confirmation that God accepts the life of the oppressed Jesus, and therefore all lives crushed by those who oppressed him. Thus, in the Risen Christ we have decisive evidence that God sides with the oppressed against the oppressor. How, then, are either blacks or whites to understand Jesus' resurrection as the liberation of the oppressed unless they consider Christ as one who in our society would be seen as a black person?

The Black Christ, then, tells the black community that God gives freedom that it has no right to deny and has a responsibility to defend. Likewise, it calls into question both the cultural system and the religious presuppositions of other Christians because Christ's blackness proclaims a freedom no one else may legitimately deny.

Concretely, to defend this freedom, "liberation" is a more adequate term than "salvation." Why? Because "salvation" has been presented as though it pertained only to another life, to another world. It has been preached as a means of giving a future hope to the oppressed, rather than as a statement that God actually stands with them as their Savior in the present. Salvation in the future permits slave owners and their descendants to continue to avoid Jesus' message about the rule of God and it discourages slaves and their descendants from acknowledging Christ's victory. The new term, "liberation," thus clarifies the gospel and the concrete responsibilities of the Christian movement in the present historical situation of racist America.

Liberation Theology: American Black Theology makes liberation an issue, but it is a distinct expression of a wide range of liberation theologies in the Third world. Black Theology expressed the historical experience of black churches in the United States as they marshalled their forces during the Civil Rights Movement of the sixties. It is important for Americans to listen to the questions being asked by the liberation theologians elsewhere, if only to overcome our own enthnocentrism. Nonetheless, personally I think American black theology is both a more immediately challenging and a more mature statement of Christian faith than other forms of liberation theology. I am perhaps showing a cultural bias. But I believe that it is necessary to ask: Might a liberal democratic society such as ours, by means of self-reform, self-renewal and the free contest of ideas, not provide a better context for liberation than some others? In such a context as ours, is it necessary to speak of class conflict, and are we better off for not having to do so? In many ways, black theology, which springs from a people who want no more or less than to share what we proclaim already to be the right of all in our society, appears to say "yes" to both questions.

Liberation theologies in the Third world, especially in Latin America, arose in the midst of churches which were at best only beginning to be influenced by native poor people. Unlike the black churches of the United States, which were created and governed by black people (and indeed were their most conspicuous grass-roots organization), the Latin American Church was imposed by a colonial government and remained dependent on foreign leadership until very recently. While the Civil Rights Movement in the United States appealed directly to an unfulfilled agenda embedded in the U.S. Constitution and political tradition, the liberation movement in Latin America had little choice but to advocate a revolutionary redistribution and restructuring of both politics and economics.

Thus, liberation implied different things because both the Church situation and the cultural situation were different. It is not fair to expect the newly emerging Church and people in Latin America to have the maturity that comes from the long tradition of black community and Church independence in the United States. If this is the case, without judging Latin American efforts, we might yet expect that the questions they raise may be more pertinent and important than the tentative solutions they propose.

Liberation theology arose in Latin America in response to the Second Vatican Council (1962-65). No part of the Catholic world made as energetic and organized a response to the social agenda of the council as did the Latin American Bishop's Conference. Staggering problems within the Church and society, encouragement from Pope Paul VI (especially in his encyclical *"Populorum Progressio"* in 1967) and extraordinary local leaders such as Brazilian Archbishop Helder Camara led to collective decisions by all the Latin American bishops meeting in 1968 at Medellin, Colombia. In the Medellin papers, the bishops declared, "The Lord's distinct commandment to 'evangelize the poor' ought to bring us to a distribution of resources . . . that effectively gives preference to the poorest" (Gremillion: p. 474). This preferential option for the poor established the context and strategy of Latin American liberation theology.

CHRIST POOR AND LIBERATOR: The bishops focused on the fact that Christ "not only loved the poor, but rather 'being rich He became poor', He lived in poverty" (Gremillion: p. 473). They called on the Church to assume voluntary poverty and solidarity with the poor. Theologians and priests tended to focus on Christ as Liberator of the poor. Thus, Leonardo Boff presents the rationale and consequences of the Church's preference for the poor:

> Jesus . . . is primarily interested in whether a person is disposed to sell all properties to acquire the field with hidden treasure; whether one is ready to sell all to buy the precious pearl (Mt 13:4-6); whether in order to enter the new order, one has the courage to abandon family and fortune (Mt 10:37), risk one's life (Lk 17:33) tear out an eye and cut off a hand (Mk 9:43 and Mt 5:29). (p. 65)

The rationale for Christian poverty is that it is the condition for building the kingdom. But the consequences are equally clear: this is a *"no* to the established order [which] does not signify asceticism but an attitude of readiness to comply with the exigencies of Jesus" (p. 65).

In Latin America the oppressed with whom Jesus and the Church are in solidarity are not a minority, but the overwhelming majority of the population. Thus, liberation theologies had to consider not only the freedom and dignity of the oppressed, but the means to achieve that freedom and dignity, an achievement that involved revolutionary changes in the society, not merely adjustments and improvements. The still unsettled debate in Latin America is over what means are compatible with the gospel of Jesus. What kind of revolutionary methods are acceptable?

BASIC COMMUNITIES AND CONSCIENTIZATION: Two approaches of the proponents of liberation theology are generally accepted. Thus, the bishops encouraged the formation of basic communities (communidades de base) and conscientization in the Medellin Documents (Gremillion: pp. 452-453). The basic communitites are relatively small, grass-roots level assemblies of people at the lowest level of the society which focus on marshalling their own resources to bring about change. These communities work together, study together and pray together somewhat like mini-parishes, but with a much more comprehensive concern for all areas of life than the average parish. They take for granted that some of the problems they face involve political action and fundamental social change. But they are particularly interested in forms of common action that will so involve the members of the community that they will come to recognize their own dignity and power.

Thus, the basic communities are linked to the process of conscientization, consciousness raising. Conscientization springs from the conviction that part of the difficulty of the oppressed is that they have accepted the oppressors' definition of who they are and what they are worth. The first challenge then is to make oppressed people aware of their self-worth. In Latin America, especially, educators like Paolo Freire argue that education must come through praxis, learning by problem-posing, rather than by theory. The method "bases itself on creativity and stimulates true reflection and action upon reality [the concrete situation of their lives], thereby responding to the vocation of men as beings who are authentic only when engaged in inquiry and creative transformation" (Freire: p. 71).

How far action to transform the social situation should go is more controversial than the need for such action. Some of the liberation theologians have been criticized for excessive reliance on a Marxist analysis of society, leading to promotion of class conflict. Others contend that these theologians advocate violent revolution. Again, the theologians have support in the Medellin Documents, which speak of "a situation of injustice that can be called institutionalized violence" (Gremillion: p. 460). The bishops contend that if the leaders in Latin America "jealously retain their privileges and defend them through violence they are responsible to history for provoking 'explosive revolutions of despair' " (Gremillion: p. 461).

Citing Pope Paul VI and the Medellin Documents, Juan Segundo argues, " 'Violence is neither Christian nor evangelical'. It is the inevitable remnant of the hominization process which makes love possible and which, insofar as it is possible, desires to be replaced slowly and gradually by love" (p. 169). Violence must be seen in a larger perspective than is often the case. "To do violence," Segundo explains, is to make the "person an instrument for obtaining something" (p. 164). Pure violence would therefore be egotism that relativizes others "so that they are seen only in terms of one's own advantage."

But pure violence is seldom if ever found in the concrete, because there are no absolute and universal egotisms. Segundo observes that concretely there is no love without violence. Why? Love attempts to establish "bonds with more and more persons." But to do so, loving persons must move out from their neighbors, from those nearest to those more distant step by step. By concentration on those nearest first, the loving person or community initially treats those at the greatest distance as "things" or "instruments" to obtain what is needed by those nearest. Violence has many forms: physical force, impersonal legislation, prejudice, the refusal to consider further issues of concern to some other human beings. In itself, it is not Christian. But as part of the project of extending love, violence is present in Jesus' own ministry and work.

CHRIST AND VIOLENCE: Although some liberationists point to Jesus' cleansing of the temple as a violent act, and others have portrayed him as a political revolutionary, theologians like Segundo make a more careful argument.

He says that Jesus "does not present himself in the guise of some extraterrestial and inhuman love" (p. 165). Instead, he liberates particular persons, selects particular persons and effectively excludes others. He even chose not to follow John the Baptist in his collision course with Herod, but to pursue his own path. In deciding not to reach out to Gentiles, as well as in deciding to attack the Pharisees he adopted popular stereotypes and prejudices which *for the moment* excluded interpersonal love. He shaped a particular concrete community, a core community to exemplify and extend an ever more, but never quite complete, universal love. The love of one person or group conflicted with attention to all the others, doing all the others the violence of making them wait for what they have a right to as persons.

The key element in Segundo's analysis is the idea that Jesus is God working within the confines of time and history. Jesus' time was not unlimited and thus he had to submit to violence from others as well as act impersonally, violently, himself. The point is not that Jesus made violence a Christian virtue or ideal. It is not. To make a universal principle that one person may be used for another's advantage is unacceptable. To use one person or group for the advantage of others *temporarily,* as part of the strategy of extending a more universal love, acknowledges the temporal limits of all human deeds and systems.

Segundo argues that temporality was at the heart of the Arian controversy in the early Church. Arius was essentially denying that God in his very Godness could have been involved in human history, that Christ could be truly and fully God, because as a human being Christ was in time and history. But Nicaea insisted that Christ was truly God, and therefore that history was an arena in which God could and did function. Thus, it is necessary to accept historically conditioned deeds and projects, not as absolutes, but as nonetheless true efforts on behalf of the rule of God, love, within the world. This implies that no deed or political effort, including both the existing systems and the revolutions that attack them, is an absolute representative of God's rule, but that what God is doing within the world is done within the limits of such efforts (pp. 154-158).

4. Jesus the Jew in his own Time and Place

Both black theologians and liberation theologians have insisted that understanding Jesus means taking his situation in Jewish life in the first century seriously. Black theology, nourished by a tradition that has been more attentive to the liberation dynamics of the Jewish scriptures, has been less inclined to show Jesus contradicting Judaism than Latin liberation theologies, where a residue of anti-semitism appears. But both place emphasis on understanding Jesus within his own cultural setting as a starting point.

Two other recent developments further the objective of placing Jesus in proper cultural context. First, a growing number of biblical scholars interpret the Bible and Jesus cross-culturally with help from anthropological studies. Second, contemporary Jewish scholars have begun to study the New Testament, clarifying how Jesus would have been and might be understood by Jews.

Cross-Cultural Studies: Why add anthropology to the sciences necessary for biblical and theological investigation? The language of the New Testament is different and requires translation. Events and understandings must be placed in order, so that we do not attribute later ideas to earlier people. Today the need for literary and historical criticism is generally accepted. But anthropology now alerts us to the truth that the same words and deeds within different cultures may mean different things.

A culture is a network of symbols and values and the primary values in one culture may be quite secondary or non-existent in another. The meaning of any particular symbol or value in a given culture is modified by how it fits into the overall cultural scheme. Thus, biblical scholars now recognize that they must become capable of thinking cross-culturally. That is, they must define a term such as "law" or "freedom" outside of the modern or Western cultural system in which we find ourselves.

A CULTURE WITHOUT INTROSPECTIVE INDIVIDUALS: If we wished to dramatize the cultural gap between the contemporary world and the world of Jesus, we need look no further than to consider how they established their identity as persons. A sense of identity may be acquired by reflection on oneself (introspection) or by interaction with others. Introspection played little if any role in the New Testament world.

Ordinarily, first century people knew who they were because their place in society was laid out for them by ties of family, group, and nationality. Their sense of who they were was constantly reinforced by feedback from others in social interaction. First century Jews were members of a family, villagers or townspersons and Israelites. Their sense of self-worth, whether they were good or bad, saints or sinners, heroes or villians, honorable or shameless, arose from judgments made by others on their actions.

By contrast the modern Western person is first of all an individual. We belong to groups voluntarily, withdrawing from them without necessarily affecting our sense of who we are. We think that we bring our personalities to the group. We think it inappropriate to be overly dependent on groups, to have our self-worth and values shaped by others. Thus, in some sense each individual has a uniquely configured system of values, and in the privacy of conscience judges the worth of individual actions. Because the modern individual considers himself and others to be such intimately defined beings, we psychologize to explain ourselves to others and to get some explanation for who other people really are.

On the other hand, when people derive their identity from the group, beginning always with cues given by others (as in the New Testament) they generate little psychological data. About the characters of the New Testament, Jesus included, we know little of their hidden thoughts or feelings. Where the modern person expects insight into how someone personally felt about something, the New Testament provides a generality or a reference to something in the tradition accepted by everybody.

For example, the modern reader expects the account of Jesus' temptations to reflect an inner crisis. Indeed, reading these accounts as internal struggles, we supply motives where they are lacking. In fact, the evangelist depicts a stereotypical Israelite. Jesus is tempted to do the same things that Israel was tempted to do in the wilderness, and he responds with citations from Scripture. Instead of revealing the inner workings of Jesus' mind and heart, we find he is depicted as the faithful Israelite.

Modern theologians have devoted a great deal of energy to the question of Jesus' messianic consciousness: Did he claim to be the Messiah? We have difficulty with this question, partly because direct claims by Jesus do not appear in the text. What is little recognized is how unlikely it would have been in the first century Mediterranean world for anybody to make a direct claim about himself. Indeed, when a title, or even a compliment, was offered, such a person would very likely deny it.

Why? As Bruce Malina points out, it was assumed in this culture that every person was born with a given position in life, and to rise above that status threatened the equilibrium of society as a whole. One accepted honors with a schooled reluctance, lest one appear to be making a personal claim. Notice how Jesus declined to be "set up as your judge and arbiter" (Lk 12:14), when brothers asked him to intervene in a family dispute. Notice also how consistently Jesus provides healing and help to those who ask, but never seems to volunteer it unasked. Even when Jesus is addressed as "Good Rabbi," he responds as any honorable man of his day, "Why do you call me good? No one is good but God alone" (Mk 10:17-18). No one made a claim or a request that might be interpreted as imposing or presuming on someone else. To act otherwise would have been seen as aggressive, disrespectful and would scarely have been taken seriously (Malina 1981: pp. 76-79). In the light of Malina's description of how the culture functioned, the reason Jesus directed attention away from himself becomes clear.

THE NON-CHARISMATIC CHRIST: We have to ask: why then was Jesus followed? In such a culture, how did one become a leader? Neither born with the right to rule, nor part of the religious or political establishment, Jesus to many moderns must be described as a charismatic leader, one who easily dominated others because of unique personal abilities. Among the characteristics of the charismatic leader is the tendency to oppose all the existing traditions, to claim personal authority over his followers and to seize and use power. For the most part, today we admire such persons.

According to Malina, this modern description of Jesus as a charismatic leader is based on ignorance of Jesus' cultural setting and denial of clear evidence in the gospel texts. Malina argues that the ancient world would not follow such a person. It preferred someone who tried to avoid leadership, even when others forced it upon him. People looked up to someone who exemplified the best within their own traditions, who demonstrated not a will to power but rather was known for "virtue," the capacity to relinquish or share power. Such a person acquired a reputation as the best representative of the people, instead of dominating and controlling them (Malina 1984: pp. 58-59).

When we take a second look at the gospels in the light of Malina's observations, suddenly Jesus' flight when the crowd appeared ready to make him king falls into place (Jn 6:15). Indeed, Jesus' reticence when Peter acclaims him "Messiah," his insistence on speaking of his own suffering and death, and his consistent theme of the rule of the Father show one who does not try to claim power.

Instead, Jesus sought to empower others to live the heart of the tradition of the prophets, of the people as a whole. What is most radical in Jesus neither contradicts nor opposes what Judaism represents. Indeed, he insisted that "not the smallest letter of the law, not the smallest part of a letter shall be done away with until it all comes true" (Mt 5:18). He did not demand power. He commanded respect because he was the embodiment of what the people themselves recognized as their own true selves. The leadership style is similar to that shown by Washington, who was sought out by others to represent them, and not that of modern charismatic leaders who cultivate the crowds seeking support (Malina 1984: pp. 56-60).

The Jewish Jesus: It is fitting, therefore, that contemporary Jewish scholars have shown keen interest in Jesus. Christian scholars, who for centuries saw Jesus in opposition to the Judaism of his day, have in recent times judged accurate portrayal of the historical Jesus a dubious project. Contemporary Jewish scholars, on the other hand, recognize Jesus as an authentic Jew. Drawing on their knowledge of Jewish contemporaries of Jesus, they evaluate gospel accounts of Jesus' ministry rather positively.

If Jewish scholars do not accept Jesus' divinity, they yet assign him a place in Jewish tradition that is extraordinary. Indeed, because they approach Jesus without accepting Christian claims about him, their delineation of his character and work is often all the more helpful to Christians who seek to understand why our Christological claims arose.

JESUS THE HASID: Christian theology has strangely neglected, perhaps taken too much for granted, Jesus' role as a master of prayer and devotion to the Father. Geza Vermes finds in the gospel account of Jesus a person who lives as a *hasid*. The *hasidim*, meaning "the devout," focused their lives on heartfelt intimacy with God.

Vermes begins with Jesus' mission "to the physically, mentally and spiritually diseased . . . He was the healer, the physician *par excellence*" (p. 58). In Jewish tradition, sin and sickness were always intimately associated. Healing required forgiveness of sin in the case of bodily illness, and expulsion of evil spirits in the case of mental illness. Jewish tradition at times saw healers and exorcists as bearers of esoteric powers, magicians. But Vermes claims that alongside this folk tradition was a more orthodox tradition going back to the prophets, notably Elijah. Those in immediate contact with God could heal without special incantations or formulas. Such holy men, *hasidim*, healed with a word or a laying on of hands through God's power. Jesus fits this hasidic pattern, which was especialy prevalent in Galilee (pp. 59-80).

From rabbinic sources Vermes concludes that the *hasidim* had somewhat tense, somewhat conflict-ridden relationships to the ordinary religious leaders, especially the Pharisees. The people saw them as a renewal of Elijah-like prophecy. They were at times more lenient, at other times more strict than Pharisees in interpretation of the Law, and were inclined to emphasize ethical issues, discounting matters of ritual. They were not simply dismissed by the authorities but were sometimes mistrusted. They were seen as links between heaven and earth with a traditional, although extra-legal authority (pp. 80-82).

JEWISH CONTRIBUTION: Vermes illustrates two typical Jewish contributions to the contemporary understanding of Jesus. First, Jewish scholarship helps the Christian understand where the problem with Jesus arose in first century Judaism. For example, Jewish scholars are less inclined to assume, as Western Christians do, that the miraculous is an overlay on authentic history. They are willing to assume that Jesus enjoyed special intimacy with God, even though they do not conclude that he is divine. This is because they are aware of parallels which they have no reason to doubt.

From Jewish accounts, the Christian begins to see that people of Jesus' own time were not doubtful, as moderns would be, about stories told about his deeds and words. They were unsettled by the appearance of someone who disturbed, without directly challenging, their understanding of the ordinary processes of religious observance. The disturbance would be greatest in the center of the religious establishment, relatively cosmopolitan Jerusalem, where Jesus and his Galileans would appear as an anachronistic revival movement.

Second, Jewish scholars, such as Vermes and David Flusser, presume that the gospels' accounts of Jesus' own attitudes may be more accurate than either later dogma or recent historical studies have been willing to admit. These attitudes have to be interpreted in their context, not in the light of later Western prejudices. Thus, while rejecting or hesitating when called "Messiah" (Vermes: pp. 129-56), Jesus never appears to deny the designation of "prophet" (pp. 87-90). Is it possible that the gospels fairly accurately depict the sources of these titles when they show "Messiah" coming only from others?

Vermes concludes that given the atmosphere of the day, friend and foe alike saw Jesus messianically in spite of Jesus' misgivings (p. 156). Jesus and his contemporaries conceived the prophet as a man of God like Elijah at work with the outcasts of the land, bringing healing and reconciliation. In contrast, the modern Westerner understands prophets in terms of the writing prophets like Amos, rather than Elijah. Thus, in modern thought prophets are social critics, sometimes seen as revolutionaries, instigators of a messianic age. The modern understanding of *prophet* is thus closer in some respects to the first century understanding of *messiah*.

Jewish studies of Jesus, then, exemplify the validity of the cross-cultural approach suggested by anthropologists. For, when the gospels are placed in the hands of people with fewer assumptions from Western Christian culture, and closer ties to the Jewish culture of Jesus' day, a fresh and rather sympathetic historical portrait of Jesus emerges. The Christian is challenged anew to permit this Jesus to have an effect on the Christian world similar to his impact on the Jewish world. To sum this up, we might begin by noting that around his words and deeds there developed a movement that moved into what was then the global village of the Roman Empire.

The Christian Mystery in the Global Village: From the beginning the experience of Christ has been the experience of God's active involvement in the future of humans and the world. God collaborating with humans through Christ has remained constant. Our vision of the intimate association humans have with Christ in the Christian movement has changed, as indeed our understanding of ourselves and our world has changed. In a world grown suddenly, and sometimes frighteningly small, the demand for dialog and collaboration has grown even as the first fruits of this process begin to be felt in the enriched understanding we now have of Christ, the Father and ourselves.

It might well appear that we have today far more questions about the identity of Jesus than ever before. Certainly, this last chapter reveals that we have now begun to face very basic questions about the ways we have expressed Christian faith since the Christian movement emerged as the focus of moral life in the Western world.

Christians now find themselves questioned and challenged. Although the questions sometimes appear hostile, real hostility is more often revealed by indifference. Those who do not question, whether Christian or not, have lost interest in Christ, have ceased to acknowledge life in the movement that began with him. People always want to know who someone is in relation to themselves, to their lives. The new questions, thus, come from those who imagine in some way that Jesus does relate to them.

Finally, as in the past, today's questions come from Christ himself. No person can be an open and closed book before others. As we are in some ways mysteries to ourselves, we always finally demand that others acknowledge that hidden dimension by being open to a reassessment of who we are. No less is true in the case of a person we acknowledge as divine and human. To a significant degree we have denied Jesus his real personhood when we have presumed to have full statements of who he is, or when we have said "Christ is the answer."

For believers, Christ must remain the question mark on our own lives and ways, the Son and Brother who always challenges us anew: What does it mean to be sons and daughters of the Father? What does it mean to be brothers and sisters in a global village? The questions "Who do you say that I am?" and "Who do you say was neighbor to the one by the side of the road?" are not only closely related, but very much alike. They can be answered only by decisions and actions that change history and human life.

WORKS CITED

James H. Cone
    1970 *A Black Theology of Liberation*. Philadelphia: J.B. Lippincott.
Robert J. Daly
    1978 *The Origins of the Christian Doctrine of Sacrifice*. Philadelphia: Fortress.
David Flusser
    1959 *Jesus*. New York: Herder & Herder.
    1969 "Jesus in the Context of History," in Arnold Toybee, ed., *The Crucible of Christianity*. New York: World, pp. 225-234.
Paolo Freire
    1971 *Pedagogy of the Oppressed*. New York: Herder & Herder.
Joseph Gremillion, ed.
    1976 *The Gospel of Peace and Justice: Catholic Social Teaching Since Pope John*. Maryknoll, NY: Orbis.
Frederick Herzog
    1970 "The Political Gospel," *The Christian Century* 87: pp. 1380-83.
Charlotte Klein
    1978 *Anti-Judaism in Christian Theology*. Philadelphia: Fortress Press.
Bruce J. Malina
    1981 *The New Testament World: Insights from Cultural Anthropology*. Atlanta: John Knox.
    1984 "Jesus as Charismatic Leader?" *Biblical Theology Bulletin* 14: pp. 55-62.

Johannes B. Metz
    1969 *Theology of the World*. New York: Herder & Herder.
Robert T. Osborn
    1973 "A Christian Mission to the Jews?" *The Christian Century* 90: pp. 1168-71.
J. Deotis Roberts
    1974 *A Black Political Theology*. Philadelphia: Westminster.
Rosemary Ruether
    1974 *Faith and Fratricide: The Theological Roots of Anti-Semitism*. New York: Seabury.
Juan Luis Segundo
    1974 *Our Idea of God*. Maryknoll, NY: Orbis.
Geza Vermes
    1973 *Jesus the Jew: A Historian's Reading of the Gospels*. New York: Macmillan.
Leland J. White
    1975 "Christology and Corporate Ministry," *American Benedictine Review* 25:1 (March 1975) pp. 54-74.

APPENDIX A
(see pp. 5 ff.)

MATTHEW 17:14-15

As they were rejoining the crowd a man came up to him and went down on his knees before him.

"**Lord**," he said, "take pity on my son: he is a lunatic and in a wretched state; he is always falling into the fire or into the water. I took him to your disciples and they were unable to cure him." "Faithless and perverse generation!" Jesus said in reply. "How much longer must I put up with you? Bring him here to me."

MARK 9:14-28

When they rejoined the disciples they saw a large crowd round them and some scribes arguing with them. The moment they saw him the whole crowd were struck with amazement and ran to greet him. "What are you arguing about with them?" he asked. A man answered him from the crowd,

"**Teacher**, I have brought my son to you; there is a spirit of dumbness in him, and when it takes hold of him it throws him to the ground, and he foams at the mouth and grinds his teeth and grows rigid. And I asked your disciples to cast it out and they were unable to." "You faithless generation," he said to them in reply. **"How much longer must I be with you?** How much longer must I put up with you? Bring him to me." **They brought the boy to him, and as soon as the spirit saw Jesus it threw the boy into convulsions, and he fell to the ground and lay there writhing, foaming at the mouth.**

And when Jesus rebuked it
the devil came out of the
the boy who was cured from
that moment.

Jesus asked the father, "How long
has this been happening to him?"
"From childhood," he replied, "and
it has often thrown him into the fire
and into the water, in order to destroy him. **But if you can do anything, have pity on us and help us."
"If you can?" retorted Jesus,
"Everything is possible for anyone
who has faith." Immediately the
father of the boy cried out, "I do
have faith. Help the little faith I
have!"** And when Jesus saw how
many people were pressing round
him, he rebuked the unclean spirit.
**"Deaf and dumb spirit," he said,
"I command you: come out of him
and never enter him again." Then
throwing the boy into violent convulsions it came out shouting, and
the boy lay there so like a corpse
that most of them said, "He is
dead." But Jesus took him by the
hand and helped him up, and he
was able to stand.**

(translation from *The Jerusalem Bible*)

APPENDIX B
(see pp. 71 ff.)

ACTS 3:12-21

When Peter saw this, he addressed the people as follows: "Fellow Israelites, why does this surprise you? Why do you stare at us as if we had made this man walk by some power or holiness of our own? The God of Abraham, of Isaac, and of Jacob, the God of our fathers, has glorified his Servant Jesus, whom you handed over and disowned in Pilate's presence when Pilate was ready to release him. You disowned the Holy and Just One and preferred instead to be granted the release of a murderer. You put to death the Author of life. But God raised him from the dead, and we are his witnesses. It is his name, and trust in this name, that has strengthened the limbs of this man whom you see and know well. Such faith has given him perfect health, as all of

ACTS 2:14-36

Peter stood up with the Eleven, raised his voice, and addressed them: "You who are Jews, indeed all of you staying in Jerusalem! Listen to what I have to say.
"You must realize that these men are not drunk, as you seem to think. It is only nine in the morning! No, it is what Joel the prophet spoke of:
'It shall come to pass in the last days, says God,
that I will pour out a portion of
    my spirit on all mankind:
Your sons and daughters shall prophesy, your young men shall see visions and your old men shall dream dreams. Yes, even on my servants and handmaids I will pour out a portion of my spirit in those
    days, and they shall prophesy.
I will work wonders in the heavens
    above
    and signs on the earth below:
    blood, fire, and a cloud of smoke.
The sun shall be turned to darkness
    and the moon to blood

you can observe.
"Yet I know, my brothers,
that you acted out of ig-
norance, just as your leaders
did. God has brought to fulfillment by this means what
he announced long ago through
all the prophets: that his
Messiah would suffer. Therefore, reform your lives!
Turn to God, that your sins
may be wiped away! Thus may
a season of refreshment be
granted you by the Lord when
the Lord sends you Jesus,
already designated as your
Messiah. Jesus must remain
in heaven until the time of
universal restoration which
God spoke of long ago through
his holy prophets."

before the coming of this great and
     glorious day of the Lord.
Then shall everyone be saved who
     calls on the name of the Lord.'
"Men of Israel, listen to me!
Jesus the Nazorean was a man whom
God sent to you with miracles,
wonders, and signs as his creden-
tials. These God worked through
him in your midst, as you well
know. He was delivered up by the
set purpose and plan of God; you
even made use of pagans to crucify
and kill him. God freed him from
death's bitter pangs, however, and
raised him up, for it was impossible
that death should keep its hold
on him. David says of him:
'I have set the Lord before me,
with him at my right hand I shall
     not be disturbed.
My heart has been glad and my
     tongue has rejoiced,
my body will live on in hope,
for you will not abandon my soul
     to the nether world,
nor will you suffer your faithful
one to undergo corruption.
You have shown me the paths of
     life;
you will fill me with joy in
     your presence.'
"Brothers, I can speak confidently
to you about our father David. He
died and was buried, and his grave
is in our midst to this day. He
was a prophet and knew that God
had sworn to him that one of his
descendants would sit upon his
throne. He said that he was not

abandoned to the nether world,
nor did his body undergo corrup-
tion, thus proclaiming beforehand
the resurrection of the Messiah.
This is the Jesus God has raised
up, and we are his witnesses.
Exalted at God's right hand, he
first received the promised Holy
Spirit from the Father, then
poured this Spirit out on us.
This is what you now see and hear.
David did not go up to heaven,
yet David says:
'The Lord said to my Lord,
    Sit at my right hand
    until I make your enemies
        your footstool.'
"Therefore let the whole house of
Israel know beyond any doubt that
God has made both Lord and
    Messiah
this Jesus whom you crucified."

(translation from *The New American Bible*)

APPENDIX C
(see pp.)

Writings of Tertullian[1]

Against Praxeas, 7

(1) . . . I affirm that from God nothing void and empty can have come forth — for he is not void and empty from whom it has been brought forth: and that that cannot lack substance which has proceeded from so great a substance and is the maker of such great substances — for he himself is the maker of things which were made through him. How can he be nothing without whom no thing was made, so that one void should have wrought solid things, and one empty full things, and one incorporeal corporal things? For although at times something can be made which is the opposite of that whereby it is made, yet by what is empty and void nothing can be made.

[Can you describe as] an empty and void object that Word of God whom scripture calls the Son, who also is designated God — *And the Word was with God and the Word was God?* It is written, *Thou shalt not take the name of God for an empty thing.* Certainly this is he who, *being in the form of God,*

1. Ernest Evans, trans., *Tertullian's Treatise Against Praxeas,* London: S.P.C.K., 1948; J.H. Waszink, trans., *Tertullian: The Treatise Against Hermogenes,* Westminster, MD.: The Newman Press, 1956.

thought it not robbery to be equal with God. In what form of God? Evidently in some form, not in none: for who will deny that God is body, although *God is a spirit*? For spirit is body, of its own kind, in its own form. Moreover if those invisible things, whatever they are, have in God's presence both their own body and their own shape by which they are visible to God alone, how much more will that which has been sent forth from his substance not be devoid of substance. Whatever therefore the substance of the Word was, that I call a Person, and for it I claim the name of Son: and while I acknowledge him as Son I maintain he is another beside the Father. [Evans: p. 138]

Against Praxeas, 8

(2) For God brought forth the Word, as also the Paraclete teaches, as a root brings forth the ground shoot, and a spring the river, and the sun its beam: for these manifestations also are "projections" of those substances from which they proceed. You need not hesitate to say that the shoot is the son of the root and the river son of the spring and the beam son of the sun, for every source is a parent and everything that is brought forth from a source is its off-spring — and especially the Word of God, who also in an exact sense has received the name of Son: yet the shoot is not shut off from the root nor the river from the spring nor the beam from the sun, any more than the Word is shut off from God. Therefore according to the precedent of these examples, I profess that I say that God and his Word, the Father and his Son, are two: for the root and the shoot are two things, but conjoined; and the spring and the river are two manifestations, but undivided; and the sun and its beam are two aspects, but they cohere.

Everything that proceeds from something must of

necessity be another beside that from which it proceeds, but it is not for that reason separated [from it]. But where there is a second [one] there are two, and where there is a third there are three. For the Spirit is third with God and [his] Son, as the fruit out of the shoot is third from the root, and the irrigation canal out of the river third from the spring, and the illumination point out of the beam third from the sun; yet in no sense is he alienated from that origin from which he derives his proper attributes. In this way the Trinity, proceeding by intermingled and connected degrees from the Father, in no respect challenges the monarchy [oneness], while it conserves the quality of the economy. [Evan: pp. 139-40]

Against Praxeas, 9

(3) ... I say that the Father is one, and the Son another, and the Spirit another ... not however that the Son is other than the Father by diversity, but by distribution, not by division but by distinction, because the Father is not identical with the Son, they even being numerically one and another. For the Father is the whole substance, while the Son is an outflow and assignment of the whole, as he himself professes, *Because the Father is greater than I*: and by him, it is sung in the psalm, he has also been made less, *a little on this side of the angels.* So also 'the Father is other than the Son as being greater than the Son, as he who begets is other than he who is begotten, as he who sends is other than he who is sent, as he who makes is other than he through whom a thing is made. [Evans: p. 140]

Against Hermogenes, 3

(4) The name of *God,* so we say, has always been with himself and in himself, but not always that of *Lord,* for the

state of being inherent in the one is different from that of the other: *God* is the name of the substance itself, that is, of the divinity; but *Lord* is the name, not of the substance, but of a power. The substance has always existed together with its name, which is *God*; but [the name] *Lord* was a later addition, since it is the name of something coming in addition. For ever since things began to exist upon which the power of a lord could operate, from that moment, by the accession of this power, he both became and received that name.

[Nor is this surprising,] for God is also a Father, and God is also a Judge, but he has not always been Father and Judge for the simple reason that he had always been God; for he could not be Father before the Son was, nor a Judge before there was sin. Now there was a time when for him there existed neither sin nor the Son, the former to make God a Judge, and the latter, a Father.

In the same way he did not become Lord before the things existed of which he was to become the Lord. He was to become Lord but once in the course of time; as he became Father by the Son and as he became Judge by sin, so also he became Lord by the things which he had made to serve him. [Waszink: p. 29]

APPENDIX D
(see pp. 109 ff.)

Writings of Origen[2]

First Principles, I, 2, 6

(1) Let us see now what we ought to understand by the expression "image of the invisible God," in order that we may learn therefrom how God can rightly be called the Father of his Son; and let us first of all consider what things are called images in ordinary human speech. Sometimes the term "image" is applied to an object painted or carved on some material, such as wood or stone. Sometimes a child is said to be the image of its parent, when the likeness of the parent's features is in every respect faithfully reproduced in the child. Now I think that the first of these illustrations may be fitly applied to him who was made "in the image and likeness of God," that is, man. Of man, however, we shall inquire more carefully, with God's help, when we come to the exposition of this passage in Genesis.

But in regard to the Son of God, of whom we are now speaking, the image may be compared to our second illustration; for this reason, that he is the invisible image of the invisible God, just as according to the scripture narrative we say that the image of Adam was his son Seth. It is written

2. G.W. Butterworth, trans., *Origen on First Principles,* London: Society for Promoting Christian Knowledge, 1936.

thus: "And Adam begat Seth after his own image and after his own kind." This image preserves the unity of nature and substance common to a father and a son. For if 'all things that the Father doeth, these also doeth the Son likewise," then in this very fact that the Son does all things just as the Father does, the Father's image is reproduced in the Son, whose birth from the Father is as it were an act of his will proceeding from the mind. And on this account my own opinion is that an act of the Father's will ought to be sufficient to ensure the existence of what he wills; for in willing he uses no other means than that which is produced by the deliberations of his will. It is in this way, then, that the existence of the Son is begotten by him. [Butterworth: pp. 18-19]

First Principles, I, 2, 6

(2) This point must above all be upheld by those who allow nothing to be unbegotten, that is, unborn, except God the Father only. Moreover, we must take care not to fall into the absurd fables of those who imagine for themselves certain emanations [projections], splitting the divine nature into parts and, so far as they have [done so], dividing God the Father. For it is not only the utmost impiety, but also the depth of folly, to entertain the slightest suspicion that such a thing could happen to an incorporeal being; nor is it at all consistent with our intelligence to think that a physical division of an incorporeal being is possible. Rather we must suppose that as an act of the will proceeds from the mind without either cutting off any part of the mind or being separated from it, in some similar fashion has the Father begotten the Son, who is indeed his image; so that as the father is invisible by nature, he has begotten an image that is also invisible. [Butterworth: p. 19]

First Principles, I, 2, 6

(3) For the Son is the Word, and therefore we must understand that nothing in him is perceptible to the senses. He is Wisdom, and in wisdom we must not suspect the presence of anything corporeal. "He is the true light, which lighteth every man that cometh into our world," but he has nothing in common with the light of our sun. Our Savior is therefore the image of the invisible God, the Father, being the truth, when considered in relation to the Father himself, and the image, when considered in relation to us, to whom he reveals the Father; through which image we know the Father, whom "no one" else "knoweth save the Son and he to whom the Son hath willed to reveal him." And he reveals the Father by being himself understood; for whoever has understood him understands as a consequence the Father also, according to his own saying, "He that hath seen me, hath seen the Father also." [Butterworth: pp. 19-20]

First Principles, I, 2, 2

(4) If then it is once rightly accepted that the only-begotten Son of God is God's wisdom hypostatically existing, I do not think that our mind ought to stray beyond this to the suspicion that this hypostasis or substance could possibly possess bodily characteristics, since everything that is corporeal is distinguished by shape or color or size. And who in his sober senses ever looked for shape or color or measurable size in wisdom, considered solely as wisdom? And can anyone who has learned to regard God with feelings of reverence suppose or believe that God the Father ever existed, even for a single moment without begetting this wisdom? For he would either say that God could not have begotten wisdom before he did beget her, so that he brought wisdom into being when she had not existed before, or else

that he could have begotten her and — what it is profanity even to say about God — that he was unwilling to do so; each of which alternatives, as everyone can see, is absurd and impious, that is, either that God should advance from being unable to being able, or that, while being able, he should act as if he were not and should delay to beget wisdom. [Butterworth: pp. 15-16]

First Principles, I, 2, 2

(5) . . . Wisdom, therfore, must be believed to have been begotten beyond the limits of any beginning that we can speak of or understand. And because in this very subsistence of wisdom there was implicit every capacity and form of creation that was to be, both of those things that exist in a primary sense and of those which happen in consequence of them, the whole being fashioned and arranged beforehand by the power of foreknowledge, wisdom, speaking through Solomon in regard to these very created things that had been as it were outlined and prefigured in herself, says that she was created as a "beginning of the ways" of God, which means that she contains within herself both the beginning and the causes and the species of the whole creation. [Butterworth: p. 16]

(6) *First Principles,* I, 2, 6 in Rufinus	*First Principles,* I, 2, 6 in Jerome
Our Savior is therefore the image of the invisible God, the Father being the truth, when considered in relation to the Father himself, and the image, when considered in relation to us, to whom he reveals the Father.	The Son, who is the image of the invisible Father, is not the truth when compared with the Father; but in relation to us, who are unable to receive the truth of God almighty, he is a shadow and semblance of truth.

[Butterworth: p. 20, n. 1]

First Principles, I, 2, 10

(7) Let us now look into the saying that wisdom is "an effluence," that is, an emanation [projection], "of the clear glory of the Almighty," and if we first consider what "the glory of the Almighty" is, we shall then understand what its "effluence" is. Now as one cannot be a father apart from having a son, nor a lord apart from holding a possession or a slave, so we cannot even call God almighty if there are none over whom he can exercise his power. Accordingly, to prove that God is almighty we must assume the existence of the universe. For if anyone would have it that certain ages, or periods of time, or whatever he cares to call them, elapsed during which the present creation did not exist, he would undoubtedly prove that in those ages or periods God was not almighty, but that he afterwards became almighty from the time when he began to have creatures over whom he could exercise power. Thus God will apparently have experienced a kind of progress, for there can be no doubt that it is better for him to be almighty than not to be so.

Now does it not seem anything but absurd that God should at first not possess something that is appropriate to him, and afterwards by a kind of progress should come to possess it? But if there was no time when he was not almighty, then of necessity those things must always have existed, in virtue of which he is called almighty; and he must always have had creatures over which he exercised his power and which were controlled by him as king and ruler. Of these we shall treat more fully in the proper place, when we come to discuss the subject of God's creatures. Yet even now, since we are dealing with the question how wisdom is a pure effluence, or emanation, of the glory of the Almighty, I deem it necessary to give warning, however briefly, to prevent anyone from thinking that the title of Almighty be-

longed to God before the birth of wisdom, through which he
is called Father; for wisdom, which is the Son of God, is said
to be a "pure effluence of the glory of the Almighty." Let
him who is inclined to believe this hear what the scriptures
plainly proclaim; for it says that "thou hast made all things in
wisdom," and the Gospel teaches that "all things were made
by him and without him was not anything made"; and let
him understand from this that the title of Almighty cannot
be older in God than that of Father, for it is through the Son
that the Father is almighty. [Butterworth: pp. 23-24]

APPENDIX E
(see pp. 124 ff.)

Reported Writings of Arius[3]

Athanasius, *The Synods*, 16

(1) And what they wrote by letter to the blessed Alexander, Bishop, runs as follows:

> ... Our faith from our forefathers, which also we have learned from you, blessed Father, is this: We acknowledge One God, alone Unbegotten, alone Everlasting, alone Unbegun, alone True, alone having immortality, alone Wise, alone Good, alone Sovereign; Judge, Governor, and Providence of all, unalterable and unchangeable, just and good, God of Law and Prophets and New Testament.

> Who begat an Only-begotten Son before eternal times, through whom he has made both the ages and the universe; and begat him, not in semblance, but in truth; and that he made him subsist at his own will, unalterable and unchangeable; perfect creature of God, but not as one of the creatures; offspring, but not as one of the things begotten.

3. Philip Schaff and Henry Wace, eds., *A Select Library of Nicene and Post-Nicene Fathers, Vol. IV: St. Athanasius: Select Works and Letters; ibid.: Vol. III: Theodoret, Jerome, Gennadius, Rufinus: Historical Writings, etc.*, Grand Rapids, MI: Wm. B. Eerdmans Publishing Co., 1978.

Not as Valentinus pronounced that the offspring of the Father was an issue [projection], nor as Manichaeus taught that the offspring was a portion of the Father, one in essence; or as Sabellius, dividing the Monad, speaks of a Son-and-Father; nor as Hieracas, of one torch from another, or as a lamp divided into two. Not that he who was before, was afterwards generated or new-created into a Son, as you too yourself, Blessed Father, in the midst of the Church and in session has often condemned.

But as we say, at the will of God, created before times and before ages, and gaining life and being from the Father, who gave subsistence to his glories together with him. For the Father did not, in giving to him the inheritance of all things, deprive himself of what he has in an unbegotten way in himself; for he is the fountain of all things.

Thus there are three subsistences. And God, being the cause of all things, is Unbegun and altogether Sole. But the Son being begotten apart from time by the Father, and being created and established before ages, was not before his generation. But being begotten apart from time before all things, [the Son] alone was made to subsist by the Father.

For he is not eternal or co-eternal or co-unoriginate with the Father, nor has he his being together with the Father, as some speak of relations, introducing two unbegotten beings, but God is before all things as being Monad and beginning of all. Wherefore also he is before the Son; as we have learned from your preaching in the midst of the Church.

So far then as from God he has being, and glories, and life, and all things are delivered unto him, in such sense is God his origin. For he is above him, as being his God and before him. But if the terms "from him," and "from the womb," and "I came forth from the Father, and I am come" (Rm 11:36; Ps 110:3; Jn 16:28), be understood by some to mean as if a part of him, one in essence or as an issue [projection], then the Father is according to them compounded and divisible and alterable and material, and, as far as their belief goes, has the circumstances of a body, who is the incorporeal God.

This is a part of what Arius and his fellows vomited from their heretical hearts. [Schaff & Wace IV: p. 458]

From the letter of Arius to Eusebius of Nicomedia, reported in Theodoret, *Ecclesiastical History,* I, 4.

(2) To his very dear lord, the man of God, the faithful and orthodox Eusebius, [from] Arius, unjustly persecuted...

Ammonius, my father, being about to depart for Nicomedia, I considered myself bound to salute you by him, and withal to inform [you] . . . that the bishop [Alexander] greatly wastes and persecutes us, and leaves no stone unturned against us. He has driven us out of the city as atheists, because we do not concur in what he publicly preaches, namely, God always, the Son always; as the Father so the Son; the Son co-exists unbegotten with God; he is everlasting; neither by thought nor by interval does God precede the Son; always God, always Son; he is begotten of the unbegotten; the Son is God himself.

Eusebius, your brother bishop of Caesarea, Theodotus, Paulinus, Athanasius [the bishop of Anazarbus], Gregorius, Aetius, and all the bishops of the East, have been condemned because they say that God had an existence prior to that of his Son; except Philogonius, Hellanicus, and Macarius, who are unlearned men, and who have embraced heretical opinions. Some of them say that the Son is an eructation, others that he is a production [projection], others that he is unbegotten. These are impieties to which we cannot listen, even though the heretics threaten us with a thousand deaths.

But we say and believe, and have taught, and do teach, that the Son is not unbegotten, nor in any way part of the unbegotten; and that he does not derive his subsistence from any matter; but that by his own [God's] will and counsel he has subsisted before time, and before ages, as perfect God, only begotten and unchangeable, and that before he was begotten, or created, or purposed, or established, he was not. For he was not unbegotten.

We are persecuted, because we say that the Son has a beginning, but that God is without beginning. This is the cause of our persecution, and likewise, because we say that he is [made out] of non-existent [things]. And this we say, because he is neither part of God, nor of any essential being. For this we are persecuted; the rest you know. I bid you farewell in the Lord. [Schaff & Wace III: p. 41]

APPENDIX F
(see pp. 128 ff.)

The Creed of Nicaea[4]

We believe in one God, the Father All Governing [*pantokrat-ora*], creator [*poietein*] of all things visible and invisible; And in one Lord Jesus Christ, the Son of God, begotten of the Father as only begotten, that is, from the essence [reality], of the Father, [*ek tes ousias tou patros*], God from God, Light from Light, true God from true God, begotten not created [*poiethenta*], of the same essence [reality] as the Father [*homoousion to patri*], through whom all things came into being, both in heaven and in earth; Who for us men and for our salvation came down and was incarnate . . . [Leith: pp. 30-31]

4. John H. Leith, ed., *Creeds of the Churches*, Garden City, NY: Doubleday & Co. 1963.

APPENDIX G
(see pp. 130 ff.)

Writings of Athanasius[5]

The Decrees of the Synod of Nicaea, 20

(1) Again, when the Bishops said that the Word must be described as the True Power and Image of the Father, in all things exact and like the Father, and as unalterable, and as always, and as in him without division (for never was the Word not, but he was always, existing everlastingly with the Father, as the radiance of light), Eusebius and his fellows endured indeed, as not daring to contradict, being put to shame by the arguments which were urged against them; but withal they were caught whispering to each other and winking with their eyes, that "like," and "always," and "power," and "in him," were, as before, common to us and to the Son, and that it was no difficulty to agree to these. As to "like," they said that it is written of us, "Man is the image and glory of God" . . .

---

5. Philip Schaff and Henry Wace, eds., *A Select Library of Nicene and Post-Nicene Fathers, vol. IV: St. Athanasius: Select Works and Letters,* Grand Rapids, MI: Wm. B. Eerdmans Publishing Co., 1978; Penelope Lawson, trans., *On the Incarnation: The Treatise De Incarnatione Verbi Dei by St. Athanasius,* New York: Macmillan Publishing Co., Inc., 1946.

But the Bishops discerning in this too their dissimulation, and whereas it is written, "Deceit is in the heart of the irreligious that imagine evil," were again compelled on their part to collect the sense of the scriptures, and to re-say and re-write what they had said before, more distinctly still, namely, that the Son is "one in essence" with the Father; by way of signifying, that the Son was from the Father, and not merely like, but the same in likeness, and of showing that the Son's likeness and unalterableness was different from such copy of the same as is ascribed to us, which we acquire from virtue on the ground of observance of the commandments.

For bodies which are like each other may be separated and become at distances from each other, as are human sons relatively to their parents (as it is written concerning Adam and Seth, who was begotten of him, that he was like him after his own pattern); but since the generation of the Son from the Father is not according to the nature of men, and not only like, but also inseparable from the essence of the Father, and he and the Father are one, as he has said himself, and the Word is ever in the Father and the Father in the Word, as the radiance stands towards the light (for this the phrase itself indicates), therefore the Council, as understanding this, suitably wrote "one in essence," that they might defeat the perversenses of the heretics, and show that the Word was other than originated things.

For, after thus writing, they are once added, "But they who say that the Son of God is from nothing, or created, or alterable, or a work, or from [an] other essence, these the Holy Catholic Church anathematizes." And by saying this, they showed clearly that "of the essence," and "one in essence," are destructive of those catchwords of irreligion, such as "created," and "work," and "originated," and "alterable," and "He was not before his generation." [Schaff & Wace IV: pp. 163-64]

Discourses Against The Arians, III, 4-5

(2) On this account and reasonably, having said before, "I and the Father are One," he added, "I in the Father and the Father in me," by way of showing the identity of Godhead and the unity of essence. For they are one, not as one thing divided into two parts, and these nothing but one; nor as one thing twice named, so that the Same becomes at one time Father, at another his own Son, for holding this Sabellius was judged a heretic. But they are two, because the Father is the Father and is not also the Son, and the Son is the Son and not also the Father; but the nature is one; (for the offspring is not unlike its parent, for it is his image) and all that is the Father's is the Son's.

Wherefore neither is the Son another God, for he was not [added] from without, else there were many, if a godhead be [added] foreign from the Father's; for if the Son be other, as an Offspring, still he is the Same as God; and he and the Father are one in [properties] and peculiarity of nature, and in the identity of the one Godhead, as has been said.

For the radiance also is light, not second to the sun, nor a different light, nor from participation of it, but a whole and proper offspring of it. And such an offspring is necessarily one light; and no one would say that they are two lights, but [though] sun and radiance [are] two, yet [they make but] one light from the sun enlightening in its radiance all things.

So also the Godhead of the Son is the Father's; whence also it is indivisible. And thus there is one God and none other but he. And so, since they are one, and the Godhead itself [is] one, the same things are said of the Son, which are said of the Father, except his being said to be Father; for instance, that he is God, "And the Word was God";

Almighty, "Thus said he which was and is and is to come, the Almighty"; Lord, "One Lord Jesus Christ"; that he is the Light, "I am the Light"; that he wipes out our sins, "that you may know," he says, "that the Son of Man has power upon earth to forgive sins"; and so with other attributes. For "all things," says the Son himself, "whatsoever the Father has, are mine"; and again, "And mine are thine."

And on hearing the attributes of the Father spoken of a Son, we shall thereby see the Father in the Son; and we shall contemplate the Son in the Father, when what is said of the Son is said of the Father also. And why are the attributes of the Father ascribed to the Son, except that the Son is an Offspring from him? And why are the Son's attributes proper to the Father, except again because the Son is the proper Offspring of his essence? [Schaff & Wace IV: pp. 395-396]

On The Incarnation, 8-9

(3) For this purpose, then, the incorporeal and incorruptible and immaterial Word of God entered our world. In one sense, indeed, he was never far from it before, for no part of creation had ever been without him who, while ever abiding in union with the Father, yet fills all things that are. But now he entered our world in a new way, stooping to our level in his love and self-revealing to us. He saw the reasonable race, the race of men that, like himself, expressed the Father's mind, wasting out of existence, and death reigning over all in corruption. He saw that corruption held us all the closer, because it was the penalty for the transgression; he saw, too, how unthinkable it would be for the law to be repealed before it was fulfilled. He saw how unseemly it was that the very things of which he himself was the artificer should be disappearing. He saw how the surpassing wicked-

ness of men was mounting up against them; he saw also
their universal liability to death.

All this he saw and, pitying our race, moved with com-
passion for our limitation, unable to endure that death
should have the mastery, rather than that his creatures
should perish and the work of his Father for us men come to
naught, he took to himself a body, a human body even as our
own. Nor did he will merely to become embodied or merely
to appear; had that been so, he could have revealed his
divine majesty in some other and better way. No he took *our*
body, and not only so, but he took it directly from a spotless,
stainless virgin, without the agency of human father — a
pure body, untainted by intercourse with man. He, the
Mighty One, the artificer of all, himself prepared this body
in the virgin as a temple for himself, and took it for his very
own, as the instrument through which he was known and in
which he dwelt.

Thus, taking a body like our own, because all our bodies
were liable to the corruption of death, he surrendered his
body to death in place of all, and offered it to the Father.
This he did out of sheer love for us, so that in his death all
might die, and the law of death thereby be abolished because, when he had fulfilled in his body that for which it was
appointed, it was thereafter voided of its power for men.
This he did that he might turn again to incorruption men
who had turned back to corruption, and make them live
through death by the appropriation of his body and by the
grace of his resurrection. Thus he would make death to
disappear from then as utterly as straw from fire.

The Word perceived that corruption could not be got
rid of otherwise than through death. Yet he himself, as the
Word, being immortal and the Father's Son, was such as
could not die. For this reason, therefore, he assumed a body
capable of death, in order that it, through belonging to the

Word who is above all, might become in dying a sufficient
exchange for all, and, itself remaining incorruptible
through his indwelling, might thereafter put an end to
corruption for all others as well, by the grace of the resurrection. It was by surrendering to death the body which he had
taken, as an offering and sacrifice free from every stain, that
he forthwith abolished death for his human brethren by the
offering of the equivalent.

For naturally, since the word of God was above all,
when he offered his own temple and bodily instrument as a
substitute for the life of all, he fulfilled in death all that was
required. Naturally also, through this union of the immortal
Son of God with our human nature, all men were clothed
with incorruption in the promise of the resurrection. For
the solidarity of mankind is such that, by virtue of the
Word's indwelling in a single human body, the corruption
which goes with death has lost its power over all. [Lawson:
pp. 13-15]

The Synods, 52

(4) . . . If we acknowledge that the Father's godhead is
one and sole, and that of him the Son is the Word and
Wisdom; and, as thus believing, are far from speaking of
two Gods, but understand the oneness of the Son with the
Father to be, not in likeness of their teaching, but according
to essence and in truth, and hence speak not of two Gods,
but of one God; there being but one Form of Godhead, as
the Light is one [with] the Radiance; (for this was seen by the
Patriarch Jacob, as scripture says, "The sun rose upon him
when the Form of God passed by," Gn 32:31). And holding
this, and understanding of whom he was the Son and Image,
the holy prophets say, "The Word of the Lord came to me";
and recognizing the Father, who was beheld and revealed in

him, they made bold to say, "The God of our fathers has appeared to me, the God of Abraham, and Isaac, and Jacob" (Ex 3:16).

This being so, wherefore scruple we to call him coessential [one in essence] who is one with the Father, and appears as does the Father, according to the likeness and oneness of godhead? For if, as has been many times said, he has it not to be proper to the Father's essence, nor to resemble, as a Son, we may well scruple. But if this be the illuminating and creative Power, specially proper to the Father, without whom he neither frames nor is known (for all things consist through him and in him); wherefore, perceiving the fact, do we decline to use the phrase conveying it? For what is it to be thus connatural with the Father, but to be one in essence with him? For God attached not to him the Son from without, as needing a servant; nor are the works on a level with the Creator, and honored as he is, or to be thought one with the Father . . .

But, whereas not more divisible, nay less divisible is the nature of the Son towards the Father, and the godhead not accruing to the Son, but the Father's godhead being in the Son, so that he that has seen the Son has seen the Father in him; wherefore should not such a one be called Coessential [one-in-essence]? [Schaff & Wace IV: p. 478]

Discourses Against The Arians, III, 29-30

(5) Now the scope and character of holy scripture, as we have often said, is this, — it contains a double account of the Savior; that he was ever God, and is the Son, being the Father's Word and Radiance and Wisdom; and that afterwards for us he took flesh of a virgin, Mary Bearer of God, and was made man. . .

The reader then of divine scripture . . . will perceive that the Lord became man; for "the Word," he says, "became flesh and dwelt among us." And he became man, and did not come into [a] man; for this it is necessary to know, lest perchance these irreligious men fall into this notion: . . . that, as in former times the Word was used to come into each of the saints, so now [again] he sojourned in a man, hallowing him also, and manifesting himself in him as in the others. For if this were so, and he only appeared in a man, it would be not at all unusual. [Schaff & Wace IV: pp. 410-411]

APPENDIX H
(see pp. 152 ff.)

Writings of Theodore of Mopsuestia[6]

Commentary on Galatians

(1) There are some people who make it their business to pervert the meaning of the divine Scriptures and to thwart whatever is to be found there. They invent foolish tales and give to their nonsense the name of "allegory." By using the apostle's word, they imagine that they have found a way to undermine the meaning of everything in Scripture — they keep on using the apostle's expression "allegorical." They do not realize what a difference there is between their use of the term and the apostle's use of it here [in Gal 4]. For the apostle does not destroy history; he does not get rid of what has already happened. He sets out things as they happened in the past and uses the history of what happened in support of his own purpose...

That is how the apostle speaks. But they act in a totally opposite way; their wish is to deny any difference between the whole of the history recorded in divine Scripture and dreams that occur at night. Adam, they say, is not Adam —

6. Maurice Wiles & Mark Santer, eds., *Documents in Early Christian Thought*, Cambridge: Cambridge University Press, 1975; James M. Carmody & Thomas E. Clarke, eds., *Christ and His Mission: Christology and Soteriology*, Westminster, MD: Newman Press, 1956.

this being a place where they are especially prone to interpret divine Scripture in a spiritual way (spiritual interpretation is what they like to have their nonsense called) — paradise is not paradise and the serpent is not a serpent.

What I would like to say in reply to them is that once they start removing bits of history they will be left without any history at all. In that case, they must tell us how they will be in a position to say who was the first man to be created or how man became disobedient or how the sentence of death was introduced. If it is from the Scriptures that they have learned their answers to these questions, it follows that their talk of "allegory" is obvious nonsense, because it is clearly irrelevant at all these points. If on the other hand they are right and what is written is not a record of things that happened but is a pointer to some other profound truth in need of interpretation — some spiritual truth it may be, to use the phrase they like, which they have grasped through being such spiritual people themselves — then they must tell us by what means they have acquired these notions. How can they assert these notions, as if they were things they had learnt from the teaching of divine Scripture? [Wiles & Santer: pp. 151-52]

Catechetical Homilies

(2) The partisans of Arius and Eunomius, however, say that he assumed a body but not a soul, and that the nature of the godhead took the place of the soul. They lowered the divine nature of the only begotten to the extent that from the greatness of its nature it moved and performed the acts of the soul and imprisoned itself in the body and did everything for its sustenance. Lo, if the godhead had replaced the soul he would not have been hungry or thirsty, nor would he have tired or been in need of food.

If, however, divine nature was sufficient for all these things, human nature which was in need of the grace of salvation from God should not have been assumed, as according to the opinion of the heretics this same godhead would have satisfied the requirements of human nature, and in this case it would have been superfluous to assume a body at all as the godhead was able to perform all its acts. This, however, was not the will of God, who indeed wished to put on and raise the fallen man who is composed of a body and an immortal and rational soul, so that "as by one man sin entered the world, and death by sin, so also the free gift and the grace of God by the righteousness of one man might abound unto many" (Rm 5:12, 15, 17). As death was by man so also the resurrection from the dead [will be] by man, because "as we all die in Adam, even so in Christ shall all be made alive" (I Cor 15:22), as the blessed Paul testifies.

Therefore it was necessary that he should assume not only the body but also the immortal and rational soul; and not only the death of the body had to cease but also that of the soul, which is sin. Since according to the sentence of the blessed [Paul] sin entered the world through man, and death entered through sin, it was necessary that sin which was the cause of death should have first been abolished, and then the abolition of death would have followed by itself. If sin were not abolished we would have by necessity remained in mortality, and we would have sinned in our mutability; and when we sin, we are under punishment, and consequently the power of death will by necessity remain.

It was, therefore, necessary that sin should have first been abolished, as after its abolition there would be no entry for death. It is indeed clear that the strength of the sin (cf. I Cor 15:56) has its origin in the will of the soul. . . It was, therefore, necessary that Christ should assume not only the body but also the soul. The enemy of the soul had to be removed first and then for the sake of it that of the body, because if death is from sin and the same death is the corruption of the body, sin would have first to be abolished and the abolition of death would follow by itself ...

Because of all this our blessed fathers warned us and said: "He was incarnate and became a man" so that we should believe that the one who was assumed and in whom God the Word dwelt was a complete man, perfect in everything that belongs to human nature, and composed of a mortal body and a rational soul, because it is for man and for his salvation that he came down from heaven. [Carmody & Clarke: pp. 94-96]

APPENDIX I
(see pp. 157 ff.)

The Interrogation of Eutyches before Patriarch Flavian[7]

Acts of the Ecumenical Councils, 1, 1, 1; 142-144

Flavian: Do you admit [Christ to be] of two natures?

Eutyches: Since I acknowledge him as my God and Lord, the Lord of heaven and earth, I have never yet presumed to theorize about his nature; I admit that I have never said that he is consubstantial with us... I confess that the holy Virgin is consubstantial with us, and that of her our God was incarnate...

Florentius: Since the Mother is consubstantial with us, then surely the son is also?

Eutyches: Please observe that I have not said that the body of God is the body of man, but that the body was human, and the Lord was made flesh of the Virgin. If you wish me to add that he who is of the Virgin is consubstantial with us, I will do so . . . but I take the word consubstantial in such a way as not to deny that he is the Son of God.

7. James M. Carmody & Thomas E. Clarke, eds., *Christ and His Mission: Christology and Soteriology,* Westminster, MD: The Newman Press, 1966.

Florentius: Do you or do you not admit that our Lord who
is of the Virgin is consubstantial and of two natures
after the Incarnation?

Eutyches: . . . I admit that our Lord was of two natures
before the union, but after the union one nature. . . I
have read of the blessed Cyril and the holy fathers and
the holy Athanasius, that they speak of two natures
before the union, but after the union and the Incarnation they speak of one nature not two. [Carmody &
Clarke: p. 113]

APPENDIX J
(see pp. 158 ff.)

The Tome of Leo[8]

... If, then, he knew not what he ought to think about the incarnation of the Word of God, and was not willing, for the sake of obtaining the light of intelligence, to make laborious search through the whole extent of the holy scriptures, he should at least have received with heedful attention that general confession common to all, whereby the whole body of the faithful profess that they "believe in God the Father Almighty, and in Jesus Christ his only Son our Lord, who was born of the Holy Spirit and the Virgin Mary." By these three clauses the machinations of almost all heretics are shattered.

For when God is believed to be both "Almighty" and "Father," it is found that the Son is everlasting together with himself, differing in nothing from the Father, because he was born as "God from God," Almighty from Almighty, Coeternal from Eternal; not later in time, not unlike him in glory, not divided from him in essence; and the same only-begotten and everlasting Son of an eternal Parent was "born of the Holy Spirit and the Virgin Mary."

8. Edward Rochie Hardy and Cyril C. Richardson, eds., *Christology of the Later Fathers*, Philadelphia: The Westminster Press, 1954.

This birth in time in no way detracted from, in no way added to, that divine and everlasting birth; but expended itself wholly in the work of restoring man, who had been deceived, so that it might both overcome death, and by its power "destroy the devil who had the power of death." For we could not have overcome the author of sin and death, unless he who could neither be contaminated by sin nor detained by death had taken upon himself our nature and made it his own. For, in fact, he was "conceived of the Holy Spirit" within the womb of a virgin mother, who bore him, as she had conceived him, without loss of virginity.

. . . But we are not to inderstand that "generation," peerlessly wonderful, and wonderfully peerless, in such a sense as that the newness of the mode of production did away with the proper character of the kind. For it was the Holy Spirit who gave fecundity to the Virgin, but it was from a body that a real body was derived; and "when Wisdom was building herself a house," "the Word was made flesh, and dwelt among us," that is, in that flesh which he assumed from a human being, and which he animated with the spirit of rational life.

Acccordingly, while the distinctness of both natures and substances is preserved, and both meet in one Person, lowliness is assumed by majesty, weakness by power, mortality by eternity; and in order to pay the debt of our condition, the inviolable nature has been united to the passible, so that, as the appropriate remedy for our ills, one and the same "Mediator between God and men, the man Christ Jesus," might from one element be capable of dying, and from the other be incapable. Therefore in the entire and perfect nature of a true man was born the true God, whole in what was his, whole in what was ours. . . [Hardy & Richardson: pp. 361-363]

APPENDIX K
(see pp.)

The Definition of Chalcedon[9]

Following, then, the holy fathers, we unite in teaching all men to confess the one and only Son, our Lord Jesus Christ. This selfsame one is perfect [*teleion*] both in deity [*theoteti*] and also in human-ness [*anthropoteti*]; this selfsame one is also actually [*alethos*] God and actually man, with a rational soul [*psyches logikes*] and a body. He is of the same reality as God [*homoousion to patri*] as far as his deity is concerned and of the same reality as we are ourselves [*homoousion hemin*] as far as his human-ness is concerned; thus like us in all respects, sin only excepted. Before time began [*pro aionon*] he was begotten of the Father, in respect of his deity, and now in these "last days," for us and on behalf of our salvation, this selfsame one was born of Mary the virgin, who is God-bearer [*theotokos*] in respect of his human-ness [*anthropoteta*]

[We also teach] that we apprehend . . . this one and only Christ — Son, Lord, only-begotten — in two natures . . .; [and we do this] without confusing the two natures . . ., without transmuting one nature into the other . . ., without dividing them into two separate categories . . ., without

9. John H. Leith, ed., *Creeds of the Churches*, Garden City, NY: Doubleday & Co., 1963.

contrasting them according to area or function . . . The distinctiveness of each nature is not nullified by the union. Instead, the "properties" [*idiotetos*] of each nature are conserved and both natures concur . . . in one "person" [*prosopon*] and in one *hypostasis*. They are not divided or cut into two *prosopa*, but are together the one and only and only-begotten Logos of God, the Lord Jesus Christ. Thus have the prophets of old testified; thus the Lord Jesus Christ himself taught us; thus the Symbol of the Fathers [Nicaea] has handed down . . . to us. [Leith: pp. 35-36]

GLOSSARY OF TERMS

Alexandria: a city on the the Mediterranean coast of Egypt, highly cosmopolitan, a major center for Diaspora Judaism and for early Christianity, noted for its learning and Platonic thought.

Alexandrian Christology: see **Christology, Alexandrian.**

allegory: a story whose details and actions illustrate or symbolize something altogether different from itself; it differs most from the **parable** in that each detail may have a specific meaning and whereas parables are often oral in their origin, allegories are almost always written.

anthropology: the study of humans; **philosophical anthropology** has investigated the nature of humanity in the most general sense, often from an ontological perspective; **social** or **cultural anthropology** has investigated the varied patterns of human life and culture, emphasizing empirical evidence; **theological** or **Christian anthropology** attempts to make a coherent statement about the meaning of human existence, using revelation as its fundamental source.

Antioch: a city in Syria, which became an important center for early Christianity; here the term "Christian" was first used; it likewise was an important Jewish center after the Fall of Jerusalem; noted for a tendency towards realism and Aristotelian thought, it competed with Alexandria for influence.

Antiochene Christology: see **Christology, Antiochene.**

apocatastasis: Greek for "restoration," which was used to refer to the restoration of all creation, including sinners, the damned, and even devils, to a state of perfect happiness. Taught by a number of Christian theologians, it has been condemned in so far as it would imply that a conversion is possible after death, calling human responsibility in this world into question.

Apollinarianism: the teaching of Bishop Apollinarius of Laodicea to the effect that the Logos took the place of a human soul in Jesus.

Aramaic: a Semitic tongue, closely related to Hebrew, which was the language of the Land of Israel in the 1st century CE.

Arianism: the teaching of Arius of Alexandria to the effect that the Son is subordinate to the Father, a Perfect Creature, immortal but not eternal.

Bible, Jewish: called in Hebrew *TaNaK*, for *Torah* (Law), *Nebiim* (Prophets), and *Ketubim* (Writings); the first two, written originally in Hebrew, were already "canonical" (authoritative) by the time of Jesus. Debate over the canonical status of some of the *Ketubim,* some of which was not originally Hebrew, continued until the end of the first century. This debate resulted in later debate among Christians over those books not received as canonical by the Jews. Although arranged differently, the Jewish Bible is the same as the Protestant Old Testament, and the Catholic Old Testament minus the deuterocanonical books.

black theology: see **theology, black**

Chalcedon: a city in Asia Minor where the fourth ecumenical council met in 451, at which the Christological doctrine of Jesus' full divinity and full humanity achieved its fullest expression.

charismatic: from the Greek *charisma*, meaning gifts; in popular religious language used to refer to those who place emphasis on the extraordinary gifts of the Holy Spirit. In the social sciences, "charismatic" designates the type of leader who, depending on his own personal magnetism, establishes a movement or community in opposition to established traditions and authority.

Christology: the study of the person and work of Jesus Christ; **Alexandrian, Logos/Sarx, Word/Flesh Christology:** the Christology of the school of Alexandria, which emphasized the unity of the human and divine natures in Christ, sometimes at the expense of the distinctness and completeness of the human nature; **Antiochene, Logos/Anthropos, Word-become-Human Christology:** the Christology of the school of Antioch, which stressed the distinctness and completeness of Christ's human nature; **Christology from below:** Christology which begins with the human existence of Jesus; **Christology from above:** Christology which begins with the pre-existing divine Son; **functional Christology:** Christology which speaks in terms of Jesus' work of salvation, rather than his nature or essence; **ontological Christology:** Christology which speaks in terms of the nature, essence or being of Christ.

consubstantial: Latinized term used to translate *homoousios*, meaning "of one substance," "one in being." At Nicaea, it was used to affirm that the Son was of the same nature as the Father. At Chalcedon, it was used to affirm additionally that the Son was also of the same nature as humans.

Diaspora: a term meaning "dispersion," referring to the Jewish communities outside of the Land of Israel.

doctrine: a statement expressing the faith of the Church; **defined doctrine:**   a doctrine that has been proclaimed authoritatively, i.e. by a general council of the Church or, in the case of Catholics, by the Pope speaking on behalf of the whole episcopate.

dogma: a defined doctrine (see above definition), which is presented as an essential element of Christian belief and thus binding on all Christians. Often, dogmatic statements are phrased in negative terms, saying, for example, "Should anyone hold such and such (supply belief to be excluded), let him be anathema (condemned)."

dualism: primarily refers to the tendency to see reality as divided into two fundamental realities: matter and spirit, good and evil, body and soul, etc., often based on the idea that a good God created and/or rules one, an evil spirit created and/or rules the other. Secondarily, it refers to the tendency to so distinguish the divine and human natures in Christ that his personhood is split.

Ephesus: a city in Asia Minor in which the third ecumenical council was held in 431, at which Nestorianism was condemned and it was affirmed that the personhood of Christ was one, meaning that it was proper to call Mary *Theotokos*, God-bearer or Mother of God, not merely *Christotokos*, Christ-bearer, as Nestorius had maintained.

eschatology/eschatological: from the Greek term meaning "last," teachings about the last things or the end of the age; in Christian theology it more specifically refers to the end of human history and human life on earth.

functional Christology: see **Christology, functional.**

hasid: designation for Jews, especially after the Maccabean revolt in the 2nd century BCE, who resisted assimilation into Hellenistic patterns of life by faithful observance and who were known for a prayerful and warmly committed faith.

Hebrew/Hebraic: of or pertaining to the ancient Hebrew people, and all their descendants, who after the Babylonian Exile (522 BCE) are increasingly called "Jews"; often used, similarly to "semitic," to designate a way of thinking and speaking in contrast to Greek or Western patterns.

Hebrew religion: a term more appropriately used to designate the religious practices and beliefs of the Israelites prior to the Babylonian Exile.

Hellenism: the cosmopolitan culture which developed throughout southern Europe, Asia Minor and the Middle East, as a result of the conquests of Alexander the Great; it designates a mixture of Greek culture with oriental patterns, which took place as virtually all peoples over this vast territory came to share a common second language, Greek.

Historical Jesus: the Jesus that may be known using the strictest canons of modern historical investigation, by which historians attempt to evaluate the documents to determine the basic facts of his life in contrast to later theological interpretation placed on his life by New Testament writers.

idealism: the philosophical tendency that affirms that the really real is what exists in the mind, in ideas, rather than in physical beings, which in some sense represents or stand for such ideas. Taking a variety of forms, idealism contrasts with the varieties of realism.

immanence: a quality of God, which emphasizes God's nearness to and immediate involvement in human life and creation. It is contrasted with "transcendence."

Jew/Jewish/Judaism: terms associated with the Hebrew people after the Babylonian Exile, indicating the fact that Israelite religion had been increasingly centered on Jerusalem, which was in Judea. A distinguishing characteristic of Judaism is the fact that the *Torah* (Books of Moses) and the Prophets were by then written and seen as authoritative, so that Judaism devoted increasing attention to interpretation of its written tradition, giving increasing importance to the scribes who performed this function. **Second Temple Judaism:** the Judaism of the period beginning with the end of the Babylonian Exile, ending with the fall of Jerusalem and destruction of the Temple in 70 CE, marked by a great deal of variety in interpretation of the *Torah* and hence the proliferation of factions and sects. **Rabbinic Judaism:** Judaism after the destruction of the Temple, marked by consensus on which books were to be received along with the *Torah* and Prophets as Scripture, the development of a great body of rabbinic writings which reached their climax in the two Talmuds, and a growing consolidation of Jewish belief and practice which makes rabbinic Judaism far more uniform (though hardly monolithic) than Second Temple Judaism. Second Temple Judaism is contemporary with the life and ministry of Jesus and his first disciples, while rabbinic Judaism and sub-apostolic Christianity developed together, often in conflict with each other.

Jewish Christians: converts to the gospel from the Jewish community in the Land of Israel and the areas close by, who maintained close links with Semitic culture. Inclined towards a functional Christology, Jewish Christians in time came to be regarded as heretical because they failed to affirm Jesus' divinity in terms acceptable to Gentile Christians.

Land of Israel: a term used from the first century BCE to designate the territory occupied by the ancient Israelites, specifically the kingdoms of Israel (northern) and Judaea (southern). At the time of Jesus they were under Roman rule and divided into the Province of Judaea (including Samaria) and the Tetrarchy of Herod Antipas (Galilee). In 135 CE, the Romans renamed the whole area "Syria-Palestina," eliminating the term "Province of Judaea" as part of their effort to crush Jewish nationalism. The territories were commonly called "Palestine" thereafter.

liberation theology: see **theology, liberation.**

Logos/Anthropos: see **Christology, Logos/Anthropos.**

Logos/Sarx: see **Christology, Logos/Sarx.**

moderate realism: see **realism, moderate.**

monotheism: philosophically, the doctrine that there exists a single, supreme, infinite, personal spirit distinct from the world that creates, sustains and pervades all reality. Biblically, the teaching that the God of Israel and the Father of Jesus Christ alone is truly God, and thus less an abstract idea than a conviction with moral consequences for believers.

Montanism: a sect of enthusiasts of the 2nd century CE, following the teachings of Montanus, who claimed to have new revelations from the Holy Spirit, of which he was in some sense an incarnation. Among these teachings were the proclamation of the imminent end of the world, a very austere morality, severe forms of penitential practice, and a diminished role for hierarchy in the Church.

naive realism: see **realism, naive.**

Nicaea: a city in Asia Minor where the first ecumenical council was held in 325, at which the divinity of the Son was affirmed against the Arian interpretation.

ontological Christology: see **Christology, ontological.**

pre-existence: the state of being of the Son or Logos before the incarnation or beginning of the earthly life of Jesus of Nazareth.

rabbinic Judaism: see **Judaism, rabbinic.**

realism: the philosophical tendency that affirms that what one knows (truth) is fundamentally what one perceives. **naive realism** tends to reduce the knowable to what is physicallly perceived. **dogmatic realism** accepts the data (percepts) of revelation as truths, i.e. as realities not to be contradicted. **moderate realism** affirms that what is known corresponds to what exists, but that in addition to some form of perception it is required that the intellect make a judgment about the perceived reality. For all practical purposes dogmatic realism is a specific form of moderate realism; realism is a position that contrasts with idealism.

Second Temple Judaism: see **Judaism, Second Temple.**

sect: a religious group diverging from the mainstream religious tradition, often characterized by an anti-world attitude, an exclusive membership, and a rather rigid way of life. *Sect* is generally contrasted with *Church*, which is thought of as more disposed to accept in some form society at large, to have an open membership and a more accomodating ethical code. Sociologists have often followed theologians in defining the sect in terms of opposition to the Church. More recently, they have emphasized opposition to society as the characteristic feature of early Christian sects, in as much as even what might be called "Church" at that time stood at best on the fringes of society. Even more recently, sociologists have argued that the term "faction" is more appropriate for both Jewish and Christian parties in the first century in as much as these "fellowships" tended to interact with each other and with the Jewish society at large with which they shared a common tradition, however much they may have emphasized one or another element in the tradition.

Semite/Semitic: a descendant of Shem, speaking one of the inter-related Semitic languages, including Hebrew and Arabic. Semitic thought and culture is often contrasted with Greek or Western thought, notably in terms of the former's emphasis on the concrete and practical rather than on the abstract and theoretical. In the modern West, *Semite* is often identified with *Jew*, hence, "anti-Semite" for those who hate Jews.

structural evil: the evil embedded in society at large, rather than created by the decisions and intentions of individuals, by which values and expectations, rewards and punishments stand in opposition to justice and true human community. Liberation theologians have emphasized structural evil in arguing that to eliminate injustice social structures rather than individual intentions need reform.

subordinationism: the teaching that the Son is not the equal of the Father, but subordinate in being to God.

synagogue: from the Greek word meaning "assembly," and thus also "the place of assembly." Developed during the Babylonian Exile as a substitute for the Jerusalem Temple, it served a wide variey of purposes including prayer, study and community life, but not sacrifice. Although it flourished in the Diaspora, and may have existed in the Land of Israel during the Second Temple Period, evidence for synagogues in the homeland before 70 CE is uncertain; after 70 CE, it became the most distinctive feature of Jewish life everywhere.

synoptic: describes accounts given "from the same point of view" and thus applies to the gospels of Matthew, Mark and Luke, in contrast to John.

Temple: a place of worship and sacrifice; in Judaism there was but one such place, the Temple in Jerusalem, erected first by Solomon, rebuilt after the Babylonian Exile, restored by Herod the Great, and destroyed by the Romans in 70 CE. Temple-centered Judaism contrasts on some important respects with later synagogue-centered Judaism, in as much as all public ritual was centralized in one place.

theology: most strictly, the study of God; more generally, all teaching about the relationship between God and humanity, comprehending what is believed and what is to be practiced by the believer. Technically, theology differs from faith or belief in as much as it reflects on faith more systematically; in this sense, faith provides the data to be analyzed and organized by theology. **black theology:**   the theology developed by American black churchmen, which attempts to counter what they contend is the inherent bias of traditional theology, a bias that made theology define the divine-human relationship with little or no reflection on the racist presuppositions of many believers. **liberation theology:** the theology developed by Latin Americans, American blacks, women and other oppressed groups, which attempts to counter the bias of traditional theology and to highlight those elements of the religious tradition that would more directly serve the cause of liberating the oppressed. **political theology:** the theology developed especially in the last half of the twentieth century which, using the insights of social science, exposes the relationships existing between religious and political ideologies in order to make theologians more self-critical. **white theology:** a term used by black theologians to describe theologies developed without regard for the structural evil present in a racist society, which implies that such theologies in fact serve the cause of the white majority in spite of the fact that the white theologians assume a stance of impartiality.

Torah: a Hebrew word, often translated as "Law," but more adequately meaning "Instruction," "Teaching," or even "Way"; used to refer to the will of God for Israel, especially as revealed to Moses. More specifically, then, the *Torah* is the teaching of Moses, which is contained in the first five books of the Jewish Bible, which are themselves designated *Torah*. The Pharisees developed the idea of a twofold *Torah*, written and oral, the oral *Torah* being all the traditions coming from Moses by which the written *Torah* was to have more immediate application and meaning in everyday life. This liberalizing trend was rejected notably by the Sadducees (the priestly party), but apparently accepted by Jesus, as well as by later Judaism.

transcendence/transcendent: a quality of God, which emphasizes that God is distant from the world and humans, "other" than anything finite or created. It is contrasted with God's "immanence."

SELECTED BIBLIOGRAPHY

I. Understanding the world of the New Testament:

Raymond E. Brown
>1984 *The Churches the Apostles Left Behind.* New York: Paulist.

W. D. Davies
>1967 *Introduction to Pharisaism.* Philadelphia: Fortress.

John Gager
>1975 *Kingdom and Community: The Social World of Early Christianity.* Englewood Cliffs, NY: Prentice-Hall.

Joachim Jeremias
>1969 *Jerusalem in the Time of Jesus: An Investigation into Economic and Social Conditions During the New Testament Period.* Philadelphia: Fortress.

Howard Clark Kee
>1980 *Christian Origins in Sociological Perspective.* Philadelphia: Westminster.
>1984 *The New Testament in Context: Sources and Documents.* Englewood Cliffs, NJ: Prentice-Hall.

Abraham J. Malherbe
>1977 *Social Aspects of Early Christianity.* Baton Rouge: Louisiana State University.

Bruce J. Malina
1981 *The New Testament World: Insights from Cultural Anthropolgy*. Atlanta: John Knox.
Eric M. Meyers and James F. Strange
1981 *Archaeology, the Rabbis and Early Christianity*. Nashville: Abingdon.
Jacob Neusner
1973 *From Politics to Piety: The emergence of Pharisaic Judaism*. Englewood Cliffs, NJ: Prentice-Hall.
1978 *There We Sat Down: Talmudic Judaism in the Making*. New York: KTAV.
1981 *First Century Judaism in Crisis: Yohanan ben Zakkai and the Renaissance of Torah*. New York: KTAV.
1984 *Messiah in Context: Israel's History and Destiny in Formative Judaism*. Philadelphia: Fortress.
Samuel Sandmel
1978 *Judaism and Christian Beginnings*. New York: Oxford Univ. Press.
Geza Vermes
1973 *Jesus the Jew*. New York: Macmillan.
1984 *Jesus and the World of Judaism*. Philadelphia: Fortress.

II. New Testament Christology:

Gunter Bornkamm
1960 *Jesus of Nazareth*. New York: Harper & Row.
Raymond E. Brown
1967 *Jesus: God and Man: Modern Biblical Reflections*. Milwaukee: Bruce.
1973 *The Virginal Conception and Bodily Resurrection of Jesus*. New York: Paulist.

Oscar Cullman
  1963 *The Christology of the New Testament.* London: SCM Press.
  1984 *Christ and Time: The Primitive Christian Conception of Time and History.* Philadelphia: Westminster.
C. H. Dodd
  1970 *The Founder of Christianity.* New York: Macmillan.
James D. G. Dunn
  1980 *Christology in the Making: A New Testament Inquiry into the Doctrine of the Incarnation.* Philadelphia: Westminster.
David Flusser
  1969 *Jesus.* New York: Herder & Herder.
Reginald H. Fuller
  1965 *The Foundations of New Testament Christology.* New York: Scribner's.
Ferdinand Hahn
  1969 *The Titles of Jesus in Christology: Their History in Early Christianity.* New York: World.
Howard Clark Kee
  1977 *Jesus in History: An Approach to the Study of the Gospels.* 2nd ed. New York; Harcourt Brace Jovanovich.
T. W. Manson
  1953 *The Servant-Messiah: A Study of the Public Ministry of Jesus.* London: Cambridge Univ. Press.
Willi Marxsen
  1969 *The Beginnings of Christology: A Study of its Problems.* Philadelphia: Fortress.
  1970 *The Lord's Supper as a Christological Problem.* Philadelphia: Fortress.

Stephen Neill
    1976 *Jesus through Many Eyes: Introduction to the Theology of the New Testament.* Philadelphia: Fortress.
John Reumann
    1973 *Jesus in the Church's Gospels: Modern Scholarship and the Earliest Sources.* Philadelphia: Fortress.
Leopold Sabourin, S.J.
    1984 *Christology: Basic Texts in Focus.* Staten Island, NY: Alba House.
Gerard S. Sloyan
    1983 *Jesus in Focus: A Life in its Setting.* Mystic, CT: Twenty-Third Publications.
H. E. Todt
    1965 *The Son of Man in the Synoptic Tradition.* London: SCM Press.

III. Christology of the Fathers and Early Councils:

Walter Baur
    1971 *Orthodoxy and Heresy in Earliest Christianity.* Philadelphia: Fortress.
Henry Chadwick
    1966 *Early Christian Thought and the Classical Tradition.* New York: Oxford Univ. Press.
Robert M. Grant
    1961 *The Earliest Lives of Jesus.* New York: Harper.
    1967 *After the New Testament.* Philadelphia: Fortress.
Aloys Grillmeier
    1975 *Christ in Christian Tradition: From the Apostolic Age to Chalcedon (451).* 2nd. ed. Atlanta: John Knox.
Hans Jonas
    1963 *The Gnostic Religion.* Boston: Beacon.

J. N. D. Kelly
> 1978 *Early Christian Doctrines.* 5th rev. ed., New York: Harper & Row.

Bernard J. F. Lonergan
> 1976 *The Way to Nicaea: The Dialectical Development of Trinitarian Theology.* Philadelphia: Westminster.

Richard A. Norris, Jr.
> 1963 *Manhood and Christ: A Study in the Christology of Theodore of Mopsuestia.* Oxford: Clarendon Press.
>
> 1980 *The Christological Controversy.* Philadelphia: Fortress.

Jaroslav Pelikan
> 1966 *The Finality of Jesus Christ in an Age of Universal History: A Dilemma of the Third Century.* Richmond: John Knox.
>
> 1971 *The Christian Tradition I: The Emergence of the Catholic Tradition (100-600).* Chicago: Univ. of Chicago Press.

G. L. Prestige
> 1963 *Fathers and Heretics.* London: S.P.C.K.

IV. Recent Christology:

D. M. Baillie
> 1948 *God Was in Christ.* New York: Scribner's

Karl Barth
> 1970 *The Humanity of God.* Richmond: John Knox.

Leonardo Boff
> 1978 *Jesus Christ Liberator: A Critical Christology for Our Time.* Maryknoll, NY: Orbis.

Dietrich Bonhoeffer
   1966 *Christ the Center*. New York: Harper & Row.
Hans W. Frei
   1975 *The Identity of Jesus Christ: The Hermeneutical Bases of Dogmatic Theology*. Philadelphia: Fortress.
Walter Kasper
   1977 *Jesus the Christ*. New York: Paulist.
H. Richard Niebuhr
   1951 *Christ and Culture*. New York: Harper & Row.
Wolfhart Pannenberg
   1968 *Jesus — God and Man*. Philadelphia: Westminster.
Edward Schillebeeckx
   1963 *Christ the Sacrament of the Encounter With God*. New York: Sheed and Ward.
   1979 *Jesus: An Experiment in Christology*. New York: Seabury.
   1981 *Christ: The Experience of Jesus as Lord*. New York: Crossroad.
Piet Schoonenberg
   1971 *The Christ*. New York: Seabury.
Jon Sobrino
   1978 *Christology at the Crossroads*. Maryknoll, NY: Orbis.
Dorothee Soelle
   1967 *Christ the Representative*. Philadelphia: Fortress.
Frans Josef Van Beeck
   1979 *Christ Proclaimed: Christology as Rhetoric*. New York: Paulist.

V. Historical and Doctrinal Surveys of Christology:

Karl Adam
   1962 *The Christ of Faith: The Christology of the Church*. New York: Mentor.

Gustaf Aulen

1960 *Christus Victor: An Historical Study of the Three Main Types of the Idea of Atonement.* New York: Macmillan.

Carl Braaten and Roy A. Harrisville, eds.

1964 *The Historical Jesus and the Kerygmatic Christ: Essays on the New Quest for the Historical Jesus.* Nashville: Abingdon.

John C. Dwyer

1983 *Son of Man & Son of God: A New Language for Faith.* New York: Paulist.

Reginald H. Fuller and Pheme Perkins

1983 *Who Is This Christ? Gospel Christology and Contemporary Faith.* Philadelphia: Fortress.

John H. Hayes

1976 *Son of God to Super Star: Twentieth-Century Interpretations of Jesus.* Nashville: Abingdon.

Leander Keck

1971 *A Future for the Historical Jesus.* Nashville: Abingdon.

John F. O'Grady

1981 *Models of Jesus.* Garden City, NY: Doubleday.

Dietrich Ritschl

1967 *Memory and Hope: An Inquiry Concerning the Presence of Christ.* New York: Macmillan.

BIBLICAL INDEX

INDEX

Other Books of Interest

from ALBA HOUSE

AQUINAS' SUMMA
An Introduction and Interpretation
Rev. Edward J. Gratsch, S.T.D.

A basic guide for students of theology and anyone interested in a modern systematic overview of Thomistic thought, this volume is actually much more than an introduction and interpretation of St. Thomas' enduring masterpiece. *Aquinas' Summa* is really an excellent, faithful and readable synthesis of the Angelic Doctor's main writings, creative mind and holy life.

In this up-to-date introduction to the *Summa*, the author has digested a vast amount of material and managed to present it in a clear, flowing and organic manner without sacrificing anything truly essential. Frequent references are made throughout the work to the *Summa's* impact on the Second Vatican Council and the New Code of Canon Law.

While other prominent authors have written voluminous studies on the *Summa*, no one in the last dozen years has offered a better compendium of Thomistic doctrine than has Father Gratsch.

$11.95

A COMPANION TO THE BIBLE
Edited by Miriam Ward, R.S.M.

"The aim of this book is to lead others to study the exciting and inspiring new approaches to the Bible. For the student who is just starting to get acquainted with the Bible and for the interested, educated non-specialist this book will provide insights and perspectives from some of the best representatives in the field.

"The authors whose essays are represented in this book demonstrate both their scholarly competence and ability to convey their scholarship to those who have not had the leisure or inclination to pursue such studies on their own, and at the same time to enrich those whose ministerial function demands an ongoing personal formation for the good of their respective congregations." *From the Preface by Miriam Ward, R.S.M.*

Contributors

Elizabeth Achtemeier	Philip King	Pheme Perkins
Paul Achtemeier	John L. McKenzie	Donald Senior
Bernhard W. Anderson	Bruce M. Metzger	David M. Stanley
Raymond E. Brown	M. Lucetta Mowry	Krister Stendahl
James Fischer	Roland E. Murphy	Carroll Stuhlmueller
Reginald H. Fuller	Jerome Murphy-O'Connor	Bruce Vawter
Cyrus H. Gordon	Gerald O'Collins	Abp. John Whealon
	Carolyn Osiek	

$14.95